MEDIA
audience
Research

3e

MEDIA
audience
Research

A Guide for Professionals

Graham Mytton
Peter Diem
Piet Hein van Dam

 **SAGE** www.sagepublications.com
Los Angeles • London • New Delhi • Singapore • Washington DC

First edition published in 1993 as: *Handbook on Radio and Television Audience Research*,
Paris: UNICEF and UNESCO
Second edition published in 1999 as: *Handbook on Radio and Television Audience Research*,
Revised and expanded edition, London: BBC World Service, UNICEF and UNESCO

This third edition published in 2016 by

SAGE Publications India Pvt Ltd
B1/I-1 Mohan Cooperative Industrial Area
Mathura Road, New Delhi 110 044, India
www.sagepub.in

SAGE Publications Inc
2455 Teller Road
Thousand Oaks, California 91320, USA

SAGE Publications Ltd
1 Oliver's Yard, 55 City Road
London EC1Y 1SP, United Kingdom

SAGE Publications Asia-Pacific Pte Ltd
3 Church Street
#10-04 Samsung Hub
Singapore 049483

Published by Vivek Mehra for SAGE Publications India Pvt Ltd, typeset at 10.5/13 Palatino by Diligent Typesetter, Delhi and printed at Sai Print-o-Pack, New Delhi.

Library of Congress Cataloging-in-Publication Data Available

ISBN: 978-93-515-0643-0 (PB)

The SAGE Team: Shambhu Sahu, Neha Sharma and Rajinder Kaur

CONTENTS

PREFACE

The original idea for this book came in 1990 from Morton Gierseng when he worked for United Nations Educational, Scientific and Cultural Organization (UNESCO). He later moved to United Nations Children's Fund (UNICEF) and both organisations backed the original two editions, first in 1993 and then an expanded edition in 1999. He, among others, had noted the lack of suitable published works on audience research and how to carry out such research. Most of what existed fell into two broad categories. First, there were mostly empirical studies done mainly in the developed world. Much of this work is dominated by the demands of advertisers. There was also a fair amount of material about research in the non-commercial public service sector. This was also mostly from the richer industrialised countries. UNICEF and UNESCO as global organisations devoted to development and human progress were keen to promote the use of audience research outside the mainly commercial world.

Second, there was a large, growing body of mostly theoretical and critical studies produced by academic scholars. A lot of this is far removed from the practical day-to-day problems and issues facing radio and television broadcasters and others who use these and other modern communications media.

There is a growing interest in audience research in developing countries. It is seen less as an expensive luxury and more as an essential tool in developing better broadcasting, better-targeted advertising and advocacy and altogether a more efficient use of all kinds of media for all purposes. With the rapid changes in communications technology, the growth of deregulation and the changes in consumer behaviour, audience and other forms of market research have become ever more vital. There is also a growing interest in using the techniques of market research in improving the effectiveness of development activity. This revised edition, like the first and second editions, is intended to be relevant to all situations, covering as it does the appropriate methods and techniques. There is, however where appropriate, a deliberate emphasis on the needs of less developed media markets.

We are indebted to many people and organisations for granting us permission to include material. The extract from *Yes Prime Minister* is reproduced by the kind permission of BBC Worldwide. The extract from *The Manual for Culturally Adapted Research* is reproduced by the kind permission of the author, Professor Scarlett Epstein.

The book is intended to help make communications more effective and worthwhile anywhere in the world. It has been an exciting project to produce something that will, we hope, be of real practical value in not only helping communicators of all kinds do their work better but also in showing the value and use of audience and market research to all those who use the media, whether in development and advocacy for the public good or for advertising in the commercial world.

The years since the publication of the second edition in 1999 have seen vast changes in all forms and technologies of human communication. And that is not all. The same technological progress has brought about huge changes to the ways we do research into media use. All forms of market and opinion research of which media research is a major part, have gone through changes every bit as complex and thorough. It is now time for a new edition of a media research book being used in all parts of the world to train people involved with audience research. The second edition was translated into several languages, including Slovak, Indonesian, French and Russian.

Readers of the previous two editions will see that even the title of the book has changed. The first two had the same title *Handbook on Radio and Television Research*. Because of the changes in the media, such a title would no longer make much sense. Media convergence means that this new edition becomes *Handbook on Media Research*. It covers all kinds of research into the audience use of all media technologies—radio, television, the Internet, mobile phones, social media and print.

The original author, Graham Mytton, left the BBC in 1998. He had headed the department responsible for global audience research since 1982. Since he left the BBC, he has concentrated on training people in audience research methods as well as managing and leading several media research projects in all continents. This 18-year period has been marked by several major changes in both the media landscape of the world and the ways in which research into media can be and is being done.

This new edition encompasses the Internet, both as a research tool and as a medium in its own right to be a topic for research, as well as mobile telephony and the social media that the mobile phone and the Internet have produced in their wake. All these innovations have had a major impact on media research.

We also realised that separating the two media, TV and radio, as discrete topics for study and teaching no longer made much sense. One major feature of modern communication is 'convergence'. The digital revolution made it possible to send and receive all kinds of media content—sound, pictures, photos, text, movies, video, books and more—and this brought about a blurring of the distinction between media. You can watch TV programmes on a computer or a mobile phone. You can do the same with radio stations, books, films, photos and more. Individuals can make and send their own videos, sounds and pictures. And, sometimes, two media are being used at the same time. Books can be read, and increasingly this is happening, on specially made devices that are in fact computers—at home or elsewhere. The old boundaries have been blurred or gone entirely.

This was first brought to the notice of *Scientific American* readers in a special edition of the magazine in 1991. Predicting the future in technology is difficult; however, the magazine was able to predict what we have seen happening in the quarter of the century since. The magazine was perhaps the first to see that computing and communication technologies would 'fuse' or converge bringing about new infrastructures that would 'profoundly reshape our economy and society'.[1] Within less than a decade, the world of communication experienced massive changes. Hardly anyone had access to the Internet when this edition of *Scientific American* appeared. The magazine carried no reference to its own email address and, of course, no website was referred to. Twenty years later, as we can see in the following chart, the Internet has become commonplace. First, a chart showing the rapid rise of the Internet use in one country, Austria,[2] and then a chart showing household access to the Internet in Europe in 2014.[3]

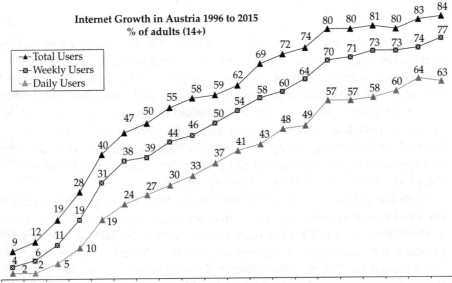

Internet Use in Europe 2014

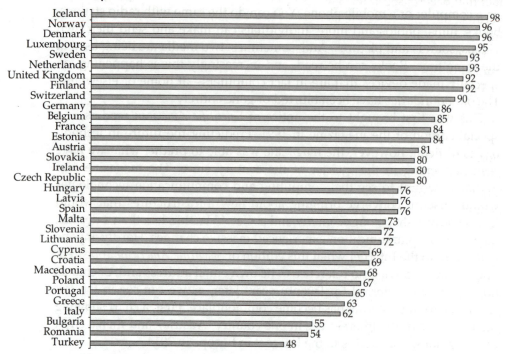

Source: Europa. Use of Internet in Past three Months.

It made more sense to turn this into a book about media research, rather than restricting it to radio and TV, and that is what we have done. To do this, the original author, Graham Mytton, brought in Peter Diem, former head of research at the national public service broadcaster, the Österreichischer Rundfunk (ORF) (Austria), who later worked for the research agency GfK, and who specialises in new media research. He also roped in Piet Hein van Dam of the technology company Wakoopa based in the Netherlands, who is a specialist in passive Internet usage metering. This new, third edition is the product of the joint effort of the three authors.

With the global growth of Internet penetration, the use of this medium for market and opinion research purposes is growing from year to year. Conventional ways of asking respondents such as by face-to-face or telephone are increasingly being replaced by Web-based interviewing. The main reason for this is cost-efficiency. In Internet-based market research, there are no geographical constraints. Also, response rates tend to be higher in surveys conducted online.[4] Finally, there is also proof for the fact that Web-based interviews produce longer and more honest answers because the respondent feels freer as he/she is not faced with a personal interviewer.

We are grateful to many people for their help and encouragement. David Bunker of BBC Audiences (the audience research department in the domestic broadcasting arm of the BBC) helped us with obtaining recent audience data in the UK. In the previous editions, acknowledgements were made to many others, to whom we remain indebted. We have especially gained insights and learned valuable experiences from colleagues in our profession of media research, and fellow members of ESOMAR[5], the Group of European Audience Researchers (GEAR), the Pan African Media Research Organisation (PAMRO) and several other professional bodies. Several people from research companies and institutes have also provided many useful links and content. We especially thank Charles Lawrie and Lyndsay Ferrigan at the joint industry committee (JIC) in the UK for radio audience research (RAJAR) for information on their methods and permission to use a page from their listener diary. We also acknowledge and thank Gerry Power and Joe Miller of M&C Saatchi World Services for granting us permission to use, in Chapter 7, some very useful desk research and analysis done by them of current media access and use in India. Gerry has also been a valued adviser to us on several aspects of the book when it was being revised.

We are very grateful to the editorial team at SAGE India for their guidance and editorial skills and especially thank Shambhu Sahu and Neha Sharma for their patience and good counsel.

All forms of market research are strengthened by professional cooperation and sharing. All of us have benefited immensely from working with others. Any weaknesses or faults that remain in this book are our responsibility. Our wish is that the book is useful, especially in promoting better use of all forms of communication by those bodies which seek to improve the lot of their fellow men and women.

Notes and References

1. 'Special Edition: Communications, Computers and Networks'. *Scientific American*, 265, no. 3 (September 1991): 30 passim.
2. http://www.integral.co.at/de/aim/ (accessed 16 July 2015). One per cent is equivalent to 73,000 people. It means that in early 2015, 6.14 million Austrians were Internet users and 4.6 million were daily users.
3. ec.europa.eu/euristat/tgm/table.do (accessed July 2013). Up to date statistics on the Internet access in many countries can be found on the websites of many countries' statistical offices. For Austria, as one example, go to http://www.statistik.at and search for Internet statistics.

4. Or at least they are better than response rates in more developed countries. In less developed countries, response rates for traditional face-to-face interview surveys remain very high—often over 90 per cent.
5. ESOMAR originally stood for the European Society for Opinion and Market Research, but it is now a fully global association with members from all continents and activities in all parts of the world.

Graham Mytton
Peter Diem
Piet Hein van Dam

Chapter 1

Introduction

Radio and television are 20th century phenomena. So also are the Internet, mobile phones and the digital revolution that emerged in the last quarter of the century. The years between 1900 and 2000 saw more changes in the technology of communications than any previous century. The electronic media have played a major role in those changes and now feature as an important part of the daily lives of most people in all parts of the world. Many of the major differences that we find in the world of the year 2000, when compared to a century before, are the direct result of the arrival and development during that period of what we call the mass media. Now in the 21st century, we are seeing further huge changes, all of which really came into being in the last two decades of the 20th century. First, the Internet, connecting computers across long distances, then the World Wide Web enabling links to be made on a global scale.

These developments were made possible by the convergence of electronic communications. Digital technology whereby all information—speech, music, text, images, moving pictures, scientific data, numbers and anything else that can be written, drawn, played, said, sung, calculated or otherwise devised and recorded—can be stored, retrieved, sent and received from anywhere to anywhere provided the appropriate equipment is available and there is access to a means of transmission and reception. Digitisation has not only brought us new media but has transformed all the existing media.

These major developments that have come to pass since the 1970s have continued the transformation of the world started in the 1920s by wireless radio.

To start with, radio reception relied on receiving sets that, with minor exceptions, required mains electricity supply. This was because, before the invention and development of the transistor, radio sets required the use of valves (or tubes as they are called in American English) and these required higher voltages than can be provided by ordinary cell batteries. Transistors did not have the same requirements and when transistor radios began to be mass produced from 1954 onwards, radio ownership spread very rapidly to all parts of the world.

By the 1980s, radio reached almost everyone, everywhere in the world. Television also grew rapidly in the last quarter of the 20th century, reaching many people in some of the very poorest parts of the world, but its spread has slowed down in places where there is no ready access to mains electricity, TV being generally more reliant on this than radio.[1] The printed press, whose history is very much longer, tracing its origins to the 15th century, is also important but its impact and reach is more varied. In some communities and areas, printed media are restricted by high levels of illiteracy and the high cost of newsprint, printing ink and machinery, and distribution.

In 2015, the world's population was estimated to be over 7 thousand million.[2] It is not easy to make reliable estimates of how many homes have at least one radio and/or TV set. The International Telecommunications Union (ITU) estimates that in 2013, there were 1.4 billion homes with at least one TV receiver. They calculate that this means around 5 billion people have access to a TV at home. This also means a household penetration of 79 per cent.[3]

Reliable statistics for households with radio are much more of a problem. The ITU admits this and does not attempt even a guess. However, one of the authors of this book has compiled a running database drawing on the latest evidence available from national media surveys and similarly reliable data and these calculations produced an estimate of about the same number of households in 2008—1.3 billion and about the same number of people reached.

The statistics for new media show that they are also very widespread and have actually grown at a faster rate than either radio or TV did when they began to be sold. Giving statistics here for Internet penetration and mobile phone access will be already out of date when the book is published. In a very useful document, available online, the ITU says the following:

> By end 2014, 44% of the world's households will have internet access at home. Close to one third (31%) of households in developing countries will be connected to the internet, compared with 78% in developed countries. 2013/14 growth rates in the developing world will be more than three times as high as those in the developed world (12.5% growth compared with 4%). Household internet access is approaching saturation levels in developed countries. The number of households with internet access in developing countries surpassed those in developed countries in 2013, and doubled between 2010 and 2014.

As you can see, there is what is often called nowadays a 'digital divide'—the gap between those who have access to the new media and those who have none. There is also a very large group of people in the world who have some access to both old and new media but use of both is limited by poverty, the lack of high-speed connection or other factors linked to underdevelopment. For example, the cost of batteries is a barrier to great use of radio. The lack of mains electricity supply or frequent power cuts prevents or limits access to and use of TV, the Internet and mobile phones. Many people who have mobile phones are often prevented from making fuller use of them because of the difficulty of finding places to recharge them.

Access to the more traditional electronic media of TV and radio is also much affected by levels of wealth. While there are very few people who are never reached by either radio or TV (they can and often do watch or listen outside the home), there remain many who have no home access to TV or radio or indeed the Internet and whose use of any electronic medium[4] is constrained by lack of electric power, the high cost of batteries and the fact that poverty means that broken or worn out sets are sometimes not replaced until better times come along.

There are also great disparities in the development of electronic media at the other end. The media are dominated by global companies that operate media services across boundaries. Most of these are based in the developed nations, especially the United States and Europe, although there is strong growth in some emerging countries, especially China, India, South Africa, Brazil, Russia and some Arab states.

The last decade of the 20th century was marked by a major trend that changed the ownership and control of electronic media in most countries in the world. In most countries in Africa and Asia as well as all countries in the former so-called Soviet bloc, all electronic media were under the direct control of the government until the late 1980s and early 1990s. The collapse of communist rule in the Soviet Union and East and Central Europe led to the gradual freeing of media controls and the disappearance of what had been until then a total state monopoly. The same process was also seen in most of Asia and Africa. Commercial and other independent operators have been licensed to own and run radio and TV stations in all but a small number of countries.

Historically, the organisation of radio and television has followed two broad patterns or models. In most of Europe, broadcasting began in the 1920s as an activity organised by the state. Radio was run either as a public service more or less independently of the government but under some kind of state regulation, or directly by the government as an instrument of the state. Thus, in Britain, the Scandinavian countries, the Netherlands, Switzerland and a few others, broadcasting was legislated as a public service provided for by a non-governmental agency, independent of political authority, but established by the state. In the communist countries and also in France and some other European states, broadcasting was run as a department of the government.[5]

On the other hand, in the United States from the very beginning, radio, and later television was organised as a commercial profit-making activity. The government was involved in the granting of licences to broadcast but in not much else.[6]

The rest of the world adopted one or the other of these two alternative but very different approaches to the regulation and organisation of broadcasting. Most of Latin America chose to take the US road. Most of Africa and Asia, formerly under European colonial rule, followed the European model. Thus, it was that in the whole of Africa, the colonial powers, mostly France and Britain, bequeathed broadcasting systems to the newly independent states that came directly or indirectly under state control. It was the same in India, Pakistan, Sri Lanka, Malaysia, Vietnam, Laos and most other ex-British and ex-French territories.

Broadcasting in most countries is now diversified if not entirely free from government control. Most countries in Europe, Asia and Africa that formerly had state or public service monopolies have now permitted independent broadcasters. Most of these operate on a commercial basis, relying on the sale of advertising and the commercial sponsorship of programmes. Some are community-based and funded by a mixture of public funds, advertising and voluntary contributions. Some seek to serve a religious purpose. There are also a few which have a partisan political purpose but these are relatively rare.

The two traditional electronic media, radio and television, have for many years played a major role in world information. Pictures and reports of events and people from different parts of the globe are carried everywhere and at great speed. We have become accustomed to seeing images of people and events from many distant parts of the world as they happen on our TV, computer, tablet and mobile phone screens, hear live radio reports, or read accounts of the same. The immediacy of certain kinds of information has come to be normal and expected. However, it does not mean necessarily that we are, as a result, better informed than we were before this era of more rapid global communication. Some argue that having access to ever more information, we are actually less well informed now than we were before the information explosion of the past two or three decades. Others argue that the main impact of the modern mass media may be less in the rapid dissemination of information and more in the wider dissemination of certain ways of seeing the world.

The electronic media may be doing rather more than merely giving information. Some see them as having an unwelcome influence. They are thought to enhance the power of the already powerful. They are criticised for lowering cultural standards and for blurring the distinctive richness of many world cultures. Critics see them as promoting false values. They are seen as being dominated by powerful nations or multinational companies and as further weakening the already weak. There is a counter view, especially about blogging and social media, that these have challenged and fundamentally changed the nature and extent of media power relationships. Whereas TV, radio and the press have indeed been under the control of the already powerful, this is not true of the new media which allow anyone to have a say. With new media, anyone can be a reporter, anyone can speak out, and nobody can be silenced. It is not the purpose of this book to ponder further or examine these claims and counter claims but we briefly mention them here so that the importance of media research can be better understood and appreciated, for without good data on what is happening, we are less able to know or understand what is happening.

There are others who see the modern electronic mass media as leading to greater violence, immorality and disrespect for tradition. TV, films and new media are often blamed for the supposed increase in crime. Many other ills of modern society have been blamed on television—rather less on radio. The Internet is often blamed for the spread of sexual crimes and for the promotion of extremist ideologies, especially in the years since 9/11.

At the same time, others view the electronic media as having mostly beneficial effects. It is argued that they make democracy possible by widely disseminating the kinds of information people need when exercising democratic choices. They cut across social and economic barriers and provide equal access to educational and other information by which people can improve their own personal circumstances.

It is not at all easy to decide who is right in this debate. Have the modern mass media had mostly beneficial or harmful effects? Put this way, the question is probably unanswerable. The fact is that modern life as most of the world knows it could not be imagined without electronic mass communication. The systems of mass communication found in the world today form part of the way in which world societies function. One might as well ask, 'Is modern society beneficial or harmful?'

A more interesting set of questions arises instead if we think about the media with these facts in mind: What role do they play in different societies? How much are they used, for what purpose and by whom? What are the consequences when the media change in some way?

While radio and TV began in much of the world as state institutions, the same cannot be said for the new media. The Internet and mobile telephony have from their beginnings been products mainly of private rather than state enterprise.

1.1 Why Audience (or Media) Research?

The questions—'Who is listening?' 'Who is watching?' 'Who is online?' or 'Who is able to send SMS messages?'—are surely not unwarranted or even remarkable questions to ask. Certainly, media owners need to know something about the people who are watching, listening, accessing content online or engaging with others through their phones. In all kinds of human communication activity, we think about the person or persons with whom we are communicating. A teacher speaks in a different manner and about different things to school children in their first year from those in their sixth year. If we speak to someone who does not speak our own language very well, we try to make allowances for this fact. We use different ways of addressing members of our own family, the local shopkeeper, the police, subordinates and superiors. Every time we speak, write a letter, make a phone call or write a book like this one, we need to make an effort to consider with whom we are communicating. If we don't know, we can do a little research to help us. When we meet someone for the first time, we tend to ask questions that might, in various ways, help us to continue to communicate by modifying in some way, if necessary, the way in which we communicate. Have we met before? Do we have certain things in common? Do we share similar interests? What can we ascertain about the other person's attitudes, knowledge or personality that would help us communicate better?

Radio and television broadcasting are peculiar forms of communication. Most of the communication is one-directional. Broadcasts are transmitted and the broadcaster may assume that what is being broadcast is being watched or listened to. Why is this assumption made and is it always justified?

Let us consider this a little further. It is a fact that a good deal of broadcasting activity in the world goes on without much effort being made to find out what is really happening at the other end! If you made a speech in a large hall full of people and slowly everyone got up and walked out, what would you do? Or consider what you would do if everyone started talking, ignoring what you were saying? You would change what you were saying, attempt to attract everyone's interest and attention, or perhaps you would stop speaking altogether in sheer embarrassment! You would certainly soon feel very foolish if you continued to speak without changing anything unless you were extraordinarily thick-skinned! And yet, a not inconsiderable amount of radio and television broadcasting in the world is like this, especially in countries where there is a state monopoly or very little competition. Broadcasting continues inexorably but no one seems to attempt to find out anything about viewers and listeners. However, there is evidence now that many broadcasters who have previously avoided finding out more about their audiences are themselves waking up to the realities of how broadcasting really works. They are beginning to take notice of their audiences, how they actually behave, what they are interested in and so on.

Audience research is more than a matter of knowing if anyone is listening or viewing, reading or going online.[7] By audience research, we mean the various methods and techniques used to find out about the audience. It covers a wide range of information-gathering exercises. For whom is a programme or service intended? Are those targets actually receiving? Do radio broadcasters, living in the cities, know what time to broadcast to farmers? They might think they do but experience shows that without research, they can get it wrong. If programmes are aimed at children, are children actually watching or listening? If educational programmes are made and transmitted, are they meeting a need perceived by the broadcaster but not by the intended audience? If the broadcasts meet an audience need, are they made in such a way that will attract the intended audience? Are they available to listen or watch at the time allocated? Are target groups familiar with programmes intended for them? What is their experience of using the programmes?

Broadcasting is one of a range of goods and services available to the public but unlike most other goods and services, no selling takes place. If you are selling soft drinks, you can easily find out on a yearly, monthly or even daily basis how many cans or bottles are being sold. If you are running a hospital, you can find out from your records how many people have been admitted over a given period of time. If you are running a bus service, you can add up the tickets you have sold and count the miles that have been travelled. Newspaper proprietors can count their sales. But broadcasters have no such easily obtained evidence of consumption or use. That does not mean it is not needed. Nor does it mean that it cannot be obtained.

Before the deregulation of broadcasting in the 1990s, the major radio and television stations in the less developed countries as well as in many industrialised countries were usually funded out of taxation or licence revenue. In this case, they are expected to provide a public service, serving the interests of the whole of the tax or licence-paying public. But how can a public service broadcasting station receiving public funds show that it is providing an adequate and appreciated public service unless it does audience research? Part of a public service station's purpose will usually be to serve certain minority interests. This also needs to be researched so that it can be established that these requirements are being met satisfactorily.

Research is essential when the main source of funds for broadcasting is advertising and programme sponsorship. How much should different time slots cost the advertisers? How many people and what kinds of people are listening or viewing at different times and to which programmes? Which is the best time to advertise if one wants to reach housewives? What is the channel listened to the most by professional people?

With the global growth of Internet penetration, the use of the online connections and methods for market research purposes is growing from year to year. Conventional ways of asking respondents such as by face-to-face or telephone are increasingly being replaced by Web-based interviewing. The main reason for this is cost-efficiency. In Internet-based market research, there are no geographical constraints. Also, response rates tend to be higher in surveys conducted online. The emergence of new methods and the differences that they have made will be more fully discussed later in this book.

1.2 About the Book

The purpose of the book was in its original form to be mainly a training manual for audience research for TV and radio with a focus on the challenges of working in less developed countries where research was needed less for commercial purposes than for development and human progress. That is still a major intention of the book. But the original book was used globally and was translated into French, Russian, Indonesian, Slovak, Lao and other languages. It became a widely used teaching manual in colleges and universities, and its use went beyond the developing world. The new edition presented now attempts to provide a comprehensive view of methods used in media research in all situations, developed and underdeveloped, and of all media from print to mobile phones—writing chronologically of two media relying on technologies that are the earliest and the latest!

Media have changed immensely in the years since the second edition in 1999. That edition concentrated on traditional forms of research. They are all included again because they will all continue to be used. But with the global growth of Internet penetration, as well as the even more rapid and more widespread growth of mobile telephony, the use of the online connections and methods for market research purposes is growing from year to year. Also, mobile phones, especially smartphones, are being used with increasing frequency and success. Conventional ways of asking respondents such as by face-to-face or by landline telephone are increasingly being replaced by Web-based interviewing and to some degree also, through mobile phones. The main reason for this is cost-efficiency. In Internet-based market research (including via mobile phones or other hand held devices), there are no geographical constraints. Also, response rates tend to be higher in surveys conducted online. The emergence of new methods and the differences that they have made will be more fully discussed later in this book.

The book follows the original structure. We begin with a review of the history of media research, especially for radio and then TV.

The book then takes the two main 'sectors' of opinion, market and media research, quantitative and qualitative methods, outlining, first, how they are done in what we can only refer to as their 'traditional' form—face-to-face using questionnaires, group discussions, in-depth interviews and similar person to person encounters, as well as research done by mail. Then, we look in detail at how these methods are being replaced and often enhanced in some important ways by the new technologies of Internet, online and mobile phone. We also show that traditional methods continue and remain essential for much research. Face-to-face surveys continue to be required and so also do real group discussions or focus groups where everyone is physically present.

A major innovation in this new edition is the whole chapter on 'passive' measurement of online media. The Internet has the facility built in to track and record everything that happens. There are major opportunities for Internet providers including social media and any example of online content provision to have data. We often meet the concept of 'big data' arising from the ability of the Internet as well as all or most other examples of digital media to provide vast amounts of data, a lot of it available in various forms to a wide variety of potential users. We aim to show how such data can be accessed, assessed and used and how they can be attributed to individuals rather than simply the hardware they use.

Notes and References

1. Radio is now growing rather more slowly than it was. Later, we will look at data from some of the poorer areas of the world that show there seems to be a large number of very poor people who do not appear to be moving into the modern world of the electronic media. The proportion of people out of touch with any modern means of communication may have stopped getting smaller.
2. Population Reference Bureau http://www.prb.org/ (accessed 16 September 2015).
3. ITU: Yearbook of Statistics 2013.
4. Throughout the book, we will be using what we think is the right way to refer to media. 'Media' is the plural of 'medium'. Radio is a medium and print is a medium. Twitter is a social medium. The Internet is another medium. Sculptors and painters talk of working in different media—it may be the medium of clay, or the medium of oil paint or the medium of collage. But in everyday speech, the word 'media' almost always refers to information, entertainment and advertising media which are mainly comprised of print, radio, television, the Internet and social media, the broad topic areas covered in this book. Medium and media have the same meaning; one is the plural of the other. In much modern usage, this fact is being forgotten. We believe this is unfortunate and robs the words of their proper meaning.
5. Sydney Head, *World Broadcasting Systems* (Belmont: Wadsworth, 1985).
6. Tom Lewis, *Empire of the Air* (New York: Harper, 1991); Sydney Head and Christopher Sterling, *Broadcasting in America*, 6th Edition (Boston: Houghton Mifflin, 1990).
7. Using the Internet and social media is a little different because these transactions can actually be measured. Transactions online are recorded as will be explained and explored later.

Chapter 2

History of Media Research

A large part of the history of media research before the advent of the Internet was focused on broadcasting. This is because of the peculiar nature of radio and television. With both radio and television, no transaction takes place that allows for anything to be counted or measured. When a newspaper is sold, it is a measurable transaction. We will still need to do research because we might well want to know who reads the newspaper, and perhaps how many read a paper even if they do not actually buy it; however even without any research, we can find out how many newspapers are actually bought. With the Internet, as we shall be explaining, every click, every page view and all other online activities leave a digital record. As we shall see, with the new interactive digital media including mobile phones as well as tablets, computers and other online devices, come ways of capturing details of activity and converting these into measurements of media use. But there has never been an equivalent way of getting data on radio and TV use. From the beginnings of radio in the 1920s, this was a problem for broadcasters. How did they know whether anyone was listening to them?

Broadcasting began in the industrialised world during the 1920s. Initially, very little of what would nowadays be recognised as audience research was carried out. Broadcasters in the early days of radio in Europe and the United States knew remarkably little about their listeners. What they thought they knew was based on unreliable and misleading methodologies.

In the early days of radio in the United States, there was no systematic audience research. Very often, it was the personal likes and dislikes of a prospective commercial sponsor—most US broadcasting was and is paid for by advertising—which determined what went on air. An advertiser might sponsor a programme from his (they were nearly all males) personal tastes and preferences.[1] But advertisers soon began to realise that they needed information that was independent of the views and opinions of the owners of the radio stations or their main sponsors and advertisers!

The first form of measurement used in the United States, used both to guide programming as well as to try to inform and perhaps impress advertisers, was obtained by counting the number of letters elicited by programmes. Other 'measurement' used by broadcasters in the early days was equally unreliable. Some radio station managers would draw a circle on a map with a hundred-mile (160 kilometres) radius around the station and determine the number of people who lived within that circle. But such a procedure is useless so far as measuring an actual audience is concerned. Differences in the transmitter power, local geography, station programming, wavelengths and numerous other factors are known to influence the size of the population habitually reached by each station, not to mention the personal preferences of the targeted audience. And the number of letters received is no measurement of anything other than the number of people who have written!

Broadcasting also began in Europe in the 1920s. In Britain, radio broadcasting began in 1922, first as a service for the purchasers of the new wireless sets provided by a consortium of manufacturers. This was very soon turned into a public corporation, the BBC, with a Royal Charter to provide radio transmissions of information, education and entertainment as a public service monopoly. The BBC started the world's first TV service in 1936, also as a public service. In Britain, no commercial broadcasting was permitted on television until 1955 and none on radio until 1973. The BBC had no audience research for more than 10 years after its establishment in 1922. Moreover, audience research did not begin without an argument about whether it was really necessary.

> I cannot help feeling more and more strongly that we are fundamentally ignorant as to how our various programmes are received, and what is their relative popularity. It must be a source of considerable disquiet to many people besides myself to think that it is quite possible that a very great deal of our money and time and effort may be expended on broadcasting into a void. (Val Gielgud, BBC Productions Director, 1930)

> I do not share Gielgud's view on the democratic issue. However complete and effective any survey we launch might be, I should still be convinced that our policy and programme building should be based first and last upon our conviction as to what should and should not be broadcast. As far as meeting public demand is concerned, I believe that the right way is to provide for a more conscious differentiation of objectives within our daily programme. (Charles Siepmann, BBC Director of Talks, 1930)[2]

These two points of view are not actually impossible to reconcile. Audience research does not aim to tell programme makers what to do. Gielgud's views were actually shared by many programme makers who felt the need to have some more reliable information on the growing audience. This information would help them to do their jobs better. It would also help those in management allocate resources better to meet their public service obligations. Siepmann's remarks seem to have been more in the nature of a caution against over-reliance on counting listeners. According to Robert Silvey, the founder of audience research in the BBC, Siepmann became a firm supporter from the early days.[3]

Audience research was formally established within the BBC in 1936. Its role has, from the outset, included serving as an instrument of public accountability as well as providing an information system for programme makers and management. There have been several special studies on particular contemporary broadcasting issues, which helped the corporation to decide on major policy issues. This function has been especially important in recent years, as the broadcasting scene has changed so rapidly in the UK.

In the United States, the process was completely different. American radio was, from the beginning, guided by one fundamental principle: people are attracted to listen if they get programmes they want to hear. All American audience measurement has derived from this basic marketing principle. Through it, the broadcasters attempt to furnish people with the programmes that sufficiently large numbers of people will want to hear, not with programmes which someone thinks they ought to listen to. The determination of the programme preferences and desires of the general public, or of target audiences within it, is a major requirement of radio and TV audience research in any broadcasting system run on commercial lines.

However, this principle is modified by an uneven consideration given to those preferences and desires. This is because two different market principles are involved in commercial broadcasting. Indeed this is also true of other communication activities that rely, at least in part, on advertising, such as newspaper and magazine publishing. There are two markets involved. These media are sometimes referred to as 'hybrid' businesses which have two distinct sets of customers whose positions *vis a vis* the respective medium are very different. Readers, listeners and viewers choose what they read, listen to or watch. Advertisers also choose where they will place their advertisements. Programmes or newspapers that appeal to large numbers of people with spending power are more likely to attract advertising and sponsorship than those which reach smaller numbers of people, or people with less spending power. Programmes or publications aimed at the poor or for minorities may be less likely to receive commercial backing. In the broadcasting world, this is the fundamental difference between public service and commercial broadcasting and it is reflected in the outlook and approach of audience research that is done for each type of broadcaster.

Some people in broadcasting, especially in public service or state-supervised or controlled radio or television, are suspicious of research, especially research using the methods of market research. This kind of opinion used to be encountered frequently: 'How can anything which helps those who are interested only in selling more soft drinks, cosmetics or baby food possibly be of interest or value to those of us who are keen to use broadcasting for the real benefit of people?' One can understand the sentiment but it is a profoundly short-sighted view. Whatever we may think about the activities of commercial firms that seek to maximise their sales and profits, sometimes perhaps unscrupulously, we have to recognise that the techniques they employ do actually work. Advertising clearly brings results; otherwise, very large sums of money would not be spent on it. It does not always work in the way intended. Indeed many expensive campaigns fail to achieve the intended results. The sums spent on advertising in the rich industrial countries are very large indeed. And because some advertising is seen to fail, large sums are spent on research designed to discover the most effective means of advertising. Can these methods not be also used for more general human benefit? The same techniques can of course be used to improve and make more effective any kind of communication. If the need is to improve broadcasting to farmers, or broadcasts to improve public health, infant nutrition, adult education or anything else, research can help. Just as it can maximise the effectiveness of advertising cosmetics, it can also do the same for more worthwhile communications activities.

Audience research can be used as a means of maximising the effectiveness of public advocacy campaigns, and of improving and enhancing education and information for effective democracy and good government. Audience research is a means of providing essential information to aid the creative process of programme making. It can be used as a means of maximising the efficient and cost-effective use of limited resources. And it can be used to test if the objectives of any educational or information campaign have been successful.

The objective may be a simple one—to increase awareness of a consumer brand—a new soft drink or a washing powder. Or it may be to make people aware of the need to protect infants in tropical areas of the world from malarial infection by getting them to sleep under bed nets. In these cases, messages via the media can be shown to increase awareness. It becomes a little more complicated and difficult to test the effectiveness of advertising or educational promotion in changing peoples' attitudes and behaviour.

When this book was first written, the Internet had only just emerged. Digital media have revolutionised world media. They have also changed the whole way in which research is done, bringing in new techniques and methods.

We have seen how audience research began in the UK. At the same time audience research began to be done elsewhere in Europe. For example, mention should also be made of the role the US-based media research scholar Paul Lazarsfeld played in the development of radio research in Austria as well as later in the United States. In 1932, he conducted more than 100,000 interviews on radio music in Vienna in 1932.[4] He also introduced the 'Stanton-Lazarsfeld Program Analyzer' for the Columbia Broadcasting System (CBS) in Los Angeles and New York in 1942 which was used to pre-test the appeal of new programmes with a randomly selected studio audience.[5]

Notes and References

1. Matthew Chappell, *Radio Audience Measurement* (New York: Stephen Daye, 1944), 2.
2. Quoted in Peter Menneer, 'Broadcasting Research: Necessity or Nicety?' *Intermedia* 12, no. 3 (May 1984).
3. Robert Silvey, *Who's Listening?* (London: George Allen and Unwin, 1974), 14.
4. Desmond Mark (ed.), Paul Lazarsfelds Wiener RAVAG-Studies 1932. Wien 1996
5. http://www.tvacres.com/commun_ads_stanton.htm (accessed 16 September 2015).

Chapter 3

Quantitative Research: Audience Measurement—General Theory and the Basics

The part of this book that dealt with quantitative research was originally one chapter; but in this edition, as this important topic of measurement has become very much more complex and varied, what was one chapter now becomes three. This first one is on the general theory of quantitative research and the various methods and approaches used. The following two chapters deal first with the measurement of traditional media—radio, TV and press—and then second with measurement of online media. This chapter focuses on the basics of quantitative measurement and all researchers need to understand what is written here. We start with the basic theory and then outline sampling, questionnaire design, interviewing and quality control.

The second chapter is on the various methods of measurement in use today. Here, we describe the several means whereby audiences are measured, mainly for TV, radio and the printed press.

The third chapter is about online research using mainly the Internet. But while other aspects of online measurement are taken up in a different way in Chapter 6 on passive online measurement, this third chapter of this part of the book is mainly about the use on the Internet to do quantitative research.

3.1 Theoretical and Practical Issues in Measuring Audiences

Introduction: Why and How Audiences Are Measured?

In this section, we look at what have become known as 'traditional' methods of audience measurement as well as taking a look at how online methods are increasingly being used. It is important to start with what have been the basic methods of quantitative research because this is where market research began and it is on its statistical bases that all measurement research is ultimately based.

Quantitative research involves the selection of large samples, usually in hundreds or in thousands. The results are expressed in percentages as well as absolute numbers. Later on we will be looking at qualitative research carried out with smaller numbers of people and where results are expressed primarily in the form of words, images and ideas.

Quantitative research is a major activity within media research in general. It is the core activity of most broadcasting audience research and the one into which most effort and money is put. This is why it occupies the largest section of this book. With radio and TV and increasingly when we consider other media of the digital age, how can we find out how many listen to, watch or access which services, which programmes or content, and when? How do we know what kinds of people are reached by this or that programme, service or other content?

The single most common kind of research activity so far as TV and radio are concerned is audience measurement. It is not difficult to see why this is so. Broadcasting is unique among the range of services and goods available to the public. It is the only one for which we have no readily available information about the users or 'customers'. When you listen to a radio station or watch a TV channel, nothing material is actually consumed. No physical transaction takes place. Sometimes we use the word 'consumers' about viewers or listeners to make an analogy with goods like food, drink and so on. The latter products are actually consumed; something physical disappears and is no more. Broadcasting is not quite like that. We can get some idea of how much beer is drunk or rice is eaten by looking at production or sales figures. We can find out how many people go to the cinema by looking at how many tickets are sold. But there is no similar way of telling how many people watch a TV programme or listen to something on radio. With the printed media, we are in a kind of halfway position. Newspapers and magazines are bought and usually thrown away within a short period (although practices can vary greatly). Printed media are something that is more obviously 'consumed'. We can usually obtain sales figures for magazines and newspapers and independent bodies often audit these so that the figures can be regarded as reliable and not reliant on the claims of the publisher. However, because a single newspaper or magazine can be read by more than one person, sales figures tell us nothing much about readership. Moreover, the growth of free newspapers or free sheets financed entirely by advertising means there are no sales figures. This is why readership surveys are carried out in most major press markets in the world. We will look in more detail later about how printed newspaper and magazine readership is measured.

TV and radio audience measurement has to rely entirely on some kind of survey instrument, for no sales transaction takes place, except in the case of the new and still very limited examples of subscription and pay-per-view television channels. Quantitative research of one kind or another is essential if we want to measure audiences for TV and radio as we know them at present. We shall describe how this is done.

Later we will describe the measures that are commonly used in audience research, especially such terms as 'Reach', 'Share' and 'Ratings'. We will also see how advertisers and broadcasters use these terms.

There are well-established methods by which we can calculate how many listen to or watch broadcasts at different times and on different days of the week. When audience measurement is carried out according to certain principles, it is usually possible to make reasonably accurate estimates of the numbers of listeners or viewers to different services and programmes. It is also possible to work out the times that they listen or watch as well as the number of minutes or hours spent on watching or listening, and the kinds of programmes that attract the most listening. Research can normally provide information about the kinds of people who form the audience for different programmes or networks at various times in the day. Research of this kind carried out over a period of time can plot trends in audience behaviour. It can show whether new programmes have increased or decreased in audience size, whether new services have achieved their audience target objectives or whether there are any significant long-term trends.

How is this done? The principles of audience measurement are not complex or difficult to understand. What we do is select a sample of the population and ask appropriate questions designed to collect data about their television viewing or radio listening.

Quantitative research of the 'traditional' kind is usually conducted using some form of questionnaire for selected respondents to answer. There are various ways to make contact with the respondent. The following are common forms of the encounter, in two types. The first involves an interviewer addressing questions to a selected respondent, while the second involves selected respondents completing a questionnaire themselves. As we shall see, there is nowadays only limited use of questionnaires in the measurement of television audiences because in most developed countries, methods that are partly passive and partly involving the respondent are used. These involve the use of automated people meters. We return to this topic in detail later.

3.2 The Basic Tools of Quantitative Research

The two basic tools in quantitative research that all researchers and users of research need to know very well are 'Sampling' and the 'Questionnaire'. As there are several kinds of both, we need to map these out in some detail.

We need to also look in fairly basic but important detail at the statistical principles involved in sampling and at the various ways in which we can make both work to the best advantage of good research.

Sampling

The questionnaire is a well-established instrument used in the process of finding out what we want to know when attempting to measure media behaviour. But as explained earlier, we need to work out who we are going to ask. We cannot ask everybody; that would be absurdly expensive and unnecessary. We need to address our questions to a selected sample of the population we seek to measure.

We first need to look into some detail at the principle and practice of sampling. How can a sample represent everyone? The principles outlined here apply to all quantitative research whatever we are seeking to measure and whatever method we then use to obtain the required data. What follows now is about the basic principles and building blocks of sampling and sampling theory in quantitative methods in the social sciences, of which media audience measurement is a part.

All branches of social, market and opinion research share the same principles of sampling that we use in audience measurement. Those principles are also used in everyday life. Experience tells us that we can draw conclusions from a few chance observations. In a market, we might ask a vendor if we can taste one orange to see if it is ripe and sweet before buying a quantity. The farmer may sometimes open a few cobs of maize to see if the whole field is ready to harvest.

It is important to choose our samples with some care. We might pick the one orange out of a whole pile that was not sweet. The farmer would be foolish to select a couple of maize cobs from a corner of the field where the maize was riper than the rest.

Theory and Practice of Sampling

The principle of sampling is to remove bias as far as possible so that the sample we achieve through our chosen method of selection is as representative of the whole as we can make it. It does not mean that it will always tell us the whole story; there are always going to be some differences between the characteristics of the sample and those of the population or universe from which it is drawn. We can reduce the magnitude and likelihood of the differences, or bias, by increasing the size of the sample. Thus, the more oranges we taste, the more maize cobs the farmer opens, the more certain we can be that the qualities represented by the sample are true of the whole lot; in other words, that the unsampled items will be the same.

The problem is that increasing the sample does not increase reliability by the same proportion. Interviewing 200 people selected at random from an area containing many thousands of people does not give us information twice as reliable as interviewing 100 people. To double the reliability of a sample, you have to quadruple its size. So, our sample would have to be 400 to be twice as reliable as a sample of 100.[1]

The point to remember is that a lot of valuable social research is based on the law of statistical regularity, which states that a small group chosen at random from a large group will share much the same characteristics. This is an important principle.

Samples and Censuses

Sometimes it is necessary to contact everyone and not to sample. Most countries have censuses of their entire populations. Many countries have a census every 10 years. The main reason for a comprehensive count of everyone within a defined geographical area is to record reliable information on a given date. But it is a very expensive activity and is really necessary only when it is a matter of accurately counting whole populations.

The very fact that censuses do take place is very important for those of us who engage in quantitative work, using samples of large populations. One of the most important aids to good sample survey research is having access to a recent and reliable census with detailed information on population size and distribution, age and gender composition, type of dwelling and other similar data. You can more easily take a sample and, above all, check that your sample really does reflect the population as a whole, or the section of it that you propose to select, when you have access to important demographic facts collected from the entire population.

Public opinion polls are well-known examples of the use of sampling to find out about the population as a whole. In a general election, everyone of voting age ought to be able to record his or her vote. But it is not necessary to have an election to know about public opinion. Between elections, we can find out the state of political opinion by selecting and interviewing a sample representative of the electorate as a whole. This is done regularly in most democratic countries. The electorate as a whole is the 'universe' which the sample will be designed to represent.

Defining the 'Universe'

The universe is defined as the population we wish to discover some facts about by taking a sample. The universe cannot be the entire population because that includes babies and infants who cannot, for obvious reasons, be questioned. In most examples of quantitative social and market research, we usually tend to sample people in various smaller 'universes' or populations. A typical choice might be to sample people aged 18 and over. Or we might want a sample of adults living in rural areas. We might want a sample of teenagers attending secondary school. Or a sample of women in urban areas aged 15 and over.[2] Such definitions of universes for research purposes are usually straightforward and simple to define and it is usually easy to determine who is included and who is excluded in the population under study.

But some populations or universes for study are less well-defined and may be constantly changing. You might want to have a sample of a particular part of a population. Just think, for example, of the following examples: the homeless population of London, the unemployed of Dhaka, Bangladesh, the rural poor of Egypt, the Afghan refugees and the displaced forest people of Brazil. Obviously some decisions have to be taken by the researcher to help define these shifting populations precisely enough to make sampling possible. In each case, the universe for study needs to be carefully and precisely defined.

Even universes that appear on the surface to be straightforward may still require care and may demand or require redefinition. For example, what do we do about people who do not live in definable households? It can be problematic, time consuming and, therefore, expensive to include the homeless in a general population survey, but leaving them out introduces a bias that can be a substantial one in countries or places within countries where homelessness is widespread, for example, Brazil or India. But what do we do about people living in institutions such as monasteries, prisons, special hospitals or other similar dwellings that are not usually defined as 'households'? In practice in most market and media research, people living in such non-household institutions are excluded for practical purposes. But again, exclusion produces a bias. Other problems are posed by media use in holiday homes or by refugees or immigrants not able to understand the local language. In such cases, all exclusions must be considered carefully and reported transparently.

Most broadcasting audience measurement research attempts to measure the radio and television behaviour of whole populations of adults and children down to a certain defined age. In most of Europe, and in most of the more developed world, the main methods of TV and radio audience measurement are based on universes of at least the entire adult population and for TV can include young children.[3] In many less developed countries, for practical or economic reasons or because of the requirements of the research, the universe may be confined to urban areas. Sometimes a few rural areas may also be covered, or in some cases, only one or two regions out of several may be selected.

Selecting a Representative Sample

In audience research in more developed countries, we are most often involved in selecting samples of the whole adult population living in households, excluding those who live in institutions.[4] We are going to look at the process of selection of such a sample. The task is to find a method as free from any bias as we can make it. The importance of this cannot be exaggerated. Bias can occur without the researcher being aware of it.

Let us use an example of sampling which is customarily performed in manufacturing industry. A company manufacturing light bulbs needs to know how reliable its manufacturing process is. To do this, batches of light bulbs are selected and tested. The company has set a minimum standard of quality and reliability. If the selected sample does not meet this, it is assumed that this is true of the rest and the whole output of that production line may be rejected and the machinery stopped for investigation. It is obviously crucially important that the information provided by the selected sample represents reality. If, after taking a representative sample of them, we find, let us say, that 97 per cent reach the required level or standard, we need to know with what confidence we can say anything about the standard of the entire output of light bulbs.

There are two main areas that we need to look at when considering the reliability of data in a circumstance like this. The first is the reliability of the sample itself. Was it truly reliable and free from bias? There are many ways in which bias can be there without us being aware of it. In a light bulb making factory, it would be necessary to take our samples at different times and on different days, especially if the machinery is operated by several different teams or shifts of people. Also, people operating machinery can behave differently at different times of the day and week. If power failure or mechanical breakdown often interrupted the manufacturing process, this would also have to be taken into account. These and other factors might mean that the quality of output was uneven.

The second factor is the size of the sample. The larger it is, the greater the degree of confidence that we would have that our sample represented the true situation. We will look in detail at this point later.

It is worth noting that methods like this are used in most mass production processes in order to monitor performance. We can sample people in a similar way ensuring that the sample is representative. Sampling is the process of selecting people (or things) to represent those not selected. Or put another way, it is the process of creating a small version of the universe under study so that the data we collect are of manageable proportions, but which nonetheless tell us something reliably about the whole. To do this, we need to devise a means whereby every unit (person, light bulb or whatever) in the universe has a more or less equal chance of being selected. This is the vital central principle of sampling. In order to carry out the discipline of sampling, and 'discipline' is an appropriate word to use, we need to devise a sampling method that ensures that we can draw a reliably random sample. For this, we need a 'sampling frame'.

The Sampling Frame

The definition of the universe can often point us very quickly to a readily available and suitable sampling frame. An electoral register, on which all eligible voters are listed with their names and home addresses, is an obviously valuable sampling frame for creating a sample of electors. All those who are electors are listed there. The register is what qualifies and defines them as voters.

But in each case of choosing a sampling frame, we need to find the relationship between the population or universe we want to study and the chosen sampling frame. Some sampling frames may not adequately cover the population we are interested in. They may not include everyone they purport to include. Electoral registers do not always include everyone who should be included. This is, however, a real and serious political problem because people may be deprived of their right to vote, with or without their knowledge, through their exclusion from an electoral register. But for political opinion research attempting to measure the opinions of those able to vote, even an inadequate electoral register, is serviceable for this purpose.

The basic question about any sampling frame is a simple one; is anyone we wish to include left out? If they are, how serious are the omissions? And can we correct any inadequacies?

Street maps may be viewed as adequate sampling frames, especially when they show dwellings. But there are three major weaknesses. First of all, maps are very soon out-of-date and omit new developments. Second, they sometimes omit illegal, unplanned, 'squatter', 'informal' or temporary housing areas. The third weakness is that even though they may show dwelling units, they usually give no indication of housing or population density. They do not tell you how many people live in each dwelling.

Let us illustrate the latter problem. We might seek to use a street map of a city which showed dwelling units on it. We might systematically select a pure random sample of these units. But while it might be a random sample of dwellings or homes and, therefore, useful if you were sampling 'households', it would be a biased way of sampling 'individuals'. One might, for example, select 10 people from one group of 100 dwellings with over 500 adults living in them. We might then select 100 from another part of the same city with only 150 adult residents. The two areas have widely different densities of people per dwelling. We know that density is correlated with social class and wealth and that such a sample would, therefore, be a biased one, especially in relation to media use.

Another kind of sampling frame often used in survey research is provided by a population census. Geographical definitions of ways in which the population was counted are produced. A census, once it has been analysed and the reports issued, will provide the researcher with detailed data, broken down by enumeration area. There is usually a simple-to-understand hierarchy of analysis in any census. Population data for the country as a whole are given, then a breakdown by region, and then by sub-region or area, right down to enumeration areas of usually no more than a few hundred people each. The precise geographical definition of each of these population units is usually described, often nowadays using Global Positioning System (GPS) coordinates.[5] Data on both population and household numbers make census results of enormous value for the conduct of well-designed quantitative research among general populations.

Sometimes no ideal sampling frame is readily available. In many parts of the world, there are no electoral registers. Up-to-date maps showing streets and houses may not exist. There may be no reliable or recent census data. You may have to create an adequate sampling frame yourself. This may seem daunting. It need not be.

Let us imagine that you need to take a representative sample of the population of a village or group of villages. A published map may not exist but with the Internet, maps are readily available and free. Google Maps are based on recent satellite images and, therefore, show roads, streets, paths and dwellings as seen from space. This valuable resource has transformed survey research in remote areas of the world. It also provides a very much more up-to-date sampling frame than was the case in the days when one relied on printed maps. You can see where people are living at or near the time of your survey. Google Maps are rarely more than three years old. You can print or download them to your computer and update where necessary. You can draw the boundaries of the area you want to survey and from which you are taking the sample.

If you have data from a census, the enumerator or enumerators of the area will have already gone through a similar process. If you can access census data down to enumeration area levels, you can usually work out where enumeration areas are on the maps that you are yourself using. What is practical usually works best and is obvious. The local geography will often make decisions about planning the sample easy. Rivers, lakes, ranges of hills and unpopulated land often make natural boundaries.

There are many other examples that could be given of sampling frames that can be used to make representative samples of any universe we have as the subject for study. Let us consider some examples.

We have written mostly about making samples of the general adult population. For this, we require a sampling frame that covers that population, which is why we were looking at censuses, enumeration areas and maps, including, especially, Google Maps because they not only show streets but also dwellings. But very often in research we want to study subgroups of any population and something more than maps, censuses or electoral registers are needed.

Here are some examples of possible universes for quantitative research and some suggested sampling frames:

Universe or Population Subgroup	Possible Sampling Frame
Nursing mothers	List of mothers visiting a mother and baby clinic
Doctors	List published by the national professional body
School teachers	Lists kept by professional body or by the schools where they teach
Children attending school	Attendance/registration lists
Farmers	Local Ministry of Agriculture lists
Subscribers to a pay TV satellite channel	List of subscribers

Sometimes a ready-made sampling frame in the form of a list of names does not exist and you will need to create one. In the case of the homeless, you may be able to gain access to the people you wish to reach through a charity that exists to serve them. But you might also need to add those who do not come into contact with that agency. One way might be to observe how many people are 'sleeping rough'—that is, those who sleep on the streets or in railway stations or other places. Note where they are to be found, make an estimate of how many there are in different places and devise a way of taking a random sample of them.

Random or Probability Samples

These are theoretically the most accurate forms of sampling. Taking a random sample means that every individual in the area of your survey or within the universe for study—teachers, children of school age, nursing mothers or whatever—has an equal or known chance of being selected. If you were taking a nationally representative sample of adults, aged 15 and over, in your country you might set about making a list of the entire 15+ population, and having done so to proceed to select names entirely at random, then find these people and interview them. This would be a true random sample survey. In practice, this is never done, at least not in an entire country. It would be extremely time-consuming, expensive and needlessly complicated.

Pure random samples are, however, possible and often used with smaller groups, especially those for whom we can obtain or create universal or comprehensive lists. For example, it is a simple matter for a company that does all its business through mail order to create a random sample of its customers. It has all their names and contact details. It is a simple matter to select a truly random sample of them. Another practical example would be sampling for a survey to be taken in a small community to measure local opinion perhaps during a local election campaign. On a small scale, randomised samples do not pose great difficulties.

If you were seeking to do a study of recent graduates from a university and you wanted to send a questionnaire to a sample of, say, 400 of them, you might first obtain a list of names and addresses from the college of all recent graduates. This would be your sampling frame. There are a number of ways you could make a random selection. One is to use a method similar to that used by lotteries. This might involve writing everyone's name on a slip of paper and mixing these very well in a drum. You would then select, without looking, let us say, 400 slips of paper to be your sample. Everyone in the drum has an equal chance of selection. We would obtain a pure random sample.

Having to write out everybody's name is little tedious. An easier alternative is to use random numbers. These are easily generated on many computer programmes. We have used a computer to produce 400 random numbers between 1 and 1,000 in the appendix of this book. You can use these numbers in any order. Each number between 1 and 1,000 had an equal chance of being chosen each time that my computer made its selection. Random numbers can easily be obtained by using 'random number generators' available on the Internet. There is a useful free site on the Internet that generates random numbers of any range you need at www.random.org

However, considerations of time and expense make the task of conduct-ing a pure random sample rather rare when covering a general population. A pure random sample opinion survey of 1,000 Zambian adult representa-tives of the adult population is theoretically possible. Everyone is supposed to be registered with the National Registration Board and a random sample of 1,000 could be made using that resource. But having made the selection, finding everyone would be a time-consuming task, let alone the problem that the records of people's addresses are always out of date. Supposing they could all be found, one would still find oneself making several very long journeys just to interview scattered individuals.

There is another problem. By the nature of random samples, anything is possible. You might actually select a sample that was unrepresentative. For example, when selecting recent college graduates, you might discover that most of those selected had been science graduates, whereas science gradu-ates were not in the majority. Your method of selection had been correct. There was no bias in your method. And yet you have a sample that is biased. It can and sometimes does happen.

Stratified Random Samples

There are various ways in which we can improve the chances of a random sample being representative without losing its randomness. Stratifying the sample has the added advantage of saving time and expense. When there are well-defined categories within a population that you need to be fairly represented within your sample, you can construct the sample accordingly while retaining the principles of randomness. You can decide on a prede-termined number to be selected within defined groups or 'strata' within the population or universe under study.

Much sampling of general populations uses this method. What happens is that we usually divide the country into sampling areas and draw up sam-pling plans in accordance with what is known about the population in each part of the country. The existing administrative boundaries are useful for this purpose. Usually we will use the population size in each area to deter-mine the number of people to be selected in each. Thus, for example, if we were carrying out a sample survey of adult Tanzanians (aged 15 and over) our 'universe' in 2014 consists of about 27 million people.[6] We may decide that a sample of 3,000 will be taken to represent the whole country's adult population. We would need to determine from the last census what the dis-tribution of our universe is between the different districts.

A sample of 3,000 in a universe of 27 million means a sampling fraction or ratio of one in nine thousand. One in nine thousand adult Tanzanians would be selected to represent the population as a whole. In a district of, say, 540,000 people, the sample would be 60. In a district of 180,000, 20 would be selected, and so on. In practice, we often over-sample in sparsely populated areas and make adjustments to the data in the analysis stage in a process called 'weighting'. A simpler alternative and one that avoids the need to apply weights is to divide the country into a number of areas each with a similar number of people. You would then take an equal sample in each. But this solution is not easy when, as is often the case, there are large areas of low population density.

Sampling of a country is often stratified by types of area, rather than using the political or administrative boundaries. If we were, for example, creating a sampling frame for a national survey of India, we might first choose to divide it into its 28 component states and seven territories. These vary in size from the state of Uttar Pradesh with just over 200 million people down to the territory of Lakshadweep with only 64 thousand.[7] You could stratify the states and territories by size. There are 19 of the 28 Indian states each with populations greater than 10 million people. In each of these states, areas could be listed by their population density. For example, cities of more than 1,000,000 could be one category. Cities and towns of between 100,000 and 1,000,000 could be another. Towns of between 10,000 and 100,000 could be another. The last category could be town or villages of less than 10,000 people. Cities, towns and villages or areas could then be selected in each of these categories to be a representative. One might choose a selection in each category for subsequent sampling. This is in reality a form of stratified sampling sometimes called cluster or multi-stage sampling. It is used when it is impractical for researchers to go all over a country to carry out research. A selection of villages, towns and cities may be chosen to represent others. You could then make a selection of the smaller states and territories and make a selection of these to be covered.

If we return to our Tanzanian example earlier, the point can be illustrated further. Our proposed sampling fraction was one person in nine thousand. In an area of nine thousand adults, this fraction would suggest that we would be selecting and interviewing just one person. But that would be time consuming and probably pointless. What we generally do is to group similar areas together in our sampling frame and select one of these to represent the others. Thus, in an area of similar sized settlements, one would group many together to add up to a larger number. Then one or two places may be selected to represent all. So, if together the population of a number of similar areas adds up to 180,000, one would select one or two sampling points and select 20 respondents in one or 10 in each of two to represent all the adults in the cluster.

Of course, there are dangers in this approach. One must be especially careful if the population is made up of many distinct ethnic or linguistic minorities. In audience research, such differences can of course be major factors in media behaviour. If such differences exist, the stratification may need to take them into account. Deliberate stratification according to ethnicity or religion or similar category can ensure that people from all significant groups are included and if care is taken, in the correct and appropriate proportions. This is one way in which careful stratification of samples can improve on pure random sampling. The latter can exclude or under-represent important minorities.

Stratified sampling, which may or may not be clustered, is thus especially appropriate when the population being studied is very varied or heterogeneous. Unstratified samples may be more suitable when the population is more homogeneous—that is, the population does not vary a great deal socially, racially, ethnically or in other major ways. A random sample may not always be relied upon to reflect all the major demographic differences in the population. A stratified sample may be a better option to ensure better coverage. We gave the case of India to illustrate a stratified sample that would ensure a representative sampling of different sizes of communities from the very large to the very small. India would first be stratified by community size. Stratified sampling by ethnicity may also be necessary if we are to ensure that all the different ethnic communities are covered in a sample, simply because ethnic groups tend to live together. We find in many countries that there is a clustering by race, religion, nationality, economic status and even by occupation.

Random Sampling within a Survey

A common method of sampling in a survey of a population is to use a 'random' 'walk'. In a given geographical area, the person selecting the sample for interview may start at one house and select a respondent. It is very important to devise a method for selection of the starting point. Nothing must be left to interviewer choice in random sampling. Interviewers may want to avoid certain kinds of housing and they must not be allowed to do so.

After the first home visited, the interviewer may be instructed to select the next house after a given interval, then to turn left at the next junction and select another house at a further given interval, and so on. An alternative scheme can be devised. What matters is that you have a process that chooses the sampled household and removes the bias that would come in if you allowed your interviewer to make the choice.

But who is to be interviewed at each house? Researchers need to be careful not to interview only the first person met. You do not want a survey solely made up of people who answer the door or greet any stranger who arrives. What we need to do is to randomise the selection of people at the household level.

At each house, the person contacted by the interviewer can be asked how many people aged 15 years and over (if that is the age definition you have decided on) live in the dwelling which has been selected. One of these people is then selected randomly for the interview. A very easy way to do this is to ask whose person's birthday is next. If that person is not present, the interviewer should make arrangements to return later to interview the selected person. This process is known as 'call back'. It should be agreed beforehand how many call backs will be attempted on any survey. It cannot be indefinite, of course. It is normal to say that there will be one or two call backs during a survey when the selected person cannot be found. If after two or three calls, or whatever number you have decided on, the person is still not there to be interviewed, a substitution is made at another house, using the same sampling procedures as before. It is very important to get this process right and to avoid the risk of interviewers biasing the sample by being able to choose themselves whom they should interview. But it is also very important to make every effort to contact the selected individual. This applies not only to face-to-face sampling but also to telephone and other forms of random sampling of individuals. Otherwise, we would be taking a sample only of people who are more easily contacted.

If all your interviews take place during working hours, you will find that many people will be out on the first and subsequent calls. It is a good idea to vary the times that you call at people's homes in order to maximise the chances of being able to interview people with the entire range of working and life patterns. And be flexible when you seek to find the missing person.

One way of selecting the respondent in each household is to use what is known as a Kish Grid. When houses or dwellings are selected, each one is assigned a number from, let us say, 1 to 9. When the interviewer meets a member of the household, he or she is then asked to list all the eligible people (i.e., all those who have the demographic characteristics you are seeking—in this case, all those aged 15 and over). All of one sex are listed first, then all of the other, from the oldest down to the youngest and each is given a number from 1 upwards. Using the Kish Grid reproduced here, the interviewer reads along the row corresponding to the household's assigned number in the left-hand column until he/she reaches the column giving the total number of eligible people in that household. The number at that point indicates the person by number who should be selected for the interview.

Address Serial	Number of Persons Listed in Household						
Number	1	2	3	4	5	6	7+
1	1	2	1	4	3	5	7
2	1	1	2	1	4	6	1
3	1	2	3	2	5	1	2
4	1	1	1	3	1	2	3
5	1	2	2	4	2	3	4
6	1	1	3	1	3	4	5
7	1	2	1	2	4	5	6
8	1	1	2	3	5	6	7
9	1	2	3	4	1	1	6

Thus, if we are at address number 7 and there are five eligible people in that dwelling, we interview the person who is number 4 on the list of all the adults in the household.

There is a problem with what we have just described. When we choose just one individual in each household, we are introducing a bias.

If, for example, one house visited has one adult and the next has six, we still interview only one person in each home. You can see, therefore, that people living in homes with several adults have a lower chance of selection than those in homes with few or only one resident.

In probability sampling, we have to endeavour, as far as we are able, to remove all sources of bias. The Kish Grid works well if we want a sample of one per household. It is acceptable as a way of providing a reliable sample of individuals if household sizes do not vary greatly. But if there is a lot of variation in household size, we may need a way around this problem that ensures that this bias is removed. One was devised several years ago by some British market researchers. What they came up with was a system whereby the interviewer would select respondents at fixed intervals 'of people'. It depended to some extent on the existence of an electoral register. These do not exist everywhere. So, we are devising a revised version of what Blyth and Marchant wrote about in 1973.[8]

At the first house selected, all adults should be listed. Then, one is chosen by some prearranged random method. Also prearranged will be a sampling interval for individuals. It should approximate to the mean number of adults per household, a figure obtainable from the most recent census. Let us suppose that it is three.

At each house sampled, a list of adults is made. It should be written in some prearranged order, perhaps alphabetically in order of names or in age order. The person chosen could, in each case, be the third person, not third in the home, but third on the running list since the previous interview. Let us illustrate. The names here are all fictitious and we have listed them alphabetically within each house.

House 1	John Smith	
	Mary Smith	☑
House 2	Aisha Ahmed	
	Anwar Ahmed	
	Suluma Ahmed	☑
	Yusuf Ahmed	
House 3	Navjot Singh	
House 4	Sam Brown	☑
	William Brown	
House 5	Ali Saleh	
House 6	Adam Maganga	☑
	Sarah Mwanza	
	Tommy Mwanza	
	Obed Phiri	☑
	Peter Zulu	
House 7	Veejay Patel	
	Yolanda Patel	☑

Note that sometimes more than one person is interviewed per household (House 6) and sometimes nobody is interviewed (Houses 3 and 5). This system, if used with a random method of household selection, will ensure a random sample of individuals also and one in which there should be little bias.

Quota Samples

Commercial market research companies often use quota samples. These are not random samples but are used when interviewers are instructed to look for fixed numbers of respondents of different categories or types. The categories are calculated in quotas that are typically of sex, age, housing type, social class, occupation or ethnicity. The interviewer is given a set of quota controls. One interviewer may be asked to select ten married women between the ages of 25 and 34 who live in a rural area. Another may be given a quota of five unmarried women of the same age group, in another area, and so on.

The selection criteria will be dictated by the purpose of the survey. If it seeks to represent the general adult population, the quotas will be based on the distribution of categories such as age, sex, social class, geographic area, and so on, in the adult population that can be obtained from census or similar sources. If our survey is of a particular group, let us say of mothers of preschool children, we may then draw up quotas to ensure a good representation of women in this category from all social groups. We would want to ensure that we did not select too many of the better off or too many who were living in towns. Quotas could be drawn up to ensure balanced representation in our sample.

Quota samples have a number of advantages that make them attractive to the researcher. They take less time than random samples. Interviewers conducting surveys using quota samples generally complete many more interviews in a day than when using any kind of random sample method requiring them to seek specific individuals according to the sampling plan. Because of less time spent and lower costs, quota samples are used in many commercial market research surveys. Interviewers are typically seen in a shopping street or mall in cities all over the world, also quite often at airports, holding a clipboard. She or he (more often female than male) will have been given a quota of interviewees to select that day. Typically, gender, age and often social class will define the quotas. The gender of the respondent usually presents no problems in the selection process, but age is a different matter. It is difficult to tell how old a person is before approaching him or her to request an interview. But the interviewer looking for a 35 to 44 year old man is unlikely to approach a man in his 80s or a youth in his teens. The interviewer can also more accurately establish the age, social status and other demographic criteria of the respondent from the first few questions in the questionnaire. If the person does not meet the criteria of the quota or meets a quota item already filled, the interview can be politely concluded and the interviewer can continue to seek out the category required.

Quota sampling is subject to many biases. For example, quotas may all be filled in easily accessible places while remoter areas are left out. Any system of sampling which leaves out certain areas or categories will distort the results if those excluded are different in significant ways from those included. If people living in remoter areas have different political opinions (as may well be possible) from those in more accessible areas, quotas which leave them out are likely to produce misleading results in an opinion poll.

The greatest weakness of quota samples is interviewer bias. According to the interviewer's social background, there might be a bias in selecting people for a survey—thus better educated interviewers or those with perhaps a higher social position might tend towards choosing respondents from similar backgrounds and avoid those who are different or seen as having lower social standing. And these tendencies can happen without the interviewer being in any way aware of what is happening.

With random methods, interviewers are given a strict scheme of selection and do not have any choice of their own about whom to interview. But interviewers using quota samples can choose the respondents, provided they meet the given criteria. The interviewer in the street or shopping mall can decide not to stop someone who appears to be unfriendly or another one who seems to be too busy. Another bias is produced by the place in which the selection is made. We might think that a street is a good place to find a good cross section of the population. But there are many people who spend little time on any street. There is the obvious case of the housebound and infirm. There are also people who spend a lot of time on travelling by car or working in factory or field. Quota samples conducted in the street are, therefore, likely to have a bias towards those who spend more time than others at the shops, those who appear to interviewers to be friendly and approachable and perhaps those who seem to have the time to stop and answer questions.

There are various ways to reduce these biases. One can vary the place where the interviewees are sought and the place of interviewee selection. Some people can be selected at homes or places of work. One can also introduce randomness into the way the quotas are filled. For example, one can start a survey using random methods where there is no choice left to the interviewer. The quotas come in when the interviewer checks what quotas have been filled and what categories are still to be found.

When conducting face-to-face audience surveys in Zambia in 1970–1972, Graham Mytton used a hybrid sampling method with the elements of randomisation, stratification, cluster and quota methods. First, he stratified the country by geographical area—rural and urban districts. All districts were visited and quotas for age and sex were drawn up for each geographical category, urban and rural within each district. Using the 1969 national census, he then worked out the number of men and women in each age group that he needed to select to be interviewed in each district, in both urban and rural areas. In each district, all towns were included. In Zambia, there are relatively few towns and it was not necessary to make a selection. When it came to the rural areas, a selection had to be made. Within each rural district, census enumeration areas were chosen at random and interviews were clustered in each. Urban districts were stratified according to the types of housing or settlement—high-density 'legal' or 'legitimate' housing, low-density housing, and squatter or shanty areas. Using a random process of selection, houses were visited and quotas were used to select the members of each household for interview. The resulting sample matched the census data by age and sex, which were what the quotas were based on. When the sample was complete, we were able to see if it matched in the other important details. We checked if it matched the language or ethnic composition of the country and found that it did so within a small margin. He achieved a representative sample fairly simply and effectively by reducing, as far as possible, interviewer bias.[9]

Telephone Samples

The telephone became an important tool in all forms of market research, including audience and readership research, during the post-World War two years in Europe and America as phone access became almost universal. Randomness of the sample is achieved by the use of what is known as 'Random Digit Dialling' or 'RDD'. This is a system, using a computer programme designed for the purpose, that selects any domestic subscriber's phone number at random and dials it automatically. Telephone companies usually provide, for a fee, a database of numbers for this purpose. The sampling frame can be all domestic telephone subscribers in an entire country, or all those living in certain geographical areas. If particular kinds of people are being sought, this part of the selection can take place when the phone call is answered. Sometimes a specialised database of telephone numbers of the kinds of people who are being sought may be available.

There are a few biases inherent in this method. One is that telephone penetration can be quite low in many less developed countries. This makes telephone sampling unsuitable in many countries, at least for any general population surveys. Another bias lies with whom the contact is made. It is obviously important not always to automatically select whoever answers the phone. One of the methods described already of selecting individuals in each household may need to be used, and every effort should be made to contact that person, with repeated calls, if necessary. A third bias is that in many countries, telephone line customers can opt to have their numbers removed from the lists used. And finally, while RDD can be used for calling landlines, it is much more difficult to use for mobile phones. This is partly because of the nature of the medium. Phone numbers for mobile phones are less long lasting. They generally come with a SIM card. They are also likely to change more often and any database of numbers in use is very much more difficult to create or obtain. In less developed countries in South America, Africa and Asia while mobile phone ownership has soared to high levels, landline phones remain accessible only to a minority. The use of mobile phones in quantitative research is dealt with more fully in Chapter 4.

Internet Samples

When this book first appeared in 1993, the Internet was new and had not spread very far. It was mostly used for sending and receiving emails. Now, just over 23 years later, the Internet is part of our everyday lives in most parts of the world. No part of the world is unaffected, the Internet is not yet universal but its growth has been faster than that of radio and television. At first the Internet required the use of a desktop or laptop computer but now the computer's small and portable companion, the mobile phone, has made an equal if not greater impact, and the effect of both home computers and mobile phones as well as tablets and other hand-held devices on market research has been massive and is continuing to make changes as this book is being put together. The changes that are transforming the whole of social, market, media and opinion research include the way that much sampling is now done. Most quantitative surveys completed now in developed countries, where the majority of people use the Internet, are done using sampling through that medium. So, what is an Internet sample and can it do what the previous forms of sampling already described can do?

The advantages of doing research using the Internet are obvious. The biggest expense in market research of any kind is labour—the necessarily large number of interviewers who have to be employed to do both the complex and disciplined work of sampling and then the sensitive and sometimes tricky work of administering a questionnaire and accurately recording the responses. Use of the telephone saves time, a lot of expensive and time-consuming travel and some of the complexities of randomising any sample. But using a phone to make interviews still involves the employment of quite large numbers of people to engage with respondents. But with the Internet, one is putting questions to respondents and it is mostly they who do the work. Costs are, therefore, very much reduced with no travel to undertake and no phone charges. Responses are automatically captured by a computer, and the analysis is immediate. No data entry is needed. The respondents (with the data-receiving computer) do almost everything for you.

It is no wonder that most quantitative research in Europe and many other more developed countries with high Internet access and use is now done online. The figures for several, mainly European countries, are given in the Preface. The use of the Internet for quantitative research is dealt in detail further. But it is worth noting here just how far online quantitative research has grown in the past few years. The following chart comes from the 2013 Confirmit report on changes in market research over the previous decade.[10]

The growth has not been equal. It is high in developed countries, but face-to-face quantitative research is still flourishing and widespread in

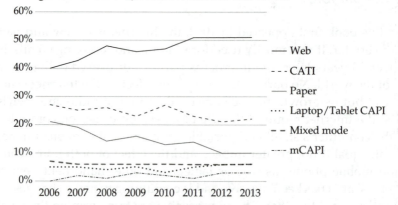

Changes in Methods of Quantitative Research 2006 to 2013

less developed countries where there is far les online access. But even here online research is beginning to grow, especially through the use of smartphones.

Market research conducted online requires the creation of so-called access panels. These are permanent address pools of persons representative of the online universe of a specific country and willing to participate in online surveys. Professional high-quality online research is conducted using access panels that have been recruited 'offline'. This typically means that respondents who have been selected by one of the traditional methods of more or less random methods already described may be asked if they are willing to become an online panel member. But in practice, many research firms use panels that are recruited 'online'. This method contains the danger of recruiting 'incentive hunters'—people who may participate in a number of panels and are doing it to earn money. Such practices are to be avoided.

Snowball Samples

There are some cases where sampling or obtaining access to respondents for face-to-face interviewing can be very difficult. Normal methods of recruitment may be impossible. Examples are in situations of conflict and emergency, situations where local culture and social norms prevent direct access to people's homes and in other situations where it may be seen as inappropriate for a stranger to approach anyone in a random manner without being formally introduced. Sometimes methods have to be used which are far from ideal and have serious problems of bias. One example is so-called snowball sampling. This technique of obtaining a sample is used when certain categories of people are difficult to make contact with, or in situations where it is not possible to do random samples in the normal way. The resulting sample may not be representative. We describe it here in this section on sampling for quantitative research, but it is more often used in obtaining respondents in qualitative research, described later. But it can also be used to recruit respondents for online panels.

Snowball sampling derives its name from the way when you start rolling a ball of snow, it becomes bigger and bigger as you continue to roll it. Snow attracts and sticks to snow. In snowball sampling, you ask people with whom you make contact to suggest others they may know in the category you are looking for. If you are looking for people who are professionals in a particular field, snowball sampling may be an appropriate way to find the numbers you are seeking. However, snowball sampling is not random sampling and is subject to unknown but probably considerable levels of bias. It should be used only when other forms of sampling are impossible. In Saudi Arabia, to give one example of its use, snowball sampling has to be used in a lot of quantitative research because in Saudi culture, it is either difficult or impossible for a stranger to gain access to any household. All contact has to be made by an introduction from another person. It means that random sampling in that country is not possible.

There is more that can be said about sampling that relates less to quantitative research and more to qualitative methods.

Sampling and Statistical Theory

How large should a sample be? This is a question often asked. It is generally true that the larger the sample, the more accurate the data ought to be. However, if the sampling method is faulty, increasing the sample size will not improve it. Worse, it may increase the skewed nature of the sample while giving the impression of greater precision.

In this section, the intention is to provide an easy guide to some of the statistical basics which lie at the heart of sampling. They are relevant and useable only in the context of probability sampling. Some statistical concepts will be introduced here. Some of these use Greek symbols. At this point, many readers may be put off. But we think you will find that the statistical bases of quantitative research are not as daunting as they may first appear to be.

The principle underlying sampling theory is the important and basic theory of 'normal distribution'. This depends on probabilities. Let us suppose an imaginary situation where we are trying to discover something about a population. We are trying to find the value of x. It could be how many people live in households with a 'smart' (i.e., Internet connected) TV set, the number of people who have been to university or the number of homes without running water. Suppose we try to find the answer by taking a series of samples of the population and ask them the relevant questions.

We will be able to plot the result—let us say the percentage of people who have been to university. If we do a series of samples, we will come up with a series of percentages, all different, at least to some degree. The true result will lie at the centre of the horizontal axis of the following graph. If we take several samples of the same universe, the results we obtain will fall within the following normal distributions. The mean of all results $\bar{x}$ should lie at the centre.

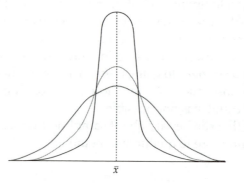

The sample that best represented reality would be one that gave us the result in the middle. But we can never be certain if we have achieved that correct result. Most of the samples we take will be on either side of this middle line. But we never know for certain how far away from the true figure we are with each individual result. What we can do, however, is to work out what the shape of the normal distribution for each sample probably is. In other words, we can say, with a reasonable degree of certainty, the likely distance, plus or minus, within which our results lie. That is what statistical probability theories let us do. That is why, as researchers, we really need to understand these things.

To calculate the range of reliability, we need to work out the shape of the normal distribution for a variable. To do this, we need to know two things, the arithmetic mean $\bar{x}$ (Greek letter Chi, pronounced kai) and its standard deviation σ. This latter Greek letter, σ (Sigma) is used to refer to the amount by which the value of x is likely to vary. When the arithmetic mean $\bar{x}$ is low and the standard deviation σ is high, the value of x varies a great deal. This is when we get a flatter shape to the normal distribution shown in the graph. When the value of is high, that is, when many of the results we get for value x are the same or nearly so and, therefore, the standard deviation σ is low, we get a taller narrower distribution and less variation in x. We will now show how we can calculate these.

When we carry out a survey to find the percentage of people who live in houses with 'smart' TV sets, we will not get the exact figure but an estimate. Another survey would in all probability provide us with a different figure. If we continued to do survey after survey, we would end up with a frequency distribution of these estimates for the percentage ownership of 'smart' TVs. It would be in the shape of a normal distribution as in the graph. The most common results would be at the middle, but some surveys would give results at either side. Some would, by the laws of chance, give us low estimates at the left-hand side of the graph. Others would, by the same laws, give us high estimates on the right.

The area under each of the curves on the graph represents the range of results for x achieved. It can be shown mathematically that 95 per cent of the estimates will lie within two standard deviations of the average, both above it and below. This last sentence is very important. Even if you find the preceding few sentences difficult, this last sentence really matters and needs to be remembered. It helps us work out how reliable any estimates from quantitative research are likely to be.

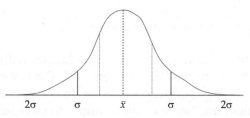

$$2\sigma \qquad \sigma \qquad \bar{x} \qquad \sigma \qquad 2\sigma$$

The areas at the two sides beyond the two σ symbols (two standard deviations) constitute 5 per cent of the area (2.5 per cent on each side). Ninety-five per cent lies between these two outer lines. We can, therefore, be 95 per cent confident that the true answer lies within two standard deviations (2σ) of the average. And this is the usual degree of confidence that we give in survey research. To illustrate, we will use the example of a survey measuring the percentage of individuals who live in homes with a 'smart' TV set.

Let us say that from a survey of 1,000 adults, we have achieved an estimate that 30 per cent of individuals have a 'smart' TV at home. We will now show how near to the true figure this estimate is likely to be. And we will do so within a 95 per cent confidence limit, the one most often used when we report the results of survey research. What we have to do is to discover the size of the standard deviation, also known as the 'standard error'.

The standard error is established mathematically by a simple formula:

$$\sqrt{\frac{x(100-x)}{n}}$$

x is the result—in this case 30 per cent—while n is the sample size. And $100-30 = 70$
So that formula becomes:

$$= \sqrt{\frac{30 \times 70}{1,000}}$$

$$= \sqrt{\frac{2,100}{1,000}}$$

$$= \sqrt{2.1}$$

$$= 1.4$$

The standard error 1.4 per cent is the value of σ. As you can see from the previous graph, there are 2 σ s on either side of the mean $\bar{x}$. Ninety-five per cent covers the area of two standard deviations from the mean.

Our estimate of 30 per cent, therefore, has a margin of $+/-$ (plus or minus) two standard errors.

$$30\% + / -2 \times 1.4 = 30\% + / -2.8$$

The true figure for individuals living in homes with 'smart' TV sets almost certainly lies between 27.2 per cent and 32.8 per cent. This may be sufficiently accurate for your purpose. What do we do if we want a margin of error smaller than this? As we noted earlier, to increase the reliability of a sample to make it twice as accurate, you have to quadruple the size. We would need a sample of 4,000 to have results twice as accurate as those given by a sample of 1,000 would. We, therefore, repeat the calculation:

$$\sqrt{\frac{x(100-x)}{n}}$$

$$= \sqrt{\frac{30 \times 70}{4,000}}$$

$$= \sqrt{\frac{2,100}{4,000}}$$

$$= \sqrt{2.1}$$

$$= 0.7$$

Using two of these values for σ, we get a +/− (plus or minus) range of 1.4, twice as accurate as before where the sample was 1,000 instead of 4,000. It means that the result is now (with a 95 per cent probability as before) between 28.6 per cent and 31.4 per cent.

In quantitative research, we have to remember though that the more people sampled, the more the survey will cost and the longer it will take to complete and analyse. Somehow, we have to find a compromise between the need for accuracy and the resources and time we have. A table giving the margins of error for findings from different size samples is given in the appendix. This table saves us the effort of working these things out. But do remember how the table was created. It is based on solid statistical theory.

The other thing we often need to do is to compare two results from different surveys with different sample or sub-sample size. You might find that between successive audience surveys of the same population, the audience for a certain radio station has fallen from 43 per cent weekly to 37 per cent. Does this represent a real or only an apparent fall? In other words, how likely is it that this result represents a real change in the behaviour of the general population and is not the result of sampling error?

There are more comprehensive and detailed books on the details of sampling and statistical theory, which those involved in fieldwork of this sort, should study. Some suggested titles are given in the bibliography. You should also note that most good computer programmes for survey analysis or statistics contain χ^2 (Chi squared) calculations and formulae.[11]

With the example we use above—the radio station whose audience has 'fallen' from 43 per cent to 37 per cent weekly reach—we need to know the sample sizes. If for both surveys, it was the same, and 2,000 people were interviewed, statistical tests show that the fall in audience is probably (95 per cent certain) real and not the result of sampling error. But if the samples had each been only 1,000 and we had the same result, we would not be able to say that the surveys had shown a real fall in audience.

Do remember though that these calculations and other statistical tests of significance or reliability work properly only with random samples. Mere size of sample is of no importance in establishing its reliability if the sample has been chosen by other means. For example, a radio station might give out questionnaires to people at a public event. It would be justified in feeling pleased if there were good responses. But it would not be justified in supposing that 2,000 replies, let us say, were any more reliable an indication of listener opinion than 1,000. This might seem surprising but it is true. The respondents are self-selected; they decide to participate and reply; they are not a random or representative cross section of the listenership. They are likely to be different from the remainder of listeners in significant ways and simply increasing the number who responds will not make the replies any more reliable.

The Questionnaire: The Art of Asking Questions

The basic instrument of the sample survey is the questionnaire. With care, we can obtain a representative and reliable sample. But if the questionnaire then used is not well constructed, the results of our research can be spoiled. Even the most carefully selected sample will be of little value if the questions asked are not well constructed or not easy to understand. There are a few basic kinds of questionnaire used in quantitative surveys.

Interviewer Administered Questionnaires

Face-to-face Interview with Printed Questionnaire: The most well established form of this is a face-to-face interview with pencil or pen and paper. The interviewer conducts interviews with selected respondents and records responses in writing on a pre-printed questionnaire. This is the traditional market research method in use for most of the 20th century. It never had nor really needed an abbreviation to refer to it but with the recent use of abbreviations in market research for other forms of interviewing, it is occasionally referred to as PAPI—Paper and Pencil Interviewing.

Face-to-face Interviews Using a Laptop or Hand-held Computer, Increasingly of the Tablet Kind: This is also known as computer-assisted personal interviews or CAPI. The questions are read out from a hand-held tablet-type computer where the questionnaire is stored. Another method is to ask the respondent to type answers into a laptop provided by the interviewer, who in turn supervises the interview. Built in to the software is a means of easily recording responses into a pre-formatted database. The software also prevents errors being made such as inconsistent or contradictory responses, questions being left out or more than one answer recorded when only one is required.

Telephone Interviewing: This usually involves the use of similar computer-based questionnaire software as in CAPI. This form of contact with the respondent is known as computer-assisted telephone interviews or CATI.

Most market research institutes are equipped with telephone studios in which a number of booths are provided to be used by interviewers. In sometimes dozens of such booths, interviewers are provided automatically with the phone numbers to call.

The above three methods involve an interviewer who is present or at the other end of a phone connection during the interaction. The interviewer is part of the event, and as we will see later, the interviewer's manner, demeanour, appearance and tone of voice is a variable to consider and can be a source of bias.

It is not unknown for telephone interviews to use paper and pencil or pen. But because computer-based questionnaires make such work so much easier, faster and, if designed well, fault free, there is no reason not to use CATI when using the phone for the administration of a questionnaire.

Self-completion Questionnaires

There are various ways to encounter respondents without the involvement of an interviewer.

Postal Paper Questionnaires: Self-completion 'interviews' involve the sending out by post or by placement at respondents' homes, or by other kinds of contacts, prepared questionnaires for respondents to complete themselves. Arrangements are made to collect the completed questionnaires or to have them sent by mail to an address. These are usually referred to as postal or mailed questionnaires. Nowadays, they have mainly been replaced by Internet questionnaires or questionnaires sent by email. But paper self-completion questionnaires are still used, for example, for customer feedback, as an alternative to Internet questionnaires where respondents do not have access to the Internet and in some other cases. Before the Internet, postal questionnaires were often used in countries with widely scattered populations for many different kinds of quantitative research. For example, in Canada, a very large country with a widely dispersed population, some market research companies used large postal panels chosen to be representative of the national population. From these would be randomly selected samples to which questionnaires would be sent by mail asking questions for different quantitative projects, often including media use.

There is one continuing and very important example of postal questionnaires in continued use today. They are not often referred to as questionnaires but rather as diaries. In several countries, radio audiences are measured through the use of self-completion diaries. This important topic is also returned to later. Diaries can also be and often are nowadays sent and completed online and many systems of radio audience measurement using a diary involve a combination of paper and online diaries, according to the wishes of, or the facilities available to, the respondent.

Self-completion Internet or Emailed Questionnaires: Sometimes these are referred to as CAWI—computer-assisted Web interviews. The problem with this acronym is the use of the word 'interview', which makes it seem that an actual interviewer is involved. In fact, Internet questionnaires have many similarities with postal questionnaires. No interviewer is directly involved. The respondent is on his/her own. Usually the questionnaire is placed on a website and the respondent is sent an email with a link (URL) to the questionnaire for him/her to follow. But occasionally, the questionnaire will be sent by email and the respondent asked to complete within the format of the file sent and to save it and return by email. This is cumbersome, prone to error and nowadays less often used.

Advantages and Disadvantages of Different Interview/Questionnaire Methods

We take the methods of respondent contact in reverse order, starting with the Internet. The Internet offers huge advantages.

The self-completion interview administered using the Internet is becoming the norm now for surveys in many parts of the world. Sometimes people in market and media research might think to write here 'most parts' of the world. But this is not yet true. It is certainly true that most quantitative research nowadays involves the use of the online methods. But this does not yet mean that this happens in most countries. Internet penetration is high in most of Europe, North America, Australasia, and in the more highly developed parts of Asia, South America and Africa. But this still leaves very large numbers of people in many countries who have no or very limited access to the Internet. And even then, access to the Internet does not mean that it can always be easily or inexpensively used. Many people in less developed areas and countries may have access to the Internet, but they may not have it at home and often one finds that it is used only at work or at an Internet café. And many of those who have Internet access at home or regularly go online at an Internet café or at work may not want to or indeed be able to use if for non-essential functions as it can be an extra cost which they cannot afford. Moreover, at work and/or at an Internet café, it may be possible or even permitted to respond to questionnaires. It may also cost the respondent some money, as in the case of those who rely on Internet cafés or libraries. In many parts of the world, the face-to-face interview remains the only realistic way to do reliable and comprehensive quantitative research.[12]

However, the advantages of using the Internet for sending and receiving questionnaires are many and obvious. Most types of surveys which have traditionally been conducted face-to-face, by telephone or by mail, can today be done online. However, using different methods usually produces some changes in results. Telephone interviewing produces some differences in responses from those carried out face-to-face. Self-completion questionnaires, whether postal or online, produce some results that are different from those obtained through telephone or face-to-face interviewing. The very situation in which the questions are put and the manner of putting them produces some differences in responses.

Here are some of the reasons for the differences. First of all, we may be dealing with changes in the universe. These differences may not be great but the universe of people who have access to the Internet and are willing and able to respond online are different from those who have no access or, if they have access, do not wish to respond to surveys through the Internet. There are likely to be demographic differences between the samples recruited or selected in different ways. Those with Internet access are likely to be younger, better off, better educated, more urbanised, and more likely to be male than female. These differences are steadily reducing in developed countries but in less developed areas, the differences remain significant and problematic.

Other differences produced by the different methodologies include the fact that the all the situations involved are different and in some cases very different. Each method involves differences in the way the questions are communicated. In the first three methods, an interviewer is involved. In the latter two, the respondent is on her/his own. In the former, the interviewer can explain if there are difficulties and misunderstandings. In the latter, there is no such possibility. This of course can produce another kind of bias because of the possibly different ways in which different interviewers may explain or present a question, whereas with a self-completion questionnaire, there is no such interviewer-led bias.

The attractions of online research are very large. Fieldwork online can be very fast. Whereas a survey involving face-to-face interviews and the selection of people in many different areas, both near and remote, can take many weeks to complete, a survey using the Internet only can produce results in a few days.

Costs online are cut to the minimum. Online surveys remove the need for interviewers, the need to transport them long distances, feed and accommodate them when they are away from base and the often high costs of printing and collating questionnaires. In an online survey, the interviewee even bears the cost of transmitting the date to whoever is doing the research.

Another major advantage of online research is that distances are irrelevant. So also are borders, the weather and other geographical factors. Surveys can include people who might not be at all easy to contact face to face. Online research also means that surveys are possible in different countries at the same time. This even makes it possible to do research in unsafe environments.

Online surveys are more convenient for the respondent who can choose when and where to respond, within a time frame which can be communicated to the respondent. Because the questionnaire is self-completed, there is no interviewer bias. The online status makes it possible to use digital technology to show pictures, play sounds, video and other material relating to the survey. Questionnaire software can be designed to prevent impossible or contradictory answers.

Some topics of a sensitive or confidential nature can be difficult to handle in a face-to-face and also a telephone interview. Experience has shown that respondents are more prepared to answer sensitive questions when faced with a questionnaire online. Experience has also shown that respondents feel more willing to be candid and they may also produce more detailed answers.

Online questionnaires have higher response rates than in telephone or face to face in Europe. Response rates for both telephone and face to face have fallen to dangerously low levels, whereby the reliability of data from traditional surveys is endangered by very high-refusal rates.

Online research has another major benefit which is as important as any other, and for some it may be its strongest attraction. Data are captured immediately. Traditional face-to-face interview questionnaires have to be entered into a computer analysis programme by a data entry person. Human error is inevitable and although it is possible to detect and correct errors, the process can be expensive and time consuming. It also causes delays. The fact that online questionnaires also allow the exact capture of the precise words of a respondent's answers to open-ended questions is another plus factor.

Reports including data tables, graphs and charts can be generated very speedily, sometimes within hours of the completion of a survey, in place of the usual days, weeks or even months.

The disadvantages are also fairly obvious and have already been noted. We are still a very long way off from a world where the Internet reaches anywhere near 100 per cent of the population. In some countries near 100 per cent coverage may be achieved soon, but there will remain many more countries which remain a long away off this level of penetration and this situation is likely to continue for many years to come.

With online questionnaires, as well as the postal ones that they have now largely replaced, it is not possible for the originator of the research to explain details to a puzzled respondent. Anyone who has had the experience of answering questions in an online survey will have come across some questions to which a response that fits the respondent is not supplied and there is no box marked 'other'. This can be very frustrating for the respondent; annoying him/her is something always to be avoided. We will come back to ways of solving this issue later.

If we are trying to measure the Internet use, online surveys are not appropriate; we know before we begin the results will be 100 per cent. Another disadvantage arises from the very fact that nobody meets anybody. In face-to-face research, a good interviewer can learn a lot that is important and valuable for a research project. He/she can observe the body language of the respondent, perhaps the condition of his/her living circumstances that may well be relevant to what is being researched and much more besides. And for kinds of research not covered in this book—product testing for example—online research offers no possibility to test products by mouth, nose or hand, or at least not without some difficulty. Products can, of course, be sent or respondents can be asked to obtain the necessary items. But personal contact may always be something that is needed for some kinds of project, even in the Internet age.

One last disadvantage is that computer users are not equally skilled or knowledgeable about how to use the facilities of their hardware. Some people may be newcomers or novices and may be put off doing anything unfamiliar or complex, requiring them to use software they are not familiar with or to do things on the keyboard or with the mouse or cursor that they have not done before. On the other hand, surveys pertaining to information technology subjects may result in over-reporting on technical matters by the many Internet users who are technology savvy. But this will bias the results if you want to know reliable information about all Internet users, not just the clever ones.

There are ways to get around some of the disadvantages and limitations of online questionnaires. One is to use hybrid methods—a mixture of more than one approach. For example, one can conduct surveys supplementing online respondents with the necessary number of interviews with a sample of those who are not accessible by this means, people sometimes called 'nonliners'. This kind of survey is called a hybrid survey.

As we shall see, problems that do arise with online questionnaires can be minimised by good questionnaire design, ensuring that all online questionnaires are self-explanatory and cover all possible responses and do not cause frustration for the respondent who wants to answer truthfully but finds that no truthful option is offered.

Designing a Questionnaire

There is a saying in English 'If you ask a silly question, you get a silly answer'. Asking questions is one of the crucial basic skills of all opinion and market research, including audience and media research. Questionnaire design is a skill that is not quickly learned. But there is a logic to it that can make it more suitable that the information being sought is provided unambiguously and in a way that can be codified and analysed.

The problem is simply put, but only with some difficulty, it is solved. Human behaviour is wonderfully varied and complex. No two people are exactly the same, even in their television and radio consumption behaviour. Opinions about anything are also very variable; no two persons think the same. We are each unique individuals and we think it is a good discipline for all market, opinion and audience researchers to remember this. This is especially so in this profession because we try to put people into categories. It is the paradox of research. In order to better understand humanity, we need to distort reality by making categories out of infinite human variety.

The process of research seeks to summarise and generalise about the immensely varied opinions, attitudes and behaviour of individual human beings. Audience research seeks to aggregate the enormously varied behaviour of thousands, even of millions of people and group them into different categories. The questions we use are designed to put people into categories that make analysis possible. In research, we simplify and, therefore, to some extent, distort reality in order to understand it, make sense of it and perhaps sometimes predict it. You could, if you had enough time, describe in detail every individual's listening, viewing and reading behaviour. It would take you an immense amount of time and you would not be helping anyone understand how people, taken as a whole, behave. Instead, we summarise an immense quantity of different individual behaviour and produce aggregate data that provide us with generalisations. The questionnaire is the main instrument that makes this possible. We put the same questions to all the sampled individuals. Their combined responses give us a picture of people as a whole.

Questions need to be precise and help the respondent provide an accurate answer. Vagueness has to be avoided. This is why many of the questions we habitually ask in every day conversations will not do in a questionnaire. For example, you might ask a friend 'What radio stations do you listen to?' Your friend may mention one station or several. Your friend might assume you mean, 'what do you listen to most' or perhaps 'what station do you most like listening to'. The question could be taken to mean 'tell me all the radio stations you ever listen to'.

Would the answer have been very different if you had asked your friend, 'What radio station do you listen to?' Would the fact that you have used the word 'station' in the singular mean that you were expecting the name of only one? Would everyone you asked this question assume it meant the same thing? These concerns about meaning do not matter much in normal conversation, but when we are carrying out research, we want each respondent to understand each question in the same way and for each question to compel the respondent, as far as possible, to give a precise response.

Asking questions about choice of radio or television station, or newspaper or magazine is a familiar requirement in media research. There are various ways in which it can be done. One approach is to ask about 'habitual' behaviour. We may ask people to say what they 'usually' do. This is not an easy thing to establish or record using a simple question. People do not always recognise habitual behaviour in themselves. Or they can sometimes report habitual behaviour rather inaccurately. They may say (and believe also) that they habitually do one thing but in fact do another more often or more regularly. Moreover, asking about habitual behaviour may mean that we forget about occasional behaviour.

Another approach is to ask about actual behaviour. Questions can be asked about media behaviour on the previous day. This is a common technique in continuous media research when a survey is repeated on a regular basis. A picture of the behaviour of the population as a whole is painstakingly built up by taking a series of 'snapshots' of, for example, radio-listening behaviour, by asking a large number of people what they listened to on the previous day. And now with new technologies, it is possible, for example, by using mobile phones, to do real-time research, say, by asking respondents about their media use over the last few minutes.

How we ask questions, the manner we use, our facial expression, even our body language can affect the way people answer. Also the order in which the questions are put and the language used in the questions can have a major and unsought influence. You can ask about the same subject in a different way and get a different answer from the same person. This was illustrated in the British TV comedy series, 'Yes Prime Minister'. Here is an extract in which Sir Humphrey, a senior civil servant, seeks to show another civil servant colleague how an opinion poll can give exactly opposite results on the same issue, in this case the reintroduction to Britain of compulsory military or national service for young people. Compulsory national service ended in Britain in the 1950s:

Sir Humphrey : Mr. Woolley, are you worried about the rise in crime among teenagers?'

Woolley : 'Yes.'

Sir Humphrey : 'Do you think there is a lack of discipline and vigorous training in our comprehensive schools?'

Woolley : 'Yes.'

Sir Humphrey : 'Do you think young people welcome some structure and leadership in their lives?'

Woolley	:	'Yes.'
Sir Humphrey	:	'Do they respond to a challenge?'
Woolley	:	'Yes.'
Sir Humphrey	:	'Might you be in favour of reintroducing National Service?'
Woolley	:	'Yes.'

Sir Humphrey Appleby then poses the questions in a rather different way. See what happens.

Sir Humphrey	:	'Mr. Woolley, are you worried about the danger of war?'
Woolley	:	'Yes.'
Sir Humphrey	:	'Are you unhappy about the growth of armaments?'
Woolley	:	'Yes'.
Sir Humphrey	:	'Do you think there's a danger in giving young people guns and teaching them how to kill?'
Woolley	:	'Yes.'
Sir Humphrey	:	'Do you think it is wrong to force people to take up arms against their will?'
Woolley	:	'Yes.'
Sir Humphrey	:	'Would you oppose the reintroduction of National Service?'
Woolley	:	'Yes.'[13]

Note the use of emotionally charged language. Also note how questions follow each other in an inexorable direction, leading the respondent, almost whatever his or her views, towards one opinion and then towards the exact opposite. Reputable researchers would not ask such leading questions, nor would they 'funnel' questions in this way, leading the respondent, virtually without an alternative, towards a particular answer.

This is, of course, an extreme example to illustrate the point, but we hope it shows how sentence structures, the choice of certain emotive phrases and words can affect response. Tone of voice and 'body language'—the physical manner of the questioner—not reproduced on the printed page, are also major factors. There are many examples one could give from market and opinion research experience where results are biased by the way questions are asked. The term 'halo effect' is used to describe the way questions can influence one another by their wording or their position in the respective context of the questionnaire.

The following questions were used in a survey of households in Delhi, India's capital city, designed to find out viewers' reactions to newly introduced cable television (CTV). (Note: Doordarshan is the name of the national Indian state TV channel.)

- Some of the CTV feature films contain sex/violence which affects the minds of children. What is your opinion about this aspect of CTV?
- Do you think that exposure to such a large number of films (through CTV) with excessive sex/violence will affect the moral/ethical values in our society?
          1. Yes   2. No   3. Don't Know/Can't Say
- It is generally believed that indiscreet showing of foreign films on CTV without removing objectionable scenes/dialogues (unlike Doordarshan which shows only classical/award-winning foreign films and even removes some objectionable scenes) is a direct invasion on our culture. What is your opinion about this?[14]

What is wrong with these questions? Many of us may agree that films containing sex or violence should not be shown on television, at least not during times when children might be watching. Others, while not necessarily approving of some things that are shown, believe that there should be no censorship and that viewers should be able to choose what to watch. But the purpose here, presumably, is to discover if viewers watch such films and what their opinions of such films are. The respondent should not be told what to think. The first two questions are very difficult to ask in a neutral way, but the effort must be made if the results are to reflect true opinions and not what the respondent feels he or she is expected to say.

The third question is very biased. A better way would be to offer a range of opinions and ask the respondent with which he or she agreed. The list of what is wrong with these questions when used in this way to measure opinion could be longer.

The point to make here is that there is a reliable way to measure opinions. That is, to use a question that offers the respondent a variety of different opinions that he or she is invited to agree or disagree with. This is a more reliable way of finding people's opinions without the questions used influencing them unduly. Try these examples of a better way of measuring opinions about films on television. You could read out the following opinions and record whether the respondent agrees or disagrees with each of them.

- Films often contain scenes which I find offensive.
- Films containing scenes involving sexual behaviour should be edited before showing on TV.

- Films containing scenes of violent behaviour should be edited before showing on TV.
- Films should be shown without censorship but with due warning of what to expect. The viewer can decide whether to watch or not.
- Foreign films provide entertainment and variety and I welcome the freedom to choose myself what to view.

In each case, the person questioned should be asked to choose his or her reply from the following categories:

- Agree strongly
- Agree somewhat
- No opinion either way
- Disagree somewhat
- Disagree strongly

An alternative and equally valid way would be to ask the respondent which of the opinion statements is closest to his or her opinion.

You could try these questions out on people. There are many possible views about sex and violence on TV and in films. What questions would give a more accurate measure of the range and strength of opinions?

It is very important that thorough attention is given to the design of the questionnaire—its layout, the order and the wording of the questions. It is often the stage in research which is most neglected. Sometimes the faults in a questionnaire are very obvious and would be noticed easily if the researcher had simply tried it out on someone. New questionnaires should be pilot tested before final use in the field.[15]

What goes into the questionnaire is determined by the purpose of the research. The designer of the questionnaire needs to keep a balance between the number of questions that could be asked and how many can be safely included. If the questions are too few to cover the requirements of the research, the project will fail. But it will also fail if the questionnaire is so long and complicated that it wearies either the interviewer or interviewee, or both. There can be a tendency to 'play safe' and include everything that might be needed. The real skill is to reduce the number of questions down to those that are essential to meet the research objectives. Generally speaking, the accuracy of replies declines as questionnaires get longer. Opinions and practices vary in the research community. In our view and from our experience, we would try to avoid a questionnaire that takes more than 45 minutes to administer, and one should plan for this to be a maximum, rather than an average.

Questions to Ask before Designing Questions

There are four important questions for the designer of any questionnaire:

Q1. Will all respondents understand the question in the same way and give the meaning intended?

Q2. Will the respondents know the answer? Can you reasonably expect them to know?

Q3. Will the respondent, even if he or she knows the answer, tell the truth?

Q4. Will the question, as put, provide the information intended?

Only if the answer to each of these questions is 'yes', should the particular question be used. If you are not sure, pilot testing should provide the answer.

We have already considered Q1—how the question is understood when using the example of how we might ask a friend to say what radio station he or she listened to. Vague and imprecise questions, which can be understood in a number of different ways, should be replaced by precise and unambiguous ones. 'What radio station do you listen to most frequently' is more precise and is likely to provide a more consistent response. By consistency, we mean that everyone can be expected to understand the meaning of the question in the same way.

Q2 may be less easy to resolve. We often ask people detailed questions about their listening to the radio or watching the television yesterday. We may also ask them what newspapers or magazine they have read that day or the previous day. Can we expect them to remember what they had read two days ago? Perhaps we can, but what about three or more days before the interview? Respondents may be unable to answer a question about household income. We often need information on levels of income in order to categorise respondents according to their level of wealth. The wage earner can be expected to know, but if the wage earner is the husband and we are interviewing the wife, she may not know what their household income is.

There is no easy solution to this problem. Experience within different circumstances and cultures will point to the best solution. Sometimes a general ranking of the household's level of wealth can be obtained by asking questions instead about household ownership of various items—bicycle, radio set, electric or gas cooker, refrigerator, analogue or digital television, motor car and so on. The more these items are owned, the greater the effective wealth of the household. There is usually less of a problem about asking questions about what people own than what they earn.

The problem of respondents not knowing the answer to some questions is added to when they may know but not be willing to say—Q3. The respondent may know but not be willing to tell you! For example, the respondent may know how much he/she earns but not be prepared to tell you! He or she may not tell you the truth, fearing, despite assurances of confidentiality that the information may be passed to the income tax authorities. The respondent may give an answer that is less than the truth.

One solution to this is not to ask for a precise figure but to show a range of income levels on a card or read them out and ask the respondent to select the category into which he or she fits. The point is to find a range between poverty at one end and wealth at the other, and to try to design each category in the range that will give you subtotals of data in each income category sufficient for the analyses you will want to do. The purpose here is not to measure relative poverty or wealth but to provide demographic data for important and relevant analysis of the data for which your research is designed—and as far as we are concerned here, this would be to help us with understanding media consumption.

- Less than €500
- Between €501 and €1,000
- Between €1,001 and €2,000
- Between €2,001 and €4,000
- Between €4,001 and €6,000
- More than €6,000

Q4 is one that you need to ask about all questions used. Will the question, as put, provide the information intended? Let us illustrate this by returning to the question of income because it contains many other problems and illustrates the wider issue of designing questions that need to cover all kinds of people in very different situations. Remember that the same question needs to be addressed to both the very rich and the very poor and all levels in between. You might think the question—'what is your current income?'—which would be acceptable, provided we can overcome the problems already addressed. But what will the respondent suppose 'income' to mean? Is it household income? Do we mean cash only? In many societies, cash is not the best indicator of real income, especially, for example, among peasant farmers.

The problem is that unless you make it quite clear what you mean, the definition of income will be provided by the respondent and there will be uncontrolled variation in how people answer. A way around this problem can be to ask those in paid employment about cash income and then to ask all respondents about their other means of income in cash or kind. The question or questions used will need to reflect the local situation. This is a good example of the importance of pilot testing and of thinking carefully about the meaning and purpose of each question and of relating the questionnaire to the cultural circumstances in which you are operating.

Not All Questions Are Answerable!

You should avoid asking questions that should not be asked. It is surprising how often this happens, even in areas where there is a lot of experience in survey research. Most common of all is the question which requires a respondent to remember something in great detail. In Europe, it is common practice in audience research to ask detailed questions in surveys about what respondents listened to yesterday. Respondents are taken through the day in clearly defined time 'slots' sometimes each as short as five minutes. But one has to doubt whether anyone can remember what they did on the previous day with this degree of accuracy. Fifteen or thirty minute time periods are in more common use.

Questions asking people in great detail about something in the past may be a waste of effort. How far back is it reasonable to expect people to remember things with a fair degree of accuracy? And does this vary according to culture and tradition? Generally, accuracy declines with the length of the period of recall. People remember what they did on the previous day better than what they did on the day before that, and so on.

This is an important issue for questionnaire design in radio and television research because it is likely that some recall or memory questions will be used; probably more than in other forms of opinion and market research. But we must not expect too much of our respondents' memories.

The degree of detail required may determine the length of the recall period. As has been noted, it is a common practice in Europe to build up a picture of daily radio listening by asking respondents in a face-to-face interview what they listened to on the previous day. With the assistance of the interviewer, most people are usually able to build up quite a detailed account of what they heard on the radio the previous day. It greatly helps if the interviewee has a detached list of times of programmes and programme sequences on the different networks on the previous day. But to ask the interviewee to remember the same degree of detail for the day before yesterday would increase the difficulty. Both the difficulty and inaccuracy increases the further you attempt to get the respondent to remember.

In audience research, we often need to measure media behaviour on different days of the week. We need, in effect, a lot of different 'yesterdays'.

This is a problem in radio audience research and it can be dealt with in one of the two ways. One way is to carry out interviews with a sample of the population every day. But this is an expensive option. An alternative is to give or send out self-completion diaries to a representative sample of the target population. These are, in reality, self-completion questionnaires, with the respondent being asked to note what times he or she listens to the radio over the next few days, to what network and so on. We will describe diaries in more detail later as they are often used in the measurement of radio listening.

In audience research, it may not be possible to obtain accurate information about day-to-day listening habits from a one-off survey. But if we consider what we really need to know, we can ask; for example, 'Have you heard programme X on the radio in the past seven days?' or 'When you last heard the radio can you remember what you heard?'

Types of Question

There are many things that the designer of a questionnaire needs to know. Some are the well-known rules or guidelines that we have outlined. Others will be learned through experience; what works in one culture or society may not work in another. A questionnaire is itself a cultural product; it is very important to make sure it is appropriate to the social and cultural context in which it is used and does not import assumptions, values or opinions from another.

Questions can be put into nine broad categories.

Open-ended or Verbal Questions: The expected response ranges from a single word or phrase to an extended comment. Let us use an example that relates to what you are doing right now. Someone could ask you, 'What are your opinions of this book so far?' If the question were an open-ended one in a questionnaire, whatever you reply would have to be written down by the interviewer. This poses problems. You might speak very fast and the interviewer would have to try to write down whatever you said, or else try to summarise it as best he or she could.

Open-ended questions can elicit a wide range of responses and can reflect a great diversity of opinion and behaviour. But a major disadvantage, among many, is that the answers can be extremely difficult to analyse and report. When you have collected all the answers—and there could be a very wide range of them—they have to be categorised somehow in order to produce some kind of summary of responses.

Another problem is that there is a high risk of interviewer bias. The interviewer may not have either the time or the space to record all that the respondent says and so has to try to summarise the reply. Interpretation is involved and this will certainly differ between interviewers, leading inevitably to bias and distortion in what is recorded and reported.

Open-ended questions are often used in a pilot test to provide the list of likely responses to be used in the final questionnaire. However, there is another important use of the open-ended question. It is often important and valuable to give people the chance to express themselves freely on one of the topics being researched. Respondents may well have something to say which is not covered by the structured part of the questionnaire. An open-ended question may be a valuable 'safety-valve' for the expression of strong opinions. This technique can be used at the end of a questionnaire and interviewees often welcome the chance to express views freely. It may not be necessary to code these responses for analysis. The experienced researcher can extract the main themes of such answers ('verbatims') by careful and extended reading.

Open-ended questions are also very often used in self-completion questionnaires when the respondent is free to write down views and opinions. In this case, there is, of course, no interviewer bias. But in both face-to-face interviews and self-completion questionnaires, open-ended questions can help to sustain interest. A long and fully structured questionnaire with preset answers and boxes to be ticked may become rather tedious for both interviewer and respondent. The respondent may have things he or she wants to say but which are not called for. So, an open-ended question can be a useful safety valve. It can also help to focus attention on a new topic if you include an open-ended question at the beginning of a new set of questions about that topic.

Online questionnaires have given new life to the open-ended questionnaire. Respondents are allowed and may be even encouraged to write exactly what they want about the matter being researched. What can then be a valuable data set of individual responses about a topic or series of topics can be analysed using one of the many word and theme analysis packages referred to later in the section on online qualitative research. Text analysis software has taken a lot of the tedious and time-consuming labour off our hands to everyone's advantage.

List Questions: With this kind of question, a list of prepared optional answers is offered, any of which may be chosen. Sometimes only one answer can be chosen, at other times, the respondent may select more than one answer, sometimes referred to as 'multipunch'.[16]

List questions are often used to measure opinions. A pilot survey carried out beforehand with open-ended questions can collect a range of opinions about something. The most common responses, simplified and summarised, can be listed on the final questionnaire. The respondent may be asked which opinion is closest to his or her own, the alternative of 'other response' also being offered and recorded where appropriate.

Use of list questions in place of open-ended questions removes the interviewer bias that is difficult to avoid with open-ended questions. It also has the advantage of uniformity of meaning, making comparisons possible. There is still space for those answers that still do not appear in the list by offering the option 'other' and leaving a space for the 'other' view to be entered.

How long should a list of options be in such a question? There is no fixed maximum, but remember that the longer the list, the greater the difficulty the respondent will have in making a choice and the more difficulty you may have in interpreting the results. A smaller number of possible answers may distort reality more but makes interpretation easier. In research, we attempt to generalise and summarise the infinite variety of human behaviour, choice and opinion in order to understand them better, quantify them and be able to explain and predict them more accurately. But all forms of quantitative research by questionnaire attract the legitimate criticism that they distort reality. They do, but only to make sense of it. This is the paradox of all quantitative research.

List questions can be used in several ways and for several kinds of information. Here, for example, is a list question from a media research questionnaire used in Namibia.

What is your main source of news? That is, where do you receive information about what is happening in the world, your country and in your area?[17]

[Interviewer instruction:] Record as many as given

Television

Radio

Newspapers/magazine

Family

Friends or neighbours

Church/mosque

Public meetings

Other (Write in) . . . .

The question can then be put asking the respondent to name the single most important source using the same list. Note that the same grid can be used with two columns to the right, the first being for all sources used by the respondent and the second for the single most important source. In the 'Other' category, the precise answer stated should be written by the interviewer or by the respondent if this is a self-completion questionnaire.

List questions may be used to measure household equipment and facilities—electric cooker, refrigerator, flushing toilet, electric light, running water, phone line, computer, and also personal and portable items such as mobile phones and similar items. In this case, obviously multiple answers may be given and recorded.

Sometimes lists are read out to the respondent. Sometimes this may not be necessary. For household facilities, for example, the interviewer may be able to see him/herself what is there. With sources of news, it is our experience that the best approach is to simply ask the question about the source or sources of news and record the answers given and not to read out the list of possible sources.

Observant readers may have noticed two things here. The question above asks, 'What is your main source of news?' As the word 'source' is given in the singular, will some respondents not think that they are to give only one? The question when asked first probably would be better in the plural—'sources'—and the word 'source' in the singular used for the second question for the single most important source. The second observation or objection lies in the explanatory sentence: 'That is, where do you receive information about what is happening in the world, your country and in your area?' You might point out that different sources would be likely to be used for different types of news. This also is likely and the solution would be to ask the same question three times for the different kinds of news topics. If you spotted either of these problems, well done. If you did not, you soon will. It is these kinds of things you need to train yourself to notice and amend. Questionnaires need to have as little ambiguity or scope for misunderstanding, or scope for different kinds of understanding as it is possible to make them.

There is a tendency for items at the beginning or end of read-out lists to be selected by respondents. This 'list order bias' effect can be neutralised by changing the order in which the list is read out, usually by rotating it, choosing a different starting point with each successive interview. This is common practice and should be adopted in all cases. Interviewers need to remember this because it would be very complex and costly to print questionnaires with rotated lists. It can and often is done automatically with Internet based questionnaires and also CATI and CAPI interviews.

Category Questions: These are a variation on the list questions. Categories are provided in order to group a range of responses. For example, when we ask respondents the educational level that they reached, there might be a wide range of responses. What we can do is to create a list in which educational levels are grouped into categories. The question asked is usually something like 'What was the level you reached in education?' The interviewer would have a list summarising the different levels from no education up to a university degree or post-graduate qualification. The response is marked accordingly. A category question was illustrated earlier as a way of collecting information about income where different levels of income were summarised into a series of categories or ranges.

Ranking Questions: These are another way of measuring views and opinions. The respondent is asked to put possible answers in rank order of importance to him/her. Respondents might be asked to rank in order of desirability a list of choices for new radio programmes or popularity of different presenters. Some detail might have to be given to help people make informed choices, but this method is often used to measure opinions and explore listeners' priorities.

You might ask respondents to say what were, for them, the most important types of programme on radio or television. Number one could be given to the most important category, number two to the next and so on. In the analysis, it is simply necessary to add the scores and the overall response with the lowest score is the most favoured. One could, of course use the numbers around the other way, giving the highest number to the most important down to the lowest number to the least important. From this, one obtains a rank order of responses which may reflect no single individual's view but is an average of all of them.

You might well use a ranking question to measure the popularity of presenters or to rank entertainment programmes. The same method could also be used for more serious purposes. Let us suppose that you wanted to know how farmers wanted to get information about new seeds or fertilisers. You might ask a question something like this:

The following are possible ways in which information about new seeds or fertilisers could be announced or made available to farmers. Please rank them in order of preference for you. Give your first choice the number 1, the next choice the number 2 and so on down to the number 7 for the information source which is the least important to you.

- Announcements on the radio
- Announcements in a farming magazine
- Information to come from agricultural extension workers in this area
- Information to be sent to you in the mail
- Information to be sent by email

- Through advertising
- Other—Please state ....

When all the replies are collected, analysis would give you a series of scores for the different possible ways of obtaining agricultural information. The one with the lowest number (nearest to the top score of 1) would be the most popular medium to supply information or the one with the highest overall priority.

A modification of the ranking question is one in which the respondent is given a set of scores or numbers to assign to a list of possibilities. With the above list, every item is given a score, even if only a low one. Instead, the respondent may be given a fixed number of points or numbers to distribute. He or she can then give no points at all to those things of no interest or importance and give more points to those things that are really wanted. He/she can even give all the points to one category if that one matters so much to the respondent.

For example, we might give the respondent 36 points to distribute among all the possibilities. He or she might distribute these evenly among three or four favourite projects and give no points at all to the others. Or, even give all the points to one if he/she cared that much for it. It is a way of capturing such enthusiasms very well.

Scale Questions: These are a little more complex than ranking questions. A common form is what is called an ordinal scale. For example, respondents may be read a statement, 'The television network should always play a feature film after the evening news' or 'Most locally made television programmes are of poor quality', and then be asked for an opinion ranging from 'strongly disagree' to 'strongly agree'.

A coding frame is provided thus:

Strongly disagree	0
Disagree somewhat	1
Neither agree nor disagree	2
Agree somewhat	3
Strongly agree	4

Note that we suggested this scheme as a better way of assessing opinions about foreign films on television in India in the example cited earlier. The order can equally well be reversed. Each point is assigned a number 0 to 4. The overall score will be a measure of opinion. This can, for ease of comprehension, be converted into a percentage. The sum of scores for each category of answer is divided by the number of responses (omitting non-responses). The resultant number multiplied by 25 gives a score out of one hundred. In the above case, the score would indicate the level of agreement and would enable comparisons to be made with similar questions or with the same question over time.

Some experts think that one should try to remove the middle position 'neither agree nor disagree' in order to obtain a clearer idea of opinion. We will use an example from a survey for the national broadcaster in Namibia to illustrate. Here, the question is designed to discover what viewers and listeners think about the National Broadcasting Company (NBC).

'In our work as market researchers, people have told us about various opinions they have concerning radio, television and the Namibian Broadcasting Corporation. Would you please tell me how much you personally agree or disagree with each of these statements by giving me one of the answers from this card? Would you say you agree strongly, tend to agree, tend to disagree or disagree strongly that the NBC . . .?'

([Interviewer instruction] Read out each statement in turn and record <u>one</u> answer for each)[18]

Statements	Agree Strongly	Tend to Agree	Tend to Disagree	Disagree Strongly
a. Understands the needs of the people				
b. Is wasting money				
c. Is educating the people of Namibia				
d. Is government controlled				
e. Is promoting the English as the country's language				
f. Is helping you with your education				
g. Is important for the country				
h. Has programmes of a very high quality				
i. Is politically neutral				
j. Represents the people of Namibia				
k. Is a parastatal				
l. Is controlled by an independent board				

Note that there is no middle position—'Neither Agree Nor Disagree'. The respondent is urged to choose one side or the other. The question uses the word 'tend' to encourage respondents to indicate which side of the argument they tend towards even if they do not hold strong views.

In the above examples, a four or five point scale has been used. There is no rule against a greater or a smaller size of scale. In our experience, four or five give the most easily analysed results.

In the Namibian case, the results, once added up and a mean score calculated, would tell the NBC on which side of the line—agreeing or disagreeing—the listeners tended to fall, and by what margin of strength. Sometimes it will be necessary to analyse results further. For example, a mean score right in the middle of the two extremes might mean that there were no strong opinions either way. But it might also mean that strongly opposing views were evenly balanced. These are rather different and you may want to know in which groups of the population the opposing and strongly held opinions were expressed. Analysis of the data should provide an answer.

Another author of this study proposes to use a 'points' scale from 0 ('very bad' or 'does not fit at all') to 10 ('very good' or 'fits perfectly') which in his opinion lends itself to measurement of a great number of phenomena—with a value of 6.5 points being the 'threshold value' above which a product becomes suitable for the market.

Quantity Questions: The response to a quantity is a number, exact or approximate, in answer to a question asking for information that can be supplied in numerical form. How many people live in your household? How many radio sets in working order are there at home? How many television sets do you have? The actual number can be recorded. You might ask the following question recording the number of items in each category that the household being visited has.

	Number in Household
Portable radio set	
Other radio	
Music/cd player (not portable)	
MP3/iPod portable personal music player	
Television	
Video recorder	
Computer	
Mobile phone	

Grid Questions: In these, a table or grid is used to record answers to more than one question at the same time. These require practice but in the end, they help both interviewer and the person who does the analysis.

For example, you might need to know what media facilities or equipment are available for use now in the home and what might be purchased or become available over the next year. Sometimes the latter is called 'intention to purchase'. We are measuring two aspects at the same time, ownership or intention to own what can be quite a long list of items. A typical grid question for this purpose might look like this:

Which of the following items does your household have now? Which of these do you think you might purchase or which might become available to you over the next twelve months?[19]

	Owned/in use now	Intention to Purchase/ Obtain within a Year
Car radio		
Portable radio		
Music/cd player/hifi		
MP3/iPod/personal music player		
Television		
Satellite dish		
Cable connection		
DVD/Video recorder		
Computer		
Mobile phone		
Landline phone		
Internet access (dialup)		
Internet access (broadband)		

It is very important to avoid too many lines and too many columns in grid questions lest respondents are 'seduced' to fill in quickly in one line ('straight liners'). As a rule of thumb, no more than 12 lines down and 6 lines across should be used. It is better to start a new grid if the number of lines exceeds the dozen.

Two Choice Questions: These are sometimes called 'binary' or 'dichotomous' questions. Some examples can illustrate the type.

- Did you listen to the radio yesterday?
- Do you have Internet Access at your home?
- Is your TV linked to a satellite dish?
- When you want to hear some music, and given the choice of listening to the radio or your own recordings which would you usually choose?

These questions, very often of the Yes/No type, are easy to handle and analyse by computer, or manually. They make 'routing' within a questionnaire relatively simple. Someone who answers 'Yes' to the question—'Did you listen to the radio yesterday?'—can then be asked further questions about radio schedules, networks, programmes and so on, while the one who answers 'No' is taken to a later section of the questionnaire. The last two-choice question provides two possible answers—radio or own recordings. Dichotomous questions make it very easy to group respondents into subgroups for subsequent analysis.

However, the two-choice question should not be overused. You might want to divide your respondents into heavy and light users of the radio. It could be tempting to use one question to determine this. Perhaps you might ask whether on the previous day the respondent listened for more or less than one hour, using this as the criterion for light or heavy listening. But this could be very misleading. A better way would be to look at listening behaviour over a longer period. If you do use two-choice questions to categorise or group respondents, make sure you use a question that defines them fairly and accurately.

Probing Questions: These are usually used only in interviewer-administered questionnaires. They may not be written into the questionnaire. But they can be standardised in order to avoid interviewer bias. For example, a standard probing question would be asking 'Anything else?' or 'Can you explain that a little bit more?' They are sometimes useful when asking people to remember something they did yesterday. When we talk of 'aided recall', it can refer to the use of additional probing questions used to aid memory about previous behaviour.

There may be other kinds of questions that might be devised but the above list covers all kinds that are normally used in quantitative market research.

Making Questions Work

The quality of the answers you get depends greatly on the way the questions are worded in the questionnaire. It is easy to forget the need to be precise and to avoid language that means different things to different people. Consider the following question and the range of responses offered:

'How much time do you spend watching television?' (Tick box).

    a. A great deal   ☐
    b. A moderate amount   ☐
    c. Not a lot   ☐
    d. No time at all   ☐

The only precise answer would be the last one. The others would have no definite meaning. All you would be measuring would be subjective opinions of the amount of time spent on listening. For one person, an hour a day would be 'a great deal' while for another it would be 'not a lot'. Never forget that the quality of research results is determined by the questions asked. If the questions are imprecise, no amount of clever statistical analysis afterwards will give the results any greater precision.

There is another kind of problem. Can you see any difficulty with the following two questions?

Q.1   Does your radio have the facility to receive FM? Yes/No
Q.2   What kind of radio do you have? (Tick box)

a.   Portable   ☐
b.   Car radio   ☐
c.   Tuner in a stereo system (with record or cd player)   ☐

How would you deal with the problem(s) you have noticed? (There are at least two.) The key thing to check is this. Do the questions work equally well for the person with ten radio sets and the person with only one? Are there clear instructions for the interviewer?

The first question would be more precise and, therefore have more use if it were: 'Do you have *any* radio with FM or VHF?' (The only problem then is that many people are not familiar with some technical terms like 'FM' or 'VHF'. It may be better to ask to see the person's sets to verify if they do indeed have the facility to receive FM broadcasts.) With the ever greater complexity of digital hardware, being able to inspect the equipment is even more valuable. (Of course, the interviewer needs to know what to look for. If you are doing research online, of course such inspections are impossible.)

The second question about the kind or kinds of radio sets at the respondent's home will not tell us about the number of sets the respondent has. If you need to know, you will have to add a question in which you ask how many of each category the person possesses.

There is another problem which is trickier but which is essential to tackle. What is meant by 'you'? Usually we need to find out about access at the respondent's homes. The person interviewed may not be the head of the household or the owner of any of the equipment asked about. He or she may not personally own any media equipment of any kind. In many cases, because of random selection within a household, we will be interviewing a youth, another relative of the head of the household or other person normally living there. We should beware of asking questions implying the ownership of radios, televisions and other household equipment in large, extended households where such things may be shared. Guard against imposing views of family structure or of the respective roles of men and women from your own background. Be ready to notice when your questionnaire, perhaps drawn up against a different background of assumptions and attitudes, does not really fit the situation. Be prepared to change it.

Sometimes questions may presume certain views. Consider the following question:

'Does your local radio station provide an adequate service?'

The presumption here is that the respondent has an idea of what an adequate local radio service would be. This question might work quite well but may need to be followed by more questions for clarity.

There is another point to look out for or be aware of. Opinion tends to lead towards leaving things as they are, and in general people tend to prefer to say 'Yes' than 'No', and they tend to approve positive statements more than negative ones. These tendencies are related. Let us use some hypothetical examples. Consider these questions:

- Do you think that the proportion of films shown on TV from other countries should be reduced?
- Do you think our TV should increase the proportion of our own country's films shown?

These are different questions of course, but each is the reverse side of the other. If you increase the proportion of indigenous material, you reduce the proportion of non-indigenous or foreign material. If respondents were logical and consistent, the support for the first proposition should be the same as that for the second. In reality, it might not be. There is a tendency in many cultures to approve of positive steps (increase, improve, enhance) and disapprove of negative ones (restrict, prohibit, prevent).

We noted above that respondents often do not understand technical terms. Avoid specialist language and try to find the words that people are more likely to be familiar with. All fields of human activities develop their own specialist language. It should be avoided in questionnaires. Broadcasters speak of 'genres' of programme. It is best in questions about 'genres' to use words like 'types' or 'kinds' of programmes. If you want to know about the 'technical quality of radio reception', avoid these words and ask how well the radio can be heard. Radio is subject to 'interference', but you may find that few people use this word. 'Can you always hear the programmes clearly?' or 'Do you sometimes find difficulty in hearing programmes' are better ways to obtain information about reception quality.

The Order of Questions

The structure and order of questions is important. 'Funnelling' is helpful here, but not in the way that Sir Humphrey did it in the passage from the TV comedy, 'Yes Prime Minister'. Good funnelling is when the questionnaire moves from the general to the more particular in a way that will not bias the response.' For example, if you asked the question 'Have you read the Daily Mail in the past seven days?' as your opening question, you might get a startled response. One would start with a general question and then focus on the particular. It might run something like this:

I want to ask some questions about newspapers and magazines. Do you ever get to read any?

(If yes) What do you read most?

Have you ever read the Daily Mail?

When did you last read the Daily Mail?

Funnelling like this is appropriate. Where there is a danger is when it comes to opinion questions; funnelling can then tend to bias response.

It is important to avoid undue influence, sometimes called the halo effect or other contamination between one question and another. In the example quoted earlier from the TV comedy show, Sir Humphrey's questions were asked in such a way as to lead almost inevitably towards a particular set of replies. What he did was not only to use biased language but also to use the juxtaposition of questions to assist the process of obtaining the response he wanted. He did this to prove his opinion that opinion research can make anyone say almost anything. There is some truth in his charge and that is why we need to be aware of the danger and take all steps to remove it. The example we used was taken from a TV comedy, but there are some examples from real life.

The order in which questions are asked can also influence and even change response. In 1939, when the Second World War began in Europe, the United States was not at first involved. There was a poll containing these two related questions:

- Do you think that the United States should permit American citizens to engage in the German army?
- Do you think that the United States should permit American citizens to join the British army?

The questions were asked in a different order in order to see if this affected the response. It did to a significant degree.[20]

		Order 1 - 2	Order 2 - 1
	Yes	22%	31%
Question 1	No	74%	61%
	No Opinion	4%	8%
	Yes	40%	45%
Question 2	No	54%	46%
	No Opinion	6%	9%

Public opinion in the United States was generally against involvement in another European war, but there was more support for the British and Allied cause than for Germany. When the question order was reversed and serving in the British forces was suggested first, there was a greater degree of support for the idea of US citizens serving in a foreign army. And note that this applied to both questions.

How can this bias be avoided, and which set of results is the truth? The answer is that probably the only way to avoid this contamination across questions in this particular case would have been to separate the two questions and put them in different parts of the questionnaire. As to which is the truth, the answer is that all the two sets of responses are equally valid but that in both cases, respondents' views as expressed have been affected by the context. If uncontaminated responses are essential, then these questions have to be separated. But the argument about what is true does not end there. Opinion polling as well as other forms of quantitative data when measuring opinions and feelings tends to show the reality that people's views are often affected by separate or discrete factors which we may or may not be aware of.

Questionnaire Design for Online Research

We now need to take a look at questionnaire design when using the Internet or emails. One of the most important things to remember is that asking questions online (as well as through a mailed questionnaire) is different in many important ways from face-to-face and telephone interviews. There is no interviewer at hand to explain things. The respondent faces the questionnaire on a screen—in most cases alone. Therefore, the design of the questionnaire is crucial. Everything must be done to make the online questionnaire not only well understood but also agreeable and interesting for the respondent. This will reduce fatigue, prevent malpractices such as 'straight lining' (filling in a multi-line matrix question in a straight line down the page) and keep respondents from breaking off in the middle of the exercise. As a result, response rates will be improved. This is very important. One of the most important resources in all media research is made up of the respondents we need to use. It must be a rule for all of us involved in questionnaire research to make the experience as enjoyable and interesting as we can. Those who abuse this and bore the respondent are doing our profession a great disservice. In fact, experience has shown that most online research appears to be done well and to heed this advice. Response rates show that generally people appear to enjoy answering questions online. Response rates in the developed world are much higher online than face to face or telephone.

The Internet actually makes it possible to do things that neither a paper and pencil questionnaire nor a telephone interview can do. And as we shall now see, there are some kinds of questions that are unique to online research because they depend on HTML computer formatting. Here are a few of these, and others are referred to elsewhere in the book.

The Slider: Unlike in the use of conventional scales (steps tagged with numbers or phrases used in paper questionnaires), by moving the slider bar which displays on the respondent's computer screen, the respondent records his/her judgement. Here is an example of a slider used for TV programme appreciation when doing this kind of research online.

Move the slider to indicate what you thought of the programme		
entertaining	══▉══	boring
good presenter	═▉════	bad presenter
nice pictures	══▉═══	dreary
informative	═══▉══	not informative

It is also possible to have sliders in different formats. The idea of the slider is to avoid any pre-conditioning of the respondent. Thus, the slider should be empty with the slider bar sitting in the centre before being operated. The polarities to be measured should be described at either end of the slider as they are in this illustration.

Drag and Drop: This technique makes good use of the ability on any modern computer to select something using the mouse and cursor to drag an item on screen and move it somewhere else. In order to select the preferred products from a series of competing offers, the drag-and-drop question is quite often used in online questionnaires and is a major advantage and advance in quantitative research using online methods. Question types that contain things to choose and rate or link to something else by moving around the screen are popular with respondents because answering the questionnaire is more fun.

As in all forms of research, extremes should be avoided. Long and dry paperwork transferred to the Web, like for like, will not make an online questionnaire work very well. You need to make best use of what the Internet can do to make the experience work well for the respondent as well as getting you the data you are seeking. An online questionnaire should be properly designed from the beginning. It should contain not only text but also some additional optical stimuli such as little images or drawings. But each individual screen page presented to the respondent should not be overloaded.

One major plus point for online questionnaires is that they can be designed to remove most errors. If a respondent has failed to answer a question, he/she will be reminded of this. If more than one answer is permitted, the questionnaire presented will allow this; but, if only one answer is being sought, it will not allow more than one to be selected. Routing of questions is automatic and quick. For example, in a sequence of questions about media use, those who answer 'No' to the question 'do you ever listen to radio'? will not be taken then to any further question about radio stations or programmes. A very large number of automated sequences can be devised that will automatically be correctly administered and in the right order. That cannot be said for face-to-face or telephone interviewing unless they are computer assisted as in CAPI and CATI explained earlier in this section.

Reliability

Reliability in this context of questionnaire design is a measure of the extent to which a questionnaire produces similar results on different occasions. A tractor that sometimes pulls a heavy load but at other times cannot even be started is unreliable. A question that produces one answer on one occasion but a different answer (from the same person or similar person with the same characteristics) on another is unreliable. But how can we ever tell?

There are various ways of testing reliability. One is to test a question on the same person on different occasions. But a better method may be to try questions out on a number of people chosen in a similar manner. A crucial question is would different interviewers asking the same question of two random samples of people get similar results? Note the use of random samples here. We can assume, with a reasonable degree of safety, that two random samples of the same universe will show the same characteristics. We can also assume that if two interviewers produce different results from two such separate samples of the same universe using the same questionnaire, then the differences arise from differences between the two interviewers or from a fault in the questionnaire that somehow gives different results in different circumstances or at different times. This is an essential point. Unless we can be absolutely sure that the questionnaire will produce the same results when applied to samples of the same population we cannot use the questionnaire to make comparisons between populations. We would say the questionnaire was unreliable. There are various ways of measuring reliability; some of them are rather complex. Usually it is through experience that we establish which questions can be relied on to give consistent results, and of course the reliability of questions can be tested for most purposes on a pilot survey.

Validity

Validity is defined as that quality in a questionnaire which ensures that what is measured or described reflects reality. Consistency of results is not enough. A questionnaire can produce consistent results, that is, be 'reliable', but still be invalid; the results may not accurately reflect reality but instead consistently get it wrong. How can we tell?

It can be quite difficult to find out. A good example of a validity problem is sometimes experienced in radio audience research. Let us suppose that we are using a face-to-face questionnaire in which the interviewer asks a large number of respondents, randomly selected from the population, about what they listened to yesterday. The process of selection and interviewing carries on over several weeks, using the same questionnaire. From the results, you would expect to be able to calculate various things about radio listening such as, the average daily audience as a percentage of the population and the average number of hours listened to per person per day. If instead you use a self-completion listening diary to another random sample of the population, we would also be able to calculate the daily audience and the average number of hours of listening. But the two sets of data will unfortunately be different; the self-completion diary method is likely to produce higher figures. Which is valid? Do diaries encourage people to overstate their listening? Do people listen more because they are filling in a listening diary? Do people who listen very little to any radio simply not bother to send in their diaries, with the result that those who do are taken erroneously as fully representative? Does an aided recall, face-to-face interview produce an underestimate? No one is certain; it is probable that any of these happen. But which is the valid measure? It is doubtful if audience researchers can ever satisfactorily answer this question, but it may not matter too much, provided that we consistently use the same method of measurement and do not compare results arrived at using different methods, because the difference in the methods may be more significant than any real difference in behaviour. There may be some distortions within each method but these are likely to be consistent over time; each means of measurement will therefore be able to tell us what we need to know.[21]

Social and Cultural Acceptability and Self-portrayal

There is always a danger that respondents will answer questions in ways that fit in with socially acceptable norms rather than with what is true. The respondent may say he/she smokes less, drinks less, listens to more 'good' programmes, reads more educational materials and so on, than is actually the case. There is no easy way around this problem. Obviously, the interviewer must ensure that all questions are asked in a wholly neutral manner and that no hint of approval or disapproval is even hinted at by his or her manner or expression. Sometimes it is possible to use different questions about the same or similar topics in different parts of the questionnaire and these can act as a cross-check.

Pilot Testing

We generally need to test a questionnaire to see if it is going to work in the way intended. In effect, what we do is to run a mini-survey. Let us suppose we are carrying out a survey to measure the impact of a radio and TV campaign on infant nutrition. Perhaps there has also been a campaign using posters and advertisements in the press. We have decided that the best method to use is a random sample survey of women with children. A questionnaire has been designed and produced. The questions cover all the areas for investigation by the research project. What is to stop us from just going ahead?

Nothing need stop you from going ahead. You may well obtain acceptable results along the lines of what was needed and expected. But there is a risk, especially with attitude and opinion questions, that some questions will not work in the way intended. Some sections of the questionnaire may be found to be unnecessarily complex. You may have made some assumptions about attitudes that are not justified. There is no point wasting resources on questions that do not work; it wastes the time and effort of everyone. Pilot testing helps you to avoid making mistakes and can save time and effort in the long run.

To do a pilot survey, it is not necessary to go to the trouble of selecting a fully random sample. But it is important to select people who will represent a wide range of possible respondents. Will the questionnaire work equally well with old and young, rich and poor, educated and illiterate, people of different ethnic backgrounds or religious affiliations, or people of different occupations and lifestyles? Here is the chance to find out. We can test the questionnaire on as wide a range of interviewees as possible. Pilot testing is also an excellent opportunity for giving interviewers experience of the questionnaire. Mistakes and misunderstandings can be corrected. It is at this early stage that the experience and skill of the interviewers can be used to improve the questionnaire. Their comments on the way that the questionnaire works in the field should always be given proper consideration.

The pilot survey is not only a way of trying out questions and training interviewers, but we can also use the exercise to see if the results provide what is needed. Sometimes even well-designed questions do not provide useful information. They may just lead to the research equivalent of a dead end. Leave out redundant questions like these and save everyone's time. Remember also the use of pilot tests with open-ended questions in order to provide a range of possible answers for list or category questions. Some writers have called this a 'qualitative preparatory stage', when essentially qualitative methods are used to prepare something—the questionnaire—for quantitative results.

When using online questionnaires, these also need to be tested to see if they work in the way envisaged. Pilot testing online is easier and quicker than with face-to-face or telephone surveys. Even the best designed online questionnaire may have unforeseen faults, ambiguities and problems. The routing (where the respondent is taken next after answers are given to certain key questions) may not work as intended, or piloting may show that some questions cause problems for some respondents. Piloting need not involve more than a handful (20 or so is usually enough) of test respondents. And it can be done very quickly. Whether face to face, telephone, postal self-completion or online, good pilot testing can save a lot of time, prevent waste and failure of some questions, and at times it will save an entire project from failure through correcting before it is too late, something that would not have worked in the way intended.

3.3 Contacting and Interviewing Respondents: Practical Issues and Key Components of 'Traditional' Quantitative Research

This next section is entirely devoted to the interview itself. It refers only to research using a questionnaire administered by an interviewer. It does not apply to self-completion questionnaires whether done by post or online.

The Interview

For face-to-face and telephone interviews, the way the encounter with the respondent is conducted plays a large part in the success or failure of these forms of research. Training and supervision of interviewers and quality control of interviews are key elements in the success of quantitative research.

The Role of the Interviewer

The manner, the tone of voice, the 'body language' of the interviewer and the relationship between interviewer and interviewee are all important. They can influence the answers given. Not only can the person being interviewed be influenced. The interviewer can interpret answers in a way determined by expectations and prior attitudes. Consider this true story from a research methods training course. Participants from various African countries were being taught the need to avoid leading respondents towards certain answers.

They were divided into three groups for a pilot study in a rural village. A key question they were to administer asked farmers to give reasons why they did not expand their agricultural activity.

Each group of interviewers was given, separately, identical instructions. Interviewers were told not to suggest answers and not to supply examples. However, before they started, the instructor casually mentioned three likely reasons. These were mentioned separately to each group and a different reason was given to each.

To the first group, the instructor suggested that the likely reasons that the farmers would give was the shortage of land, labour and equipment.

To the second group, the instructor suggested that they would hear their respondent farmers group say that it was lack of money, seed and fertiliser.

To the third group of interviewers, he suggested that they would find their respondent farmers saying that it was the lack of roads and the distance of markets.

The interviewers selected, at random, a number of farmers. The most frequently stated set of constraints in the responses were identical with that mentioned casually by the instructor to each of the three groups. The interviewers, who had been given to expect that the problem was the shortage of land and labour, recorded this as the most common reason given by the farmers. Those who had been told to expect the lack of money, seed and fertiliser recorded this as the most common reason, and those who had expected transport difficulties recorded that this was the main constraint.

The 'casual' remarks of the instructor had influenced the results. It may have been that despite the firm instructions, interviewers confronted by the difficulty of asking an awkward question of a stranger, actually helped the person to answer or interpreted responses in the expected way.[22]

Even when the interviewer scrupulously follows the rules and says nothing apart from reading the questionnaire verbatim, there is still a tendency for the interviewer's expectations to have an influence on the way responses are interpreted and recorded. There are two ways of minimising this bias. The wording of questions needs to be as neutral as possible to avoid giving the respondent the impression that certain answers are expected. Second, interviewers need to be thoroughly trained to maintain a self-critical awareness of the twin dangers of influencing interviewees, and of a subjective interpretation of responses.

The manner and tone of voice, even the 'body language' or posture of the interviewer can be a big influence. Let us imagine you are asking questions about plans to change a TV service, or it might be a proposal to open a commercial popular music radio station, or it could be a question about the current government in power. In each case, you may have very strong views yourself. It may be hard to ask questions in a tone of voice and manner that does not communicate these views to the respondent. But it must be done, otherwise your results may be distorted and give a false reflection of reality.

There are other ways in which interviewer bias can intrude. For example, the interviewer may think it is pointless to ask all questions to everyone. One might think it is not necessary to ask questions about TV viewing of very poor people, or assume by a person's demeanour or appearance that he or she was illiterate and skip over any questions about readership of books, newspapers or magazines. But beware of making any assumptions about anyone. Appearances can be very deceptive and assumptions are often wrong. Many poor people do actually watch a lot of TV. Some people may appear to be uneducated but may in fact be otherwise. Some apparently poor people have access to mobile phones, satellite TV and more. The golden rule in research is 'don't ever make any assumptions about anybody, anywhere'. Sooner or later your assumptions will be wrong. The danger is that you may not notice and record a lot of false information.

Politeness and courtesy are very important. The interviewee is giving his or her time to provide information. It may be ultimately of benefit to him or her or even to the community, but at this stage, this may not be at all clear or certain. The interviewer needs to treat the person interviewed with care and respect. One problem that can interfere with this is social class or caste. In many cultures, it is difficult to avoid the bias which can be brought into the situation by differences in social status between the interviewer and the interviewee. It is often the case that the interviewer comes from a higher social class than the person being interviewed. The reverse can also happen. Both can affect the reliability of the answers given.

Class difference can produce a range of feelings among interviewees ranging from resentment to deference, with varying degrees of unease and even embarrassment. There are various ways of dealing with this problem. One is to recruit interviewers from all social backgrounds and use them where appropriate. But this is not always a practical solution. There are no rules about this; each circumstance requires different sets of solutions. Research fieldwork supervisors need to be alert to the problem and choose and train their field workers to be sensitive to it. Often one finds that the best team of interviewers are made up of people who seem relatively class-less and who may appear so to most people being interviewed. But what-ever one writes here will not be of much help in a general sense. Conditions and circumstances vary enormously between cultures, and experience is the best guide.

Different ethnic and religious backgrounds can also play an important part in affecting response. In some societies, it is not possible for a man to interview a woman at all, or at least the woman's husband or other close rela-tive may have to be present. Such considerations of social propriety can also affect the response. A woman may say rather different things in response to a strange man, especially if a close male relative is present than she might say to a woman with no one else present. This even applies in what we might think is the relatively 'safe' area of broadcasting. In 1985, in a survey conducted for the BBC in Pakistan, the research agency carrying out the interviewing found that among Afghans living in refugee camps, some men said they did not like their wives to listen to the radio when they were not present. Women did in fact sometimes listen to the radio, whether or not their husbands knew or approved. It was, therefore, important to be sure to interview women not in the presence of their husbands. It was also essential to use women interviewers when interviewing women respondents. This is often a way of making research among women in some Moslem communi-ties go a lot more smoothly.

There are some useful rules for administering questionnaires that all good interviewers should follow.

- Introduce yourself in a friendly way and explain in simple terms what the research is for.
- Always say how long the interview is likely to last.
- Explain that the information given is confidential and anonymous. (There may be occasions when anonymity and confidentiality may be waived, but this can be done only with the prior permission of the interviewee.)

- Check back at the end of the interview with the respondent and ask if there are any points of uncertainty or if he or she has any questions.
- Do not waste the interviewee's time or in any other way abuse the privilege he or she has granted you by agreeing to be interviewed.

Ghana Broadcasting Corporation's audience research department reported some interesting problems when their interviewers went out into the field to select random interviewees. Evidently, 'gifts' are required for some of them. For example, some old women demanded tobacco before being interviewed. Often it is essential (and at least courteous) to secure the help of a village chief, which may require the provision of 'the usual customary drink'.[23]

Checking Interviewers

During normal survey conditions, one should look out for major differences between the results obtained by different interviewers. If it is obvious that these differences arise from the fact that they have been interviewing people in different locations with people from different lifestyles and backgrounds, then all may be well. But if interviewers are mostly interviewing people drawn at random from the same universe, their results should be broadly similar. If they are not, it can be an indication that one or more of the interviewers are biasing the responses. Remember that while the questionnaire is constant, the interviewers and enumerators are not. To what extent do one interviewer's responses differ from another's because of their different ways of administering the questionnaire? Our aim should be to reduce such interviewer bias to an absolute minimum.

This is why the training of interviewers is so important. They work on their own almost all the time. In most quantitative fieldwork, it is usual to have a team of interviewers under the management of a supervisor who not only directs the fieldwork but is responsible for quality checks. Sometimes he or she will attend interviews but obviously, this can happen at only a small proportion of them. The supervisor will also be involved in some check-backs, which we will explain shortly. But most interviews are neither supervised nor back-checked. A great deal of trust is put in interviewers and it is vital that they are highly motivated, well-disciplined and responsible individuals. The job of interviewing involves skills that need to be learned. One of the most important skills to develop is that of consistency. Interviewers need to do everything in the same way with each respondent so that the differences between them are entirely due to genuine differences and not something produced by the differences in the way questions have been put. This is how we produce results that capture the respondents' realities in a consistent and reliable way.

But how can we test interviewer consistency? If we are involved in a very large-scale survey in which each interviewer may be responsible for many interviews, inconsistencies and differences between results can be spotted at an early stage. It may be noted that interviewer X has a significantly larger number of responses of a particular kind while in other respects, the people interviewed were similar. One would need to investigate. But matters should not be allowed to get to that stage. It is best to note such matters in the field. In most cases, inconsistency and unreliability can be detected very quickly by appropriate methods of quality control. These take place while the survey is going on if we want to avoid additional problems later. Most of all, adequate quality control prevents a survey having to be repeated later when it becomes clear at the data-processing stage that the results are not reliable. It should be noted that it is important that each questionnaire form has to record the identity of the interviewer, as well as the time, date and place of the interview.

Interviews generally need to have a supervisor, but it is impossible for supervisors to be present at every interview. The supervisor should be present for at least a few of all interviewers' sessions with respondents, checking that the sampling procedures, the administration of the questionnaire and the recording of the responses are all in order and as instructed. The supervisor should be able to notice errors, inconsistencies, inappropriate behaviour, and so on. It is also common practice for a proportion of interviews to be 'back-checked'. The supervisor will revisit a selection of respondents to check that the recording of answers was done accurately. The services of an interviewer who was found to be unreliable may be dispensed with, unless, of course the fault can be corrected through further instruction or training. Persistently faulty interviewing should always lead to the dismissal of the interviewer concerned.

One way to check interviewer quality is to include time controls in face-to-face interviews where laptops or hand-held devices are used: extremely short interviews point to interviewers 'rushing' questionnaires. In online surveys, the same principle can be applied to self-administered questionnaires.

Checking and Editing of Questionnaires

The supervisor who goes out into the field with the team of interviewers should continually check through all questionnaires as they are completed. He or she needs to look out for inconsistencies, omitted questions and other errors. Sometimes it may be necessary to go back to the interviewee to put things right. Certain checks can be, and often are, built into the question-naire so that most inconsistencies can be spotted at the time by the inter-viewer and corrected by checking with the person being interviewed. But if this fails, the supervisor should be able to spot the error and, if needed, go back to the respondent and check for a correction.

Checking and editing also involves making sure that the questionnaire is ready for data entry—the point when the results are entered into a com-puter file for analysis. The supervisor can also use the checking process to determine whether the interviews are going well, that the interviewers are administering the questionnaires correctly and that all the answers are being recorded correctly. Questionnaires usually contain routing instruc-tions. The supervisor can easily see if these are being followed correctly.[24]

Back Checking

As we noted earlier, it is good research practice to specify a certain per-centage of interviews that will be back-checked. It may be decided that 5 per cent of all interviewees will be recontacted by the supervisor to check on the reliability and accuracy of the data as recorded by the interviewer. The drawbacks here are, first, the time factor and, second, interviewee fatigue. The person interviewed in the first place may not take too kindly to being bothered again especially with questions he or she has only recently answered. However, the cooperation of interviewees can usually be ensured by a simple explanation of why it is necessary. It is usually not necessary to check the whole questionnaire, but the supervisor will usually check a few key or difficult questions to ensure that interviews have proceeded properly. The main purpose of back checking is as a check on interviewer reliability and consistency. Much survey research around the world is con-ducted by commercial survey research agencies and you will find in their specifications for survey research that they always build in back checking into their research proposals.

Some Common Problems Encountered in Field Research and Some Solutions

At the end of any research project in the field, it is very important to find out about the experiences of the field researchers. The interviewers and their supervisors will have a good deal of important information about the project itself, problems with fieldwork, sampling difficulties and the like. They will be able to provide information that will help in the analysis and interpretation of the results. 'Debriefing' the field force will also provide valuable information to assist in the better design of future projects.

Few things ever operate perfectly. This is very true of field research when so much can be unpredictable. The weather, political upheavals and crises, civil disturbances and unrest and other events, usually unforeseen, can interrupt or influence the research in unpredictable ways. Those in charge of the research have to decide what influence or effect any events may have had on the results. When reporting any research project, one needs to relate results to prevailing circumstances.

A few years ago, during an audience survey in the capital city of a less developed country, certain problems were reported. These were not unusual problems; they are encountered in many countries, both industrialised and less developed, but tend to be encountered more often in the latter.

It was sometimes impossible to use a Kish grid because the household member first contacted would sometimes be suspicious that it had to do with security or taxation. Some interviewers reported that it was often difficult to find men over 24 years of age at home. Two or three visits at arranged times had to be made. Then, the person selected would often not turn up because of a general distrust of strangers in a city beset by both terrorism and an arbitrary police force.

When researching in the areas of higher income, it was often a household employee who opened the door. Sometimes, despite a careful explanation of the purpose of the research, the employee or servant would be reluctant or even refuse to call someone else to be interviewed. Sometimes the interview would be conducted through the intercom without the front door even being opened.

Contacting and interviewing people at lower socio-economic levels of this city was relatively easy. However, there was another problem familiar to anyone who has commissioned research in less developed areas. Other people in the household tried to influence the answers of the persons selected, even answering for the respondent at times. One interviewer reported that this was a persistent problem, even when she made it clear that personal answers were sought. In about half the cases, she reported that interviews had to be abandoned. The problem was said to be most acute with women aged 40 and over with low levels of education. When interviewing such women, other members of the household, very often the husband, would seek to intervene and 'assist'.

Some interviewers reported that questions about one of the radio stations seemed to create certain expectations in some respondents that they would receive some present if they said they listened. Evidently, the radio station in question had recently engaged in some promotional activity, rewarding people identified as listeners. Consequently, there was probably some over-claiming of listening to that station.

Educational levels were sometimes difficult to establish reliably. Young respondents, both male and female, sometimes claimed university educa-tion when they were obviously not telling the truth. Interviewers estab-lished whether the claim was accurate by adding a question asking the name of the university.

We welcome this solution invented on the spot by the interviewer to overcome a problem. Asking a supplementary question to ascertain the reli-ability of a reply is acceptable, provided that the interviewer does not make the respondent feel inadequate or foolish. This obviously requires experi-ence, tact and sensitivity. The interviewer needs to consult the supervisor about any such problem and to agree on a solution. This should be recorded in the field notes.

Addresses of some respondents were difficult to establish in some shanty areas. Dwellings were not numbered and were not in named streets. This made it difficult or impossible to trace the person interviewed for back check-ing. How can we answer the problem of identifying dwellings in shanty areas? The same problem is encountered in many rural areas of the world. The solution is to ask at the dwelling as to how it could be found again. Usually people locally have a way of identifying dwellings, very often by the name of the owner or head of household. GPS can also be used now that this is made so very much easier and inexpensive with most smartphones. And of course, GPS works everywhere even when there is no actual phone signal.

Once again there are no absolute rules. The skill of good field research, in audience research or in other fields, is to find appropriate and effective answers to problems as they come up. Then, having found a solution, one should keep a record of it. Supervisors, and very often interviewers also, need to keep a fieldwork diary to record anything out of the ordinary, prob-lems encountered, how they were dealt with and so on. Interviewers and supervisors develop skills and knowledge from their experience. These can be an immensely valuable resource.

There may be various ways of mitigating or removing some of these problems. These will depend largely on local circumstances. Here are some suggestions. Suspicions of the reasons for research are enormously difficult to overcome. Sometimes it may be necessary to give a careful account of the purpose of the research and to make a very big effort to build confidence. It may be necessary to do this at each selected household.

This can, of course, be very time consuming. There are sometimes short cuts that can help. People may be very suspicious of the police, government officials and the like, but there may be a local person who is trusted by everyone. It may be a religious leader, an elder of a village or a respected local figure such as a chief. If the purpose of the research is carefully explained to that person, his or her word of reassurance may help remove suspicion. This is more difficult to achieve in cities where there may be less social cohesion, more anonymity and less prominent or widely accepted opinion leadership.

The presence of other people at the face-to-face interview is more problematic. In western societies, where individualism is seen as of some importance, most opinion and market research interviews are conducted away from the presence of other people. It is simply not possible to ensure this in many parts of the world. Does it matter? The textbook response is to assert that it does matter because people will not always give their own personal views or be completely frank and honest when neighbours and relatives are listening. But if we accept that, it is usually impossible to interview people as isolated individuals because they do not live in that way, so to attempt to insist on one-to-one interviews may be unrealistic and pointless.

If the reality is that people's individual behaviour is always influenced by others, we should not seek to create a false and unfamiliar situation in an interview. On the other hand, when one is seeking the views and researching the behaviour of women in some societies where they take a subservient role, it may be worth trying to ensure that interviews take place without the presence of a man.

One has to make a sensible and practical judgement. It is important to explain patiently and carefully that the interview is not a test. There are no correct or incorrect answers. It should also be made clear that it does not matter in the least if the person being interviewed does not have an answer to a question.

3.4 Media Professionals and the General Public: Different Perspectives

People who work in the media have perspectives and outlooks about their output that are, not surprisingly, different from those who do not work in the media. It is an obvious thing to note and there is nothing surprising about it. However, it is sometimes quite difficult to persuade broadcasters and journalists that their audiences tend to have a very different outlook and view of the way the media work from those who work in the media.

Radio and television producers, journalists and media managers inhabit a world of separate and rival programmes, networks and identities. The audience do not share those perceptions. While media people might think that a station identity or programme and name are of great significance, members of the audience are very often oblivious to these things. In research, we sometimes find that people have only a vague idea of what programmes and networks they listen to or watch. They are sometimes just as vague about what newspapers or magazines they read. Or they may simply get it all wrong. Just as the brand name of 'Hoover' may be applied to all vacuum cleaners or 'Thermos' to all vacuum flasks, so also can viewers, listeners and readers confuse radio, television and newspaper titles and apply these to other channels and sources. In one media survey in Ghana, a respondent said that he listened to the BBC 'from many countries—from America, South Africa, Germany and Britain'. It took some time for the interviewer to realise that he was using the term 'BBC' to apply to any international radio broadcasting, rather like 'Hoover' can mean any or all vacuum cleaners.

Such kinds of errors may be uncommon, but the fact that they do occur points to the need for care and alertness. In radio and television audience measurement, when using the diary or interview method, we may need to use 'prompts'—that is, titles or phrases likely to help respondents recall and identify correctly what they watch or listen to. In both diaries and face-to-face interviews, it is sometimes necessary to give not only the 'official' name of a radio or television station but also other names by which it may be popularly known. And this applies to online research as well.

The same thing applies to magazine and newspaper titles. Very often, these are not clearly distinguished from each other. There may be several magazines with titles like 'Farming Monthly', 'Farming Today', 'Modern Farming' or 'The Farmer'. It is not surprising that some respondents may make mistakes in accurately reporting what they read. It is much the same with the names of individual radio and television programmes. It is often a painful thing for producers to realise but the audiences for many quite popular shows often have only a limited knowledge of the actual titles. In such cases, the presentation of programme titles, network names and the like will be helpful. Also with readership research, it is common practice to have the mastheads or title pages of publications to show to respondents.

3.5 Translation of Questionnaires into Different Languages

In most countries of the world, on any survey with national or major regional coverage at least, you will normally need to administer any questionnaire in more than one language. For example, in two recent media surveys in South Sudan, the questionnaires were produced and printed in both English and Arabic.

Similar practices are routinely adopted elsewhere. For example, in Morocco, it is usual to print all questionnaires in both Arabic and French. In Cameroon and Canada, both English and French are used and printed in the questionnaires. In India, a common practice is to print questionnaires in three languages—English, Hindi and the main other language of the area being surveyed. A national survey in India will usually use several versions of the same questionnaire, but since this is an immensely complex operation, national surveys in India are not very common. A good deal of market and media research in India is state-based, relying on state-wide surveys, which may later be brought together into compilations of data for the whole country. But even state-based surveys in India usually have questionnaires printed in three languages—the main language of the state, English and Hindi. But in most of these countries, other languages have to be used for many respondents. In Zambia, when one of the authors was doing national audience research during the period 1970 to 1973, a questionnaire in English was used, but it was translated by the interviewers as required into seven other languages.

If we remember how crucially important the wording of questions can be, having the questionnaire carefully translated into every language that is going to be needed would seem to be the correct way to proceed. But it does increase costs considerably, as also does the need to pilot test each language version of the questionnaire.

The challenge of languages is best dealt with in two ways. In many cases, it is simply not possible to provide printed translations in all the languages that are going to be needed. Moreover, it is even less likely that there will be either time or resources to pilot test questionnaires in every language. The solution, a compromise between research perfection and the realities of limited time and resources, is to ensure that there are agreed, printed and tested versions of the questionnaire in at least the major languages. The interviewers in the survey team will usually speak these major languages between them and of course language knowledge is an important recruitment criterion. The ability to speak fluently more than one language is a major asset on any interviewer's CV. Sometimes it may not be necessary to print all the questionnaires in different languages. But the interviewers can be provided with translations in various languages on separate sheets of paper to use as necessary.

For the lesser languages (lesser in terms of the numbers who speak them), interviewers can be taken on especially for the purpose in the respective areas where these languages are used. These interviewers will need to be thoroughly trained in the purpose of the research and the meaning and intention of all the questions. You have to make every effort to ensure that the words used in verbal translation of what is written on the question-naire are appropriate. Back-checking interviewers who speak a language not known to the supervisor poses a major problem. Solutions have to be found which are appropriate to the local conditions.

An established way of checking translations is to back-translate. Let us suppose that we are running a media survey in Peru. For any national survey, the questionnaire will normally be prepared and tested in Spanish. But we will also need a version in the main indigenous language Quechua. After translation, we would give the questionnaire to another Quechua speaker who has not seen the Spanish original nor been involved in any way with the research. This person would be asked to translate into Spanish. This 'back translation' can then be compared with the original and any discrep-ancies investigated and corrected, where necessary.

The same or similar method can also be used in the field by tape-recording interviews and getting these back-translated into the original. However, this practice is cumbersome and expensive and should be avoided, if possible.

No solution to the challenge of multilingualism is perfect. But the issue arises in most countries and the professional researcher needs to be aware that different languages carry with them different meanings and emphases. All these are related to the all-important question of culture and the need to make all research sensitive to the differences between people and the need to adopt appropriate procedures in our research. This is easier when you are dealing with a piece of research focused on a community or area rather than something on a larger regional or national scale.

Notes and References

1. See the section on sampling under Section 3.1 'Theoretical and Practical Issues in Measuring Audiences'.
2. The starting age for sampling for general population surveys varies somewhat between coun-tries. Interviewing children requires the permission of their parents or guardians. It is com-mon practice to omit children under the age of 15 or, in some countries and instances, 18. There are ethical considerations surrounding the interviewing of children. Go to www.esomar.org and select codes and guidelines. ESOMAR is the main international professional organisation for all forms of market and opinion research.
3. The restrictions on interviewing children do not apply when measuring TV audiences using people meters. These systems usually measure viewing down to the age of 4.
4. Audience research was developed in Europe where most TV viewing and radio listening occurs in the home. In other parts of the world, out of home viewing and listening is some-times very widespread, and household based sampling may not give an adequate picture of viewing or listening behaviour. Such viewing will be measured by questionnaires and diaries, but not by way of people meter systems.

5.   Another major addition to quantitative research facilities from the digital age is the ability to locate every home visited in any survey by using global satellite positioning now available on smartphones.

6.   Up-to-date population figures for all countries of the world are available free at www.prb.org

7.   http://www.mapsofindia.com

8.   W.G. Blyth and L.J. Marchant, 'A Self-weighting Random Sampling Technique', *Journal of the Market Research Society*, 15, no. 3 (1973): 157–162.

9.   Graham Mytton, *Listening, Looking and Learning* (Lusaka: University of Zambia, 1974).

10. A Decade of Innovation: The Confirmit 2013 Market Research Technology Report accessed online at https://www.confirmit.com/. Similar data can be found in the annual ESOMAR *Global Market Research* report. We also accessed the 2014 ESOMAR report which showed that in 2014 more than 60 per cent of global quantitative research was done online. www.esomar. org (accessed 16 July 2015).

11. Chi squared is a very important technique for testing the significance of quantitative data results. Readers who find this section difficult will be helped by looking for more on the Internet. Put 'chi squared' into any good search engine and you will find many simple explanations of what many of us can find hard to understand.

12. Graham Mytton has in recent years conducted or been involved in major media measurement surveys in countries as diverse as East Timor, the Gambia, Sierra Leone, South Sudan, Sudan, Tanzania and Nigeria. In none of these countries could these surveys have been done with any other method than that used—face-to-face questionnaires. He used pencil and paper; CAPI would of course be possible and is often used now in all countries.

13. Jonathan Lynn and Antony Jay, *The Complete Yes Prime Minister* (London: BBC Books, 1989), pp. 106–107.

14. Rajeshwar Dyal, *Cable Television: Glitter or Doom* (New Delhi: Indian Institute of Mass Communication, 1992).

15. For more on pilot testing, see Section 3.3.

16. The latter word derives from the time when punched cards were used for data input.

17. This derives from a questionnaire used before the Internet had become a significant medium in Namibia. Today, it would have been included in the list as also would 'social media'. Namibia All Media and Products Survey questionnaire, 1996.

18. Dyal, *Cable Television*.

19. The two questions need to be asked one after the other. First record what the respondent says is there to be used now and then ask what is likely to be purchased or become available over the next year.

20. Maurice Duverger, *Introduction to the Social Sciences* (London: George Allen and Unwin, 1961), pp. 148–149.

21. For a fuller examination of the audience measurement problem, see Peter Menneer, 'Towards a Radio "BARB"—Some Issues of Measurement', *ADMAP* February (1989): 42–45.

22. D.J. Casley and D.A. Lury, *Data Collection in Developing Countries* (Oxford: Clarendon Press, 1981), p. 95.

23. Ghana Broadcasting Corporation, Audience Research Department internal memorandum. n.d.

24. Computer programmes can be used to facilitate this process. With computer-assisted telephone interviewing, it is automatic.

Chapter 4

Audience and Media Measurement Research Methods in Use Today

Media measurement is something that is in constant and continuing demand. The strongest call for it comes from advertisers, but media owners also play a growing part in the demand for accurate and timely measurement of audiences for the different media.

In radio and television, programmes and schedules often change, there are seasonal variations caused by changes in weather and in the human behaviour associated with it. Many radio and television stations, therefore, need regular or continuous research to be able to know how the audience behave—what they choose, when they use media and why. Similarly, advertisers have campaigns that last for a certain period of time. Newspaper and magazine publishers have special promotions and special editions. They launch sales campaigns from time to time. They may see sales rise or fall. They will also, however, want to know what the readership reaction has been.

Online media users and advertisers also demand data, but as their needs are met in a different way and one that relies mainly on the devices and techniques of the Internet, much of this topic is left to Chapter 6 which focuses on this important area for research. This chapter will focus mainly on the measurement of 'traditional' mass media—print, radio and television.

How is measurement typically done for these media? We will look first at TV and radio. The challenge here is to provide something on a continuous basis. One-off or ad hoc surveys are useful and often done but they soon become out of date. Generalisations from a single survey about TV and radio consumption habits and behaviour or about readership or awareness of advertising campaigns may be reliable for a while, perhaps for as much as a year. Much depends on how fast the media and audiences are changing. But broadcasters and publishers need up-to-date information and usually expect it more frequently than annually. And perhaps even more so, advertisers need to have data which are up to date on which to base decisions on their future campaigns and on the allocation and placing of their commercial 'spots' on television or radio.

Various methods are currently used in media research. We will deal first with the methods mostly used in radio and television audience research, although some of these are also used for readership research.

4.1 Self-completion Diaries

A sample is selected to represent the population as a whole, over a certain given age. Those selected are invited to keep a diary of listening or viewing usually on a weekly basis. A precoded diary is provided, listing stations and timings. An example of a current radio diary is given in the Appendix.

Each diarist is provided with instructions. Sometimes the diary is handed over personally by a research field worker who can explain what needs to be done. The selected individual is asked to enter his or her listening activity. Most diaries are kept for seven days but can be for longer or shorter periods. Diary keepers are often recruited by mail or telephone, a less expensive option than through personal contact by a fieldworker, but the latter is probably the required method in most less developed countries. In some cases, diaries can be provided online for those who have the capability to complete a diary in this way and to send it online.

There are many recognised weaknesses of the diary method. People can forget to record all their listening activities. They may complete the task at the end of the week, just before it is to be sent by post to the audience research headquarters or research agency. By this time, the respondent may not have an accurate recall. Respondents can make mistakes in time, programme, channel or some other aspect of their listening or viewing activity.

But there are other kinds of errors that are not merely errors of omission. The respondent may record what he or she intended to do, not what actually happened. The respondent may fill in what usually happens rather than what did actually happen. Diary keepers also can try to please or impress by the listening or viewing behaviour that they report in the diary, a conditioning element that is less common in most other research methods.

Another major problem is one that is unique to the diary. People who listen to little radio or watch little TV may be reluctant to keep a diary about something they do not often do or something they do not really care about. And yet, if our diary method is to be the representative of the whole population, the diary-keeping sample needs to be a representative of people with all existing levels of radio and TV consumption. This includes those who listen or watch very little, and of those who may watch or listen to nothing during the period they are asked to keep a diary.

What about the person who never listens to radio or watches television? These will be encountered when first contacts are made with prospective diary keepers. The field worker placing the diaries should keep a record of those who say they do not listen to radio or those who do not watch TV. When someone is contacted who never listens to the radio, this fact is recorded. While trying to find 1,000 television diary keepers, it may be that one encounters 100 such people for whom keeping a diary would be a pointless exercise because they never watch television. In this case, one could 'return' the diary immediately and enter the data as a nil-viewing response. Or we can, when projecting the results to the adult population as a whole, make the necessary allowance for the fact that for every 1,000 viewers who watch any TV, there are 100 more (in this hypothetical case) who watch none. Thus, if 20 per cent of the diary keepers had seen a particular programme, we could not say 20 per cent of the population had seen it. We know that those who never watch need to be accounted for. In this case, we could say that for every 200 people who watched it, 900 did not. The audience in the population as a whole would be calculated as follows:

$$200 \div 1,100 \times 100 = 18.2\%$$

This is an obvious and easy adjustment to make. Other distortions occur with diaries and are more difficult to cope with. How do we overcome the problem of illiteracy?

We do not wish to exclude illiterate people from our research. We cannot assume they are non-listeners or non-viewers. If the percentage of illiterates in the population is small (less than 5 per cent), it may not matter very much to exclude them. But if the proportion is larger, we must either avoid the diary method or find a way around the problem. In the Zimbabwe All Media and Products Survey (ZAMPS), the standard method of media measurement in that country, the diary method is used to record detailed information about radio and television use. Many Zimbabweans, especially of the older generation and living in rural areas, are illiterate. ZAMPS includes illiterate people in the sample. When fieldworkers find that a selected individual is either unable to read or write, or who would have some difficulty in filling in a diary, they ask for a neighbour, friend or another member of the household to complete the diary for them. This is an imaginative and appropriate response to the problem. If this solution is not possible, and it may not be in all cultures or circumstances, the diary method should not be used where there is widespread illiteracy. It is important that illiterate people should not be excluded from research, especially as the media behaviour of illiterates may be significantly different from that of the literate. Moreover, a good deal of broadcasting activity is specifically targeted at the less well educated and those with no education at all. Both radio and television can be powerful and effective media capable of reaching the disadvantaged and it is important for this reason that research is designed to include them.

Another recurrent problem with diaries is that it is often difficult to recruit a representative number of people from lower socio-economic groups or classes. And those who are recruited are less likely than others to complete the diary and send it in. This introduces serious distortions in the results for which allowance should be made. This can be done at the analysis stage. For example, if 35 per cent of the population is in lower socio-economic class but only 25 per cent of the diarists and only 15 per cent of the responses sent in come from people in this group, one would 'weight' or increase the value of the results of these 15 per cent to be 35 per cent of the sample and, thus, to reflect the appropriate proportion in the population as a whole. At the same time and by the same process the responses from over-represented socio-economic groups would be weighted down to appropriate proportions. However, one should still make every effort to find sufficient respondents from all socio-economic groups and ensure, as far as it is possible that their diaries are returned.

There are various ways of encouraging maximum response. One way is to offer rewards for the return of completed diaries. These do not have to be substantial or expensive. Or a small number of larger prizes could be offered in a draw in which all respondents participate. Only a few will be rewarded, but the rest may feel sufficiently encouraged to return their diaries diligently with the hope of being lucky.

It may also help to enhance regular participation if diarists are asked to say something about the programmes—for example, to rate their opinions in terms of their 'quality'. This possibility gives the diarists a feeling of doing something perhaps more worthwhile than merely recording that they heard or saw.

Some research companies find that it is a sufficient inducement to tell respondents that by taking part in the diary research, they become part of the ratings of television or radio programmes. Respondents like to feel important, and why not! The only slight problem with this is that some respondents might feel induced to report listening or viewing in not an entirely honest way, or even to increase or change their viewing or listening behaviour because they know it is being measured.

While there are all these disadvantages or weaknesses of the diary method, many of which can be overcome, there are also many advantages.

The diary method has the great advantage of being less expensive than the main alternatives. The recruitment of the diarists usually requires interviewers to go out into the field to select the respondents. But no long questionnaires have to be administered. The diarists do most of the work for us. In some cases, the chosen respondent may be asked to complete only one week's diary and another selection of respondents is then made for subsequent weeks. In other cases, the same respondent can be asked to complete subsequent weeks diaries, and this also helps to keep costs down. Costs can be further reduced by use of online questionnaires. These, as explained elsewhere, cut the costs incurred with paper diaries that often need to be hand checked for errors (errors are excluded by online questionnaire software) and remove the need for data entry as this is automatic.

The diary method can be made to work in most circumstances. It has the enormous advantage of making it possible to plot day-to-day listener and viewer behaviour. This is virtually impossible with single face-to-face interviews, the method described later. Another great advantage over face-to-face interviews is that people who are difficult to contact in normal face-to-face interviews may agree to fill in a diary. People who spend a lot of time away from home or who work long hours are hard to contact for a personal or telephone interview. But they may agree to complete a diary.

As noted earlier, the diary method is consistently likely to record higher levels of listening than the face-to-face aided recall method—or indeed any type of metered data, which will be described later. However, allowance can be made for this, and it has been established that, provided allowance is made for under-represented groups and for non-listeners or non-viewers, diaries can give a fairly accurate picture of broadcasting media use.

How do we deal with a person who may listen to the radio or watch television on only a couple of occasions during the selected week? His or her viewing or listening behaviour is of equal importance if one is seeking to build up a truly representative and reliable picture of the behaviour of everyone. Response, even from low users of radio or television, can be improved by the way the diary system is administered. The fieldworker should emphasise, when explaining the whole process to the respondent, the fact that the diary of an occasional listener or viewer is of equal interest and importance.

Of course, all postage costs for returning the completed diary must be paid by the organisers of the research. In some cases, especially where postal services are unreliable, completed diaries can be collected by fieldworkers. In these cases, they can be checked for errors and ambiguities when contact is made at the person's home. As mentioned earlier, some existing diary systems are moving some of their panellists to online diary keeping where this is possible.

4.2 Television (and Radio) Meters

We can use electronic technology to record very accurately just what any radio or TV is tuned to, and exactly when it is switched on or off.

The two technologies for radio and TV are rather different. Let us take TV first, where meters to capture TV behaviour have been in use since the 1970s, although as we shall see, radio meters go back to the 1930s.

At first, the TV meters were capable only of recording what TV channel was tuned to. It was not until ten years later that the people meter was devised. This not only recorded what the TV set was receiving but who was in the room to watch it.

A meter can be attached to the TV set or sets and can be so designed as to keep an accurate record of what happens to the TV over a period of time. Further developments allow the meter to record the presence of visitors, capture data on time-shift viewing, measure digital channels and, now, the use of the Internet to watch TV.

The idea of attaching a meter to a receiving set predates the arrival of TV by a few years. The first meter was in fact designed to record radio listening in the early days of radio in the US. Radio began what many have called the electronic age. It was appropriate that, at a very early stage, someone should have suggested an electronic means of measuring the audience. Just a year after the first radio audience survey using face-to-face interviews conducted in March 1928 in the US, the invention of a meter device was announced. But commercial use of meters for audience measurement in the US did not happen until 1935. This was before the invention of successful magnetic tape-recording apparatus. The information that needed to be recorded—dates, time and radio channel or network—had to be marked onto a moving paper tape rather like a barograph—a machine for recording barometric pressure. There were many problems with it, not the least of which were power failures, blown fuses and disconnections, which were not uncommon occurrences in these early days. The patent for these 'Audimeters' was acquired by the market research company AC Nielsen, still a major big name in market and media research today. The system was gradually improved and developed until in 1942, there were 1,300 meters in 1,100 homes in the US. The system went into decline when in the 1950s car radios and portable radios came into common use and listening on these sets increased to the point when meter data from static radio sets became unreliable. At that time, Audimeters had to run on main electricity and could not, therefore, be used on portable and car radio sets outside the home.

These early meters were very limited in what they could do and the data they recorded. They provided information about stations tuned in to and the time and days. But they provided no information about who was listening.

> ...the record shows the audience flow only in terms of homes. Nothing is revealed concerning the people who listened. For example, the recorder may show tuning to three consecutive programs in a given home. But there may have been no actual flow of audience; for the first may have been listened to by a child, the second by a man and the third by a woman.[1]

Radio meters have come back and are in use today in some countries. We will look in some detail about them later in this section.

TV has been less portable than radio, and so meters to measure its use were developed. And today meters are used for television audience measurement in most countries in Europe and in Japan, China, India, Australia, New Zealand, the US, Canada, South Africa, Brazil and an increasing number of countries in the developing world. Meters on TV sets in selected homes are used to provide data on viewing patterns and behaviour.

The first television meters recorded only the time and the network to which the set was tuned. They did not record whether anyone was actually watching what was on the television, nor did they record how many people were in the room watching the set, nor anything about those people. They were in fact very similar in their limitations to the early meters measuring radio use in the US.

This situation changed when 'people meters' were introduced. These not only record time and network tuned in to, but they also require people to press a button on the meter to record their presence in the TV room. A different button or number can be assigned to different members of the household. There are also buttons or numbers to record the presence of visitors to the household who may be watching. In this way, at least theoretically, the people meter can record not only the time of viewing and the programmes and channels being viewed, but also who was watching and their demographic characteristics—age, sex, occupation, etc. In some meter systems, additional buttons are used to record programme appreciation. By giving the panellists the role of 'programme judges', panel fatigue is reduced.

There has been, and still is, some scepticism about whether the meter records real viewing behaviour. The respondents have to remember to record their presence in the room and their departure from it. And being present in a room with a television set switched on is no guarantee that the programmes are actually being paid attention to or watched. Experience and research has shown that the number of persons having forgotten to press their button while viewing TV is more or less equal to the number of persons who have pressed their button while not being present in the room. It is an imperfect way to measure behaviour, but so also are all methods that rely on people remembering to do things as a routine. The weaknesses seem relatively small and the system is likely to continue to be widely used until something else replaces it.

One may ask at this point about how everything about people meters relates to what has been said about the principles of sampling and representativeness. Obviously, a meter is not like a questionnaire. But the selection of households for the placement of meters follows the principle of sampling outlined earlier. The aim is to find a sample of television households that will accurately represent the population of television households in the country or region being researched as a whole. What usually happens is that a research agency first completes an 'establishment survey' to determine the nature and composition of television households as well as of households with no television. Data are collected on the size of households, number of television sets, income, class, age and sex distribution and, where relevant, ethnic and other demographic data. Data are also collected on the proportion of the population which has the access to cable or satellite services. And with the growing importance of the Internet and the arrival of online TV services and 'smart' TV sets that can access video content online establishment surveys now need to find out how many homes have these facilities also.

A model of the television owning population is built up. From this model, a household panel is constructed in which all the significant population groups are represented and in the correct proportions, from single person households to large family households, from poor households perhaps with only one television set to wealthy households with many sets, cable or satellite connection and broadband access with home cinema and 'smart' TV. Also, the existence of 'second' or 'holiday' homes needs to be taken into account. The agency then selects households that socially, geographically and ethnically, and in such matters as household size, number of sets, wealth, age and sexual composition, represent the population as a whole.

In fact, the model is neither perfect nor comprehensive in modelling the entire TV audience. It cannot be, for the people meter cannot yet, for obvious practical reasons, be used in institutions like hospitals, schools, hostels, monasteries and prisons where a large number of people may be watching a single set. People meters cannot be used in hotels, bars, community centres or cafes where, in some countries, a lot of television viewing takes place. People meters exclusively record viewing in households. In countries where a lot of viewing takes place outside the home, they do not record the whole situation thoroughly; a lot of TV viewing is, thus, never measured in these circumstances. Moreover, the factors that led to the demise of the early radio meters (see below) have begun to raise questions about the efficacy of the existing television people meters. TV has become portable. You can watch it on your smartphone, tablet, laptop or personal computer. At the time of writing this book, ways are being developed to measure these kinds of viewing as well using technologies that will be consistent with current measurement methods. The new metrics made possible by online technologies may enable the accurate measurement of online television viewing. This possibility is beginning to be used and is addressed in the chapter on passive online measurement. These new methods (again driven by the advertising industry) comprise the recording of the reception of TV content transmitted online—be it in the form of Internet broadcasts viewed live ('videostreaming') or in the form of time-shift reception ('catch-up TV'). The result is new 'currencies' such as 'streamview' (i.e., contact by the videoplayer with a piece of content for at least one second) and 'volume' (use time in seconds). Measurement is affected by a combination of server-based clickstream data and user-related information gathered by an online panel. At the moment, measurement of Internet TV is possible only for stationary PCs. Even more than in on-air TV broadcasting, reception of Internet TV (IPTV) is highly fragmented, with only a few programmes really scoring ('fat hat') and hundreds of others remaining barely noticeable ('long tail').

In some countries, households may be excluded from the panel of households with metered sets if nobody in the household knows any of the languages used on the main domestic TV channels.

Presently, people meters in use are connected to the telephone system and/or to an Internet connection. At fixed times, usually in the early hours of morning, the research agency's computer automatically 'calls' by telephone or via a broadband link to each household. (The ringing tone is suppressed so as not to wake anyone in the household!) This method means that meters are difficult to use in households where there is neither phone line nor Internet link. Various solutions can be employed, ranging from the use of mobile phones to the collection of data from computer memories in the unconnected households.

TV meters for audience measurement are used in many countries outside the industrialised West, including China, India, the Philippines, South Africa and various Latin American countries. It should be noted, however, that in most of these less developed, less urbanised countries, television meters tend to be used mainly for measuring audiences in the urban areas (agglomerations).

4.3 Radio Meters

The original radio meters failed in the US when radio became a portable medium, especially after the arrival of the transistor during the 1950s. The then existing technology for radio meters made them cumbersome and suitable only for static use in the home. And so, for the next 50 years, radio audience research relied either on subjective (active) day-after recall or on the keeping of a radio listening diary by selected respondents.

The transistor made radio portable. Eventually, the same technology, using silicon to create tiny circuitry, advanced to the stage where it became possible to make meters similarly portable. It became feasible for technical methods to be developed for the objective (passive) measurement of radio services being listened to without requiring any difficult or complex action by the respondent or listener.

There are two methods in use. One, developed and used by the US-based media research company, 'Arbitron' is about the size of a smartphone. It is carried by the respondent. The device 'hears' whatever he/she hears. By arrangement with all radio broadcasters in the areas where the meter is used, there is an inaudible code embedded in the sound of the radio stations so that the meter is able to record what station is being heard and at what time(s). The other technology, 'Mediawatch', was developed in Switzerland, by a collaboration between the Swiss public broadcaster and the Swiss watch company Swatch. The system (invented originally by the head of audience research at Swiss public radio and television, Dr Matthias Steimmann) was bought by the research company GfK. By means of tiny electronic gadgetry inside a specially made wristwatch, sound samples are picked up from the air, stored and transmitted to a centre for evaluation. The samples lasting for four seconds are compared to all available output from all radio stations in the areas where the devices are being used. Analysis of data from the meter will provide a detailed account of what radio stations were heard by the respondent carrying the device and at what times. As with the people meters for TV, the data for radio listening are collected by a central computer. The respondent is required to dock the meter in a special home device which is connected to a line—usually a phone line—and data are captured when the respondent is resting.

Note: The Mediawatch can basically measure all radio stations which can be received in the area covered by the sample. It can also be used for measuring TV channels and even for recording other media use such as newspaper reading. The Arbtiron device can also measure TV viewing but in both cases the devices rely on 'hearing' the sound of the TV in the presence of which the wearer is at the time.

The important strength of this way of measuring a radio audience is the fact that it does not demand much from the listener. This kind of passive registration of a person's exposure to radio sound is much more precise than any subjective recall. All on-air exposure to radio signals can be measured—regardless of whether such signals are noticed consciously or not—as when you might be in the vicinity of a radio in restaurants, shops, in someone else's car or home—listening to something you did not choose yourself. That kind of listening is rarely recorded by recall or diary methods. However, the radio meter is unlikely to become widely used as it is not capable of measuring listening on headphones because it cannot 'hear' the sound. One can also argue that accidental listening is not the 'real thing'. If one does not want to listen to a radio station but is doing so only because the listener is hearing someone else's choice it is not the same kind of media use as that measured in ways that involve a response from the listener. You can see the argument here. The advertisers may well be interested in this accidental listening. For the creators of the programmes such accidental listening is of hardly any interest.

Moreover, and this is probably even more of a disadvantage, the technology is expensive and has enough drawbacks to make it not worth the expense. Another practical consequence of employing the Mediawatch was that it dramatically lowered radio ratings—especially in those timeslots when recall measurement scored highest. It is not surprising that interest in such measurement by radio operators was minimal.

There have been other experiments with radio meters in recent times, none of them making major inroads into the world of radio audience measurement. The fact is that the two technologies have been designed for radio (although they can also measure TV viewing) and radio is not the medium with the biggest advertising spend by a wide margin. This fact has worked against the technology being successful. This situation is not likely to change; radio's advertising revenue is unlikely to grow much now if at all with the stiff competition from online advertising as well as television. At the time of writing, it seems uncertain that radio meters, despite their advantages in getting away from the faulty memories of listeners, will ever become more than an interesting footnote in media research history. The radio meters have not made the advances that many expected of them or hoped. They have restrictions in what they can measure. For example, they do not lend themselves well to recording radio use when it is heard on headphones. And there has been a growth in this form of radio listening now that many smartphones, music players and the like have radio-listening facility. With this technological change, more and more radio listening is done on the move, the sound is heard only by the user, the meter 'hears' no radio.

4.4 Personal Interviews

Audiences can be, and in some cases are, measured by questionnaires administered by an interviewer to respondents selected in a standard kind of representative survey. There are two basic methods. Either the interview takes place face-to-face or it is conducted over the telephone. There are many variations in approach with each.

Telephone Interviews

The use of the telephone in audience research is found mainly in more developed countries where there is a high level of ownership of telephones. In some places, it is now essential to use telephones; security systems on apartment buildings and other restrictions on access to people's front doors make personal visits for face-to-face interviews either hazardous or impossible.

Both the advantages and disadvantages of interviewing by telephone are obvious. On the plus side, telephone interviewing takes less time than conventional face-to-face interviewing. Interviewers stay in one place and are provided with special equipment both for making the telephone calls and for recording the respondents' answers. Computer software packages are now available for telephone interviewing which facilitate the immediate input of data so that results are ready as soon as all interviewing has been completed. The interviewer has a keyboard and screen on which the questions appear. No time is taken nor is money spent in travelling or looking for the next respondent. Normally many more interviews can be conducted in the same time. Back checking is done by the supervisor calling a certain proportion of all respondents.

As explained briefly earlier, the randomness of a telephone sample can be achieved through RDD, a system that selects subscribers' phone numbers at random and dials them for you automatically. The person who answers the phone, who could be a child or a visitor, may not be the one who is interviewed. The same random selection procedures described earlier may be used to select a household member. When the selection has taken place, the interviewer will explain the purpose of the phone call, assure confidentiality and say how long the interview will last. Telephone interviews need to be very much shorter than face-to-face interviews. Even half an hour could be regarded as too long on the telephone. Refusal at this stage should be avoided, if possible.

Telephone interviews have some major disadvantages. Even in the wealthy US, about five per cent of television households have no telephone. In most countries, the proportion of television households having no telephone is of course higher. The method is unsuitable for surveys of the general population in countries where landline telephone penetration is very low. However, surveys using the telephone can be appropriate where particular groups of people are the target for research. Telephone interviewing could be an appropriate way of assessing the use of satellite television in many African and Asian countries. People who have satellite dishes also tend to have landline and/or mobile telephones. However, it needs to be remembered that RDD, while fairly straightforward to do with landlines, is much more problematic for mobile phones for reasons explained earlier on Page 34.

Another disadvantage of telephone interviewing is that it is not a very suitable means of obtaining a lot of detailed information. Respondents sometimes resent and reject an unexpected phone call from a complete stranger, especially if it turns out to be a long one or if it occurs during meal times. What is more, if one just happens to be enjoying ones favourite radio or television programmes, one may especially resent being interrupted to answer questions about it!

Ironically, it was this factor which was, for some users of research, the most attractive feature of the method. Telephone interviewing could be used to determine what people were actually listening to or viewing at the moment the telephone rang. It was as near as you could get to an exact measure of real behaviour.

Various techniques have been used, from time to time, in the US, for audience research using the telephone. One method is known as 'telephone coincidental'. A very short questionnaire is used:

'What were you listening to on the radio when the telephone rang?'

(If the respondent named a radio 'programme' or 'presenter' rather than a radio 'station' a second question was then asked:)

'What station was that broadcast over?'

(If, however, the respondent named a station in response to the first question, this was the second question asked:)

'What was that station broadcasting?'

(A further question was then put:)

'Please tell me how many men, women and children, including yourself, were listening when the telephone rang.'[2]

The American audience research pioneer C.E. Hooper used this method from 1934. It is fairly easy to find fault with the questions! As worded here, they seem to assume not only that the person who answers the phone has a radio but that he or she was listening. These two facts could bias replies. But the procedure seemed to work reasonably well.

A similar technique was also used later for television:

'Do you have a television set?'

'Were you or anyone in your home watching TV just now?'

'What programme or channel?'

'How many men, women or children under eighteen were viewing?'

'Who selected the programme?'[3]

Telephone interviews are nowadays used in Europe for some audience research but not so much for coincidental measurement as for the method in far more common use, known as 'telephone recall'.

Basically this involves a conventional interview using a questionnaire which asks respondents to recall either what they listened to yesterday, or for the 24 hours preceding the call. Many variations can be used, but typically telephone recall interviews ask about:

- The time the radio (or any household radio) was in use the previous day.
- What was heard during those hours?
- The station or stations listened to.

There is a lot more that could be written about the use of the telephone in media research. It remains very difficult to obtain an unbiased sample. There can be a high refusal rate—usually very much higher than for face-to-face contacts. This is probably the weakest point of telephone interviewing.

The method is especially suitable in large countries where long travel distances may be needed. Telephone interviewing is very suitable in countries where it is difficult or impossible to gain access to people via their front doors. For example, it is nowadays extremely time consuming and, in some places, positively dangerous to attempt door-to-door surveys. The telephone survey is very widely in use where this is so. Obviously, telephone penetration has to be very high for it to be a useful method for general population surveys.

In most developed countries, telephone penetration is now over 90 per cent of households. But telephone surveys can be used in countries where telephone penetration is very low if one seeks to reach a sample of people in the income brackets where telephone ownership is high. Moreover, telephone interviewing can be used to supplement face-to-face interviewing in those areas and with those people where front-door access is difficult or impossible. For example, in the more prosperous areas of some cities in some poorer countries, security is such that access to interviewers arriving on foot is virtually impossible, in, say, the so-called gated communities. Telephone surveys may have to be used in such cases.

Even where telephone penetration is very low, it may still be possible to use telephone interviewing for all kinds of respondents. For example, there are often telephones in villages or in poorer areas of cities and towns. These phones may be in cafés or hotels, community centres or the houses of local officials. It may well be possible to devise ways of using these phones and calling selected people to the phone for interview. A procedure for selection would be needed to remove or reduce bias. We are not aware that this method has been used, except in Russia where many apartment blocks have pay phones on each floor, shared by all occupants. There some research agencies have devised a way of using these phones to make reliable representative samples and do telephone interviews. The same methods could be used elsewhere. The advantage of speed, cost efficiency and the fact that literacy is not required make the telephone method very attractive where resources are limited. Using telephones for research in poorer countries is a challenge for ingenuity. But the major weakness of bias arising from high refusal rates remains a matter of concern.

With the massive rise in mobile phone use, we need to consider the use of this medium for interviewing. Mobile telephony has greatly increased the proportion of the world's population who use a phone. And in nearly all countries today, mobile phones far exceed landline phones in number. Globally, the ITU estimated that in 2005, there were 1,243 million landline phones. Nine years later, the estimated number of landline phones had fallen a little, to 1,147 million. But over the same period, mobile phone numbers had grown from 2,205 million to 6,915 million. These are of course unevenly distributed, but even in very poor countries, mobile phones are in widespread use and the number continues to grow. Some examples from the ITU data illustrate this. In Brazil, an estimated 78.5 per cent of individuals use a mobile phone. The equivalent figure for Egypt is 74.1 per cent, Kenya 59.8 per cent, Ghana 47.7 per cent, Senegal 64.4 per cent and Indonesia 34.5 per cent.[4]

But the problem with the use of mobile phones for research purposes is that RDD is not really possible. The reason is that phone numbers for mobiles are far less static than for landline. SIM cards have the numbers but can be used for very short periods. There are always huge numbers of mobile phone numbers currently not in use. Many are in use for very short periods. Moreover, there are no national lists of mobile phone numbers as there are for landline numbers. It does not mean that mobile phones cannot be used for telephone interviewing, but the challenge is a difficult one. How do you obtain a comprehensive list of all or nearly all available and used personal mobile phone numbers? The answer seems to be, for the most part and in most countries, 'You cannot'!

Face-to-face Interviews

The sample to be contacted and interviewed is chosen by one of the methods outlined in the section on sampling. Many audience research departments of non-commercial public service broadcasting have traditionally used face-to-face interviews in which people are asked about listening yesterday.

Face-to-face interviews are probably the most practical method for use in most of the less developed countries. The method is not only least expensive but is also usually the only feasible method in areas of high illiteracy and low telephone penetration. Meters have to be excluded from consideration in many countries because of the high costs involved as well as the usually under-developed state of the local advertising market. In most developed countries, much of the costs for meters are paid by advertising-related funding.

The BBC Daily Survey of radio listening (and for some years, of television viewing also) began as the Continuous Survey in 1939. At one time, 2,500 people were selected every day of the year and interviewed face-to-face in their homes about what they had listened to on the radio and watched on television the previous day. It continued until 1992.[5]

In the US, the advertisers clamoured for day-by-day and hour-by-hour ratings. They wanted to know, if possible, how many people were listening to commercial announcements between programmes. But in Britain and almost all other European countries, there was a monopoly of broadcasting allocated by the state, either to a state-run broadcasting service or to the one run on behalf of the public by a public body like the BBC. There was no radio advertising in most European countries. In Britain, the BBC existed to provide broadcasting as a public service. No one demanded to know how many middle-class women were at home listening at precisely 2.10 PM on a Wednesday! But advertisers and programme sponsors involved in commercial broadcasting, both then and now, do want to know just that kind of detailed information.

However, public service broadcasters did want to know quite a lot about the public behaviour and opinions. Programme planners—the people who decided to place a light entertainment programme after the evening news, or light music in the early evening or more serious talks and features in the early afternoon—wanted to know about public listening habits in quite a lot of detail. BBC planners had, over the early years between 1922 and 1938, gradually devised a daily pattern of programmes. Did it suit the listeners? Were any groups seriously disadvantaged? Early research had shown senior management at the BBC just how out of touch they were with the daily habits and lifestyle of the British public. The results of an early survey were something of an eye opener to the middle- and upper-class hierarchy at the BBC who had believed that nobody ate their evening meal before 8 PM. They were 'staggered to learn that most people had finished their evening meal by 7.00 PM'.[6] This had major implications for programme scheduling; managers realised that they had, in this respect, been getting things wrong for some 15 years. Would they find that in other respects, they were badly informed about audience behaviour and tastes?

Interestingly the stimulus to providing more systematic and reliable data on listening in Britain was the Second World War. There was a major disruption of social and economic life. As Silvey put it, 'programme planners found themselves very much at sea'. It was decided that a fully representative sample survey should be conducted to find out facts about the population in respect of its use of the radio. After this initial survey took place in October 1939, it was decided that similar research would be needed on a continuous basis and the Continuous Survey, later to be known as the Daily Survey, was born. Its objective was to estimate the actual audience for each programme. It began in December 1939 and continued until August 1992 when it was replaced by a self-completion diary system that was shared with commercial radio services that emerged in the 1970s.[7] Between 1949 and 1981, it was also the vehicle by which television viewing was measured. This is now done by a people meter system in cooperation with commercial television. It was the emergence of commercial radio that eventually led to the demise of the Daily Survey. The requirements of the commercial broadcasters could not be fully met by aided recall of listening yesterday, employed by a continuous survey of this kind. This is mostly because a questionnaire which only records the listening or viewing of the previous day does not provide figures for weekly reach or weekly share and cannot be used to plot changes in listening or viewing behaviour of individuals over several days. These can all be provided by the diary and meter methods. The diary method is the one now used by both BBC and commercial radio for radio audience measurement, while the meter system is in use in most developed countries for television audience measurement.

The Daily Survey was based on the assumption that people could give an accurate account of their listening or viewing behaviour on the previous day, especially if the interviewer reminded them of what the programmes had been and at what times. The questions were limited to a single day, the previous day. A day has, for most people, a natural beginning and end. People can be taken through the day from when they woke up to when they went to bed and to sleep.

A major task, as with all interviews, is to try to ensure honest and accurate answers. A lot of attention was given to training interviewers. She (most interviewers on surveys of this kind in Britain are women) would need to be in full control of the conversation. Everything said to the interviewee, from the introduction and explanation at the beginning to the thanks at the end, was prescribed and was the same for all interviewees. Silvey's account sets the scene and approach very well.

'I am working for the BBC, finding out what people listened to yesterday. Will you tell me what you listened to yesterday, please?'

The interviewer followed this question immediately with another:

'For instance, did you happen to switch on when you got up yesterday morning?'

This was followed by another question if the respondent was unsure:

'Well what time was that, do you remember?'

Having found out what time it was, the interviewer would consult the details with which she was supplied and follow with:

'That was when ... (programme title) ... was on. Did you hear that?'

It should be noted here that until 1973, the only radio broadcaster in Britain was the BBC. The interview would then continue quite rapidly with the respondent being taken through the day.[8]

Silvey had some important observations to make about the process, which are worth noting. They are still valid today.

> This rapid approach was calculated to convey the impression to the informant that the interviewer was businesslike and that the interview would not take long and also to encourage him to regard the encounter as a friendly challenge to him to see if he could remember something as recent as yesterday's listening. If he took it in this spirit, the focus of his attention might be diverted away from a possible preoccupation with the impression his replies were making on the interviewer. He would have told her all she wanted to know almost before he had realised he had done so.

It should be pointed out here that later on, the interviewers stopped the habit of identifying themselves as being from the BBC. Silvey claims it made no difference, but in this respect, he was certainly mistaken. It is bad practice for interviewers to identify themselves in this way. Independence is vitally important.[9]

To start with, the sample for the continuous survey was 800. That was the number selected and interviewed everyday. Originally, it excluded children under 16 but later included children down to the age of four, who would be interviewed with the assistance of a parent. Originally, the sample was selected in the street. Interviewers were instructed to select by quota a given number of people of each sex in four age groups. No one was omitted if it turned out that they had not listened at all on the previous day. The idea was to get the whole picture, and not listening at all was a part of the whole daily situation that was being measured.

The survey throughout its 53-year history has usually included extra questions at the end designed to answer contemporary issues for the broadcasters and planners. For example, at the beginning of the Second World War, there was much controversy about how the bad news of the progress of the war was being reported and about the continuation of light and humorous entertainment. In 1940, the news was regularly about disaster for the allied powers as one country after another fell to the Axis powers and British forces had to retreat. Some said that in view of the situation, it was inappropriate to have light entertainment programmes. The question was asked:

'When the news is grave do you think the BBC should cut down on variety programmes?'[10]

A clear majority (over 60 per cent) said 'No' and only 20 per cent said 'Yes'. Moreover, further analysis showed that most of those who had said 'Yes' did not listen to entertainment or variety programmes.

Another recurring issue was 'vulgar' jokes in comedy sketches on variety programmes. Many letters were received complaining of poor taste, a theme that has continued in listener mail to this day. Questions on the Daily Survey were used to find out what the listening public as a whole thought. As is often the case, letter writers were shown to be unrepresentative of general opinion. As a general rule, it seems safe to assume that those who write do not represent those who do not.

4.5 Research among Specific Target Groups

Often one may not want to obtain data from the general population. For example, specific media may be aimed at certain groups. Farmers, school teachers or pupils, people in the medical profession, rural development workers, children, members of ethnic, linguistic or religious minorities, people with disabilities and many other groups form targets for special programmes or broadcast services. They can be researched in such a way as to provide data just about them. For example, one could organise a survey among children to find out specifically about their reading, listening and viewing habits and preferences. If they are included in a general population survey, there may be enough children in the sample to provide the data that you need. But there may not be enough, and in any case, the normal coverage by survey may not include people younger than teenagers. Also, you may have some special questions just for children. In these cases, a specially designed survey among children may be called for.

The general survey may provide information on other subgroups, like professionals, farmers, members of ethnic or linguistic minorities, housewives and students. But very often, the subgroup in which there is interest will not be represented sufficiently in a general survey. For example, many public service broadcasters in Europe seek to provide services for members of ethnic and linguistic minorities. These will be selected in the normal way during surveys of the general population. They will be found among households with TV meters, and they will be among those who are asked to complete diaries. But normally their numbers in such samples will more or less reflect their proportions in the population as a whole, and there may be too few for separate analysis. For example, an ethnic minority accounting for five per cent of the population will normally form only five per cent of any representative sample. If that sample is, let us say, 1,000 or 2,000, the subsample of those from the ethnic minority would be only 50 or 100, respectively. These numbers would be a little too small to do any further detailed analysis. When you want to understand the media habits of minorities, especially designed surveys of these minorities may need to be carried out.

4.6 Survey Research for Small Stations

Can small radio stations with limited funds do their own surveys? Certainly they can, provided that they follow certain basic guidelines and rules. But remember that poor research can be worse than no research at all. It can give spurious validity to data that can be quite wrong.

The main disadvantage of a station doing its own survey research is that there is a loss of independence; when an outside body does the research, the results may have greater credibility. The experience of Australia seems to have a wider relevance. Although there is a regular system of radio audience measurement, this is mainly confined to the large cities. Australia is a vast country and there are many local and regional stations not covered by this research 'omnibus'.[11] But many of these stations are non-commercial and cannot afford to commission research in their area from a research agency. Some of these small stations do their own surveys and the national broadcaster, the ABC, has provided them with guidelines on how to go about it, mainly advising the use of telephone surveys.[12]

4.7 Readership Research

The oldest medium to which we refer here is the printed word. Mass printing and circulation from the printing press began in the 19th century and the popular press became the world's first mass medium. And the printing press is still with us, despite the many technological changes we have seen since the arrival of broadcasting, and more recently, the Internet and digital media. People read newspapers, watch television, listen to the radio, go online, read blogs and participate in social media to be involved, to be informed, entertained, follow their favourite football team, learn about new films, follow fashion or popular music and much else besides. There is much in common between the various media. They each may carry news, comment, entertainment, sport and a lot of other popular content. Some media carry material designed to appeal to minority interests and tastes. Nearly all carry advertisements. Money from advertising and sponsorship provides by far the greatest amount of funds for all these media. And it is advertising which drives and usually pays for much of the research that is done. In turn, it is this research which provides quantitative value to the advertising that is placed on the various media platforms available to the advertiser.

But as with all other media, newspaper and magazine writers, journalists, editors and managers are also interested in the behaviour, reactions and motivations of readers. When there is no research into readership of magazines and newspapers, the only way an advertiser can evaluate a purchase of space for an advertisement is from sales figures and publishers' claims. In some countries, this is still all that there is. Publishers will usually tell advertisers how many copies they print. But there is often a large gap between what is printed and what is sold. And publishers are in no position to tell us anything about how many people read each copy of the paper or magazine sold or what kinds of people they are. Then there is, to add to the complexity and challenge of measuring readership, the arrival in many countries of free newspapers or 'freesheets' paid for by advertising.

The quantitative methods used to measure readership are based on the same principles as those that have been described for measuring television and radio audiences. The main method used to measure readership has for many years been the face-to-face interview in a general adult population survey. The measure derived from this and the currency most often used in many countries is 'Average Issue Readership (AIR)', which is an estimate of the number of people who will have read on average an issue of a newspaper or magazine.

Various methods have been used to achieve this. The more common approach is to read out a list of magazine or newspaper titles, sometimes with a show card reproducing the images of the title or front pages, sometimes referred to as 'mastheads'. Respondents are then asked when they last looked at, browsed through or read any issue. Michael Brown, a leading expert in this field, describes how an AIR estimate is then made:

> The number claiming contact within a period of time preceding the day of the interview and equal in length to the interval between successive issues (the previous seven days, for example, in relation to a weekly magazine) is taken as an estimate of AIR. This technique is usually referred to as the recent reading (RR) method.[13]

This system is still in widespread use in many parts of the world. The main problem is that people may not always remember accurately what they read or when they last read it.

Another method is to ask respondents about what they read yesterday. This method enables comparisons to be made with other media contact, including radio and television use. It does not make such great demands on memory as the previous method described here. It also fits in well with radio and television measurement and enables a fair comparison to be made between different media. However, it does require very large daily samples to be taken for accuracy, especially if we are measuring readership of weekly, and even more so, of monthly publications, and it probably causes under-estimates of readership of non-dailies.

It should be mentioned here that readership surveys can also be used to establish data about the attention to sections of a paper, judgements of quality of contents or form, and so on.

Reading frequency is also often measured in surveys. Respondents are asked to estimate how often they read a particular publication by asking them to answer a question which gives a scale with labels such as 'most issues' or 'at least once per week' (for a daily paper) or 'occasionally'. Questions may be phrased to pick up habitual behaviour or they may relate to a fixed period such as 'within the last month'. The problem with such questions, like the same questions with radio and television, is that people can tend to overestimate their frequency of readership. Questions can also be asked about how long respondents spend reading a particular paper or magazine. The problem with all these questions is making reliable and meaningful comparisons with other media. Readership research depends very greatly on respondents' own version of what they do. With radio and television research the same often applies, as we have seen with many of the methods used. However, there is no equivalence in readership research of the people meter method now extensively used to measure TV viewing in most developed markets. These methods measure not what people say they watch but what actually happens with TV sets in people's homes.

Just as questions about both broadcasting and print media may be asked in face-to-face interviews, both media may be included in a self-completion diary. Indeed it is quite common for a diary, primarily used for radio or TV audience measurement, to include questions which ask the respondent to record his or her newspaper or magazine readership each day. The main purpose is to compare the use of different media.[14]

Newspaper and magazine readership can, of course, now be measured through online research and this method is growing in many countries. Lately, there are projects to harmonise the use of printed media (newspapers, magazines) with that of electronic media (TV, radio, Internet) by means of so-called cross-media studies. In the form of day-budget surveys, the volume of time devoted to each medium is measured. In order to arrive at a common contact currency for all media, results must be weighted on the basis of rules stipulated by the relevant joint industry committees (JICs).

Notes and References

1. Chappell and Hooper, *Radio Audience Measurement* (New York: Stephen Daye, 1944), pp. 219–220. The word 'flow' is used to describe how audiences move between programmes and networks. It is usually expressed as a measure of where the audience came from and where it goes after each programme or daypart. See the Glossary.
2. Hugh Malcolm Beville Jr., *Audience Ratings* (New Jersey: Lawrence Erlbaum, 1988), p. 88.
3. Beville, *Audience Ratings*, pp. 98–98.
4. http://www.itu.int/en/ITU-D/Statistics (accessed March 2015). The World in 2014: ICT Facts and Figures.
5. For an account of the Daily Survey, see Silvey, *Who's Listening*, p. 64.
6. Ibid., p. 65.
7. The radio measurement system in the UK continues to use diaries. The system is run by a Joint Industry Committee or JIC called RAJAR. For a description of the service and to see some data go to www.rajar.co.uk
8. Silvey, *Who's Listening?* p. 92.
9. Ibid.
10. Ibid., p. 97.

11. The word 'omnibus' is often used in commercial market research to refer to regular quantitative surveys for which there may be several clients. One questionnaire carrying questions for these different clients is used. Media omnibuses, which carry questions solely about the media and for media clients are sometimes used. See the glossary.

12. Dennis List, *Radio Survey Cookbook* (Adelaide: Australian Broadcasting Corporation, Audience Research Department, 1990). The reputation of this excellent training manual, produced specifically for local Australian radio stations, soon spread and the ABC received requests from many countries around the world. Dennis List decided therefore to produce an international edition, designed mainly for use in developing countries. Realising that telephone interviews were not suitable in many countries, he focuses attention in the new edition on other simple and low-cost methods. The late Dennis List was an independent research consultant and a revised and expanded version of his training book is now available online, which is called 'Know Your Audience'. Go to the audience dialogue website http://www.audiencedialogue. org/index.html. The book may be purchased online or you can request a free downloadable version. But enquire through the site.

13. Michael Brown, 'Media Research', in Robin Birn, Paul Hague and Phyllis Vangelder, *A Handbook of Market Research Techniques* (London: Kogan Page, 1990), pp. 334–345.

14. For details of how readership is measured in Europe see Readership Measurement in Europe, 1996, Report on Newspaper and Magazine Readership in Europe (Amsterdam: ESOMAR, 1996).

Chapter 5

Quantitative Online Research

This section is devoted to this new area of quantitative research made possible by online (Internet and mobile phone) facilities that have emerged over the past few years and especially since the last edition of this book. The use of online quantitative methods is fast replacing other quantitative methods in more developed countries, and it is also beginning to make differences in the less developed areas. Here we aim to show how new digital media have made possible new methods that have transformed market research over the early years of the 21st century.

5.1 Measuring with an Internet Sample

In many ways, the new quantitative methods made possible by the Internet have much in common with what they are replacing. They aim to do the same kind of thing, especially to provide data on a defined universe. For example, the online opinion polls run by the company YouGov[1] aim to achieve through an Internet-only panel what previous opinion surveys using face-to-face or telephone interviews have been doing for many decades. This section will look at how, through the recruitment and use of panels like those of YouGov as well as several other similar agencies, the Internet is now providing the main means of measuring opinion, media use, use of or access to consumer goods and services and many other aspects of human life in more developed countries. Online surveys have replaced telephone and face-to-face interviewing, and also postal panels. But as we shall see, although Internet or online methods are rapidly replacing face-to-face and telephone methods in much quantitative research, audience measurement for radio and television continues to be based on current methods of diary, face-to-face or telephone interviewing and meters.

If we, for a moment, leave media research to one side and look at the whole of market and opinion research, the use of online methods for all kinds of research is very advanced and well established. In its 2014 annual review of trends in global market research, the international professional body,

ESOMAR showed that around 61 per cent of all quantitative research spending is now for online projects. Given the fact that the cost of online surveys is very much lower than face to face, it means that an even higher percentage of quantitative measurement projects is now online. Telephone, face to face and postal methods account for 16 per cent, 12 per cent and 4 per cent, respectively. The report noted the very high level of use of online methods in such countries as Japan, Bulgaria, Sweden, Canada and the Netherlands, but it noted that many fast growing markets in Asia and Africa still relied heavily on methods using human contact, including face-to-face interviews. Countries that retain a high proportion of research work being done face to face included Kenya, Bolivia, Honduras, Bangladesh and Indonesia.[2]

The attraction of using the Internet for quantitative research is simple to explain. It is very fast, much less expensive than face-to-face, telephone interviewing or sending questionnaires to postal panels; the questionnaire programmes used are designed to reduce or remove interviewee and interviewer error and there is immediate data capture. It is not surprising that in such a short time, online quantitative research has become so widespread.

But how can the principles of sampling and representativeness that have been explained previously be applied to the Internet? How do we take a sample that is representative using something that is completely different from the use of maps, electoral registers and enumeration areas of a census or anything like that? We do not have an adequate sampling frame for the Internet or any part of it. So, we have to try a different approach. The aim has to be to create an 'analogy' or model of the universe we wish to represent.

The basic principle is to create this model or analogy of the chosen universe that is as much like the real one you want to gain data from and which can stand as its reliable and valid representative. What we need to create is an online panel including a very large number of people who are as far as possible representative of the population that you would otherwise want to access through some form of random sampling. What we are trying to do is to create an online panel that is as much like the whole universe or population that we wish to study or ask questions of. This new online panel consisting of many thousands of recruited individuals is what is used to take our samples from.

The task is to recruit a very large number of Internet users who are representative of the intended universe as far as possible who then form the Internet panel for the purposes of research. But doing this satisfactorily is a difficult challenge because although the Internet is now very widespread in most counties, it still does not reach large subsections of many countries' populations. Even in the wealthier and developed countries, Internet use is significantly lower among those aged 70 and over. And in most developing countries, users of the Internet using home computers are still in a minority.

The mobile phone is, in these less developed countries, much more widespread than computers, so much so that in many of the poorest countries in the world, a majority of the adult population now have some access to a digital mobile phone. There will be more on that important topic later. But we have to remember here that even if we include people with Internet-capable smartphones and similar devices able to participate in online research, there are still very large numbers in many countries in the world which remain out of any contact with online media of any kind.

But the trend is clear. The future of market, opinion and media research will be increasingly reliant on online methods, and this is perhaps truer for quantitative research than qualitative. But more on that is talked about in a later chapter.

Another company that has successfully recruited Internet panels for quantitative research is GfK. The Austrian part of this global market research company was able to build a national panel of respondents it could use for research by careful recruitment and selection. The panel members' individual demographic characteristics are known and appropriate samples for research can be carefully selected by panel management software. Precautions are taken so that respondents are not invited too often to answer a questionnaire. As with sample surveys done face to face using random sampling of residences and of people at each residence, it is possible with online research to boost particular subgroups who need to be over-represented if they are of special interest to the topic of the research. As with traditional quantitative research, the results can be corrected for the general population by weighting. The over-sampled segments will be down-weighted again to conform to the actual composition of the universe.

But what about those sections of the population who are under-represented? Those among these groups who do access the Internet are likely to be different in many important ways from those who do not. Older people who are regular Internet users are probably different in several other important respects from others in the same age group who do not use the Internet at all. It is, therefore, dangerous and unreliable for us to rely on panel members to represent others. To use the jargon—'Onliners cannot represent Nonliners'. This difficulty can however be overcome by supplementing online research with face-to-face or telephone interviewing among the missing categories of respondents.

One additional factor that has boosted the use of the Internet for quantitative research is that response rates in Internet panel surveys are much higher than for both telephone and face-to-face research in developed countries. While in most developing countries refusal rates for participation in face-to-face surveys are still very low (typically less than 10 per cent), the refusal rates in developed industrialised countries can be from 40 per cent to as high as 70 per cent.[3]

In order to achieve high response rates, online panels must be carefully managed. Panel members are given incentives and these have to be carefully administered. The questionnaires used must be well designed and must follow the special requirements of online research.

Panel Recruitment

What happens is that an access panel is created, often referred to as an online address pool. A well-recruited and well-managed online address pool or access panel stands at the heart of professional online research. Good recruitment practice is essential in creating representative samples. And after the pool or panel is created, the work does not stop there. Careful panel maintenance and a practical incentive system are decisive to achieve and maintain high response rates. Panel management software is required to assist panel managers with their tasks.[4]

Recruiting through Traditional-type Surveys

Many practitioners believe that the highest quality level for pool recruiting for online panels is achieved by doing it offline. By this is meant collecting email and home addresses of Internet users willing to participate in online surveys through telephone or face-to-face studies. Of course, this method is expensive and usually involves using research companies which still conduct a large number of representative telephone and/or face-to-face interviews. It is important here to note that neither face-to-face nor telephone quantitative research are likely ever to disappear entirely since the new forms of research including using the Internet need it for recruitment and for other reasons. And let us not forget another obvious example of a long-term need for face-to-face research. People meter research relies on the regular provision of basic demographic and related data obtainable only with proper randomised surveys of the population. The same applies to online research. We would not, for example, ever know how representative our online panel were if we could not go to data collected by means other than online.

An efficient way to recruit panel members is to include questions like these at the end of suitable regular general population surveys done by a research company:

'Do you use the Internet?'

'Would you be willing to participate in online surveys from time to time?'

This method helps to maximise the representativeness of the online pool, because it is the only way of also recruiting persons, who are not as active as heavy Internet users, to the pool: By doing so, one is able to create interest for online research in target groups that never would do something like this proactively. Nevertheless, Internet panels are likely to be skewed towards the younger and more educated segments of the population. Another bias is due to the fact that heavy Internet users are more likely to sign up. These circumstances must be taken into account of and where possible corrected for.

Recruiting Using Online Methods

In many cases, offline recruiting will not be sufficient to build a panel of sufficient size. The alternative or additional method is to do online recruiting. The research company or institute may try to find partner sites on which ads (buttons or banners) can be placed, inviting visitors to join the address pool. Potential panel members found in this way will be redirected to the panel management welcome page. There, respondents begin their double-opt-in routine. This means that they formally declare their willingness to participate in online surveys. Newcomers to the panel are pointed to rules about the confidentiality of data under the international professional body for all forms of market and opinion research, ESOMAR.[5] They are given information about incentives to be earned by participating in surveys and asked to complete their personal profile (age, occupation, education, leisure habits, purchasing interests, etc.). Naturally, the institute can also put a recruiting button on its own homepage or on a special landing page connected to the panel management software.

One must be careful in online recruiting not to collect addresses of 'incentive hunters' or 'multi-panellists' who are more often than not 'routine answerers' or 'straight liners' (persons filling in matrix questions without thinking and in a straight line down). Such self-recruited panel members will not represent ordinary Web users.

Snowball Recruitment

Snowball samples were described in the earlier section on sampling methods. The method can be used to recruit online panel members by asking the existing contacts to recruit others known to them who meet the required criteria. One can, for example, offer incentives to the existing panel members for nominating candidates. This can be done by a special button in the panel management software. In such cases, precaution must be taken in order to keep panel members from trying to earn additional points/money by 'shovelling in' masses of addresses. Such attempts can be dealt with in various ways—for example, by restricting the number of addresses each panel member may suggest to only a few per month.

Potential respondents recruited in one of these ways will be approached by email or phone and will be asked to fill in a basic profiling questionnaire. When using snowballing as a recruiting option, one has to be very careful and strict in checking the personal data of the recruited persons. Incentives should be paid only to the recommending person after a certain time of active participation of the new recruited panel member. Special care must be taken about bias resulting from recruiting persons of similar interests, background, culture, class, etc.

Purchase of Email Addresses from External Vendors

This method should be used only if there is no other way. Although a widespread practice, using addresses bought from commercial vendors contains the risk of bad quality. In some cases, those candidates are recruited who may be incentive hunters and who are members of several similar online panels. Panel members might be asked to fill in several surveys per week, which will most probably result in negligent behaviour. In all, response rates tend to be low—also due to a loose relationship in large panels between panel management and respondents.

Other Methods of Recruitment

Other ways to recruit panel members are to book advertisements (online and offline) or use social networks like Facebook, Linkedin or other communities. Meanwhile, not only young people but also older 'netizens' (Internet users) can be recruited in this way. If it is possible to put the invitation link on a popular site (e.g., of a high circulation newspaper), the response rate may be quite satisfactory. As will easily be understood, all these methods can produce unseen or unknown biases.

Incentives

It is accepted practice among research institutes that run Internet panels that the most efficient way of rewarding respondents is a 'points' system. Respondents collect in accordance with the amount of online work they complete. After having reached a certain number of points, the panel member is sent vouchers redeemable in a large number of different shops in the country where the members live. An average online questionnaire completed, to give as one example, in Austria, will result in the respondent receiving points worth from 1 to 2 Euros ($1.35 to $2.70). A reliable and attractive rewards system is crucial for response rates and data quality. This is a major difference with online questionnaires. With face-to-face and telephone surveys, incentives are not usually on offer.

Lotteries are also an alternative—especially when offering attractive prizes. Another form of rewarding is the promise by the institute to donate a certain sum to a charity institution if the respondent fills in the survey properly. In this case, the panel management will have to produce some kind of proof to show that this happens. Finally, it is also possible to offer the results of the respective surveys to respondents. This can be especially suitable and effective when doing online research in the business-to-business sector of research (this is research among professional and similar groups, the result of which will be of genuine value and use to the participants).

Optimising and Retaining Panel Size

In large countries such as Russia, Poland, India or Ukraine, large panel sizes may be necessary, in order to be able to sell regional studies. Normally, the size of the online pool should be in proportion to the number of interviews per panel member per year. For example, assuming the online pool comprises $N = 25,000$ members, sending out 100,000 online questionnaires annually would mean a theoretical average workload of just four surveys per year per member. But usually not all pool members have the same chance to be called up for surveys because some segments of the panel will be more important for some purposes than others—but the problem remains that respondent fatigue can arise due to a lack of required activity. On the other hand, panel members should not be invited for too many surveys per year, because otherwise there is the danger of non-participation or negligence in filling in questionnaires.

For this reason, it is necessary to observe carefully the development of return rates among members of the panel. Another factor to keep in mind is the administrative cost of panel management. In order to keep respondents happy and active, it is advised to create a community (or 'club') spirit among panel members by occasional lotteries, a club magazine or interesting news displayed on the pool platform—such as results of surveys or other interesting projects. Panel maintenance should be entrusted to a person who has a personal feeling for panel members and is able to stay with the job for a longer period.

Panel Rotation

If a panel is as representative as we can achieve, it will reflect the dynamics of society. In other words, panel members will marry and get divorced, and they will move house or change jobs. They may have to go to hospital, and some of them will die. All these events can cause 'natural' rotation—panel members who have to leave or just decide to leave must be replaced by appropriate new persons.

But there is also deliberate, planned rotation, sometimes referred to as 'artificial' rotation. This is required so as to keep the panel fresh and active. In practice, panel members are most reliable during the middle of their 'lifetime'. In the initial period—right after recruitment—they may still have some difficulties in fulfilling their obligations. At the end of their career, they may become a little negligent or may lose interest altogether. An annual general panel update, that is, a renewal of the personal profiles of all members, shows the actual number of active pool members. This is an opportunity also to update the list of or personal possessions or other facts about the respondents' lifestyle, purchasing interests and other similar features if each in individual. At this point, it may be decided to let go of some panel members who have served long enough and for them to be replaced by new panel members. It can make this process easier if when panel members are recruited it is explained that it will be for a set period, which may or may not be renewed.

Panel Quality Assurance by Respondent Verification

Panel management software can do many useful processes with an existing panel. It can tell, for example, if you have duplication by building a unique profile of each respondent based on the characteristics of both the user and his/her device. The software can create a unique digital fingerprint for each respondent, which is tracked constantly. By deploying these measures in real time, it is possible to ensure the integrity of a sample. The software can identify inattentive or fraudulent respondents, such as 'speeders' (fast survey takers who are careless about what they are doing), respondents with strange grid behaviour (e.g., straight lining, diagonal/extremist completion and similar patterns of behaviour) indicating that they are probably just ticking boxes without reading any of the actual questions properly. There are also respondents who exhibit contradictory behaviour or responses and these can be detected and checked automatically; for example, by checking the way text is entered (e.g., no answers, incoherent answers, too few characters, nonsense numbers, etc.)

Respondents with Inattentive Behaviour

At the end of a completed questionnaire, the respondent's engagement with the study can be evaluated in terms of his/her overall satisfaction with the survey experience, interest in the subject, perceived length of the activity of answering the questionnaire, whether the questionnaire was clear and easy to complete and whether it was repetitive or maintained interest and engagement.

5.2 Quantitative Research Using Mobile Phones and Similar Devices

The rapid spread of mobile phones, smartphones, tablets and other handheld mobile telecommunication devices all over the world has in recent years brought about the possibility of quantitative research through mobile devices. While asking a person to answer questions over a conventional mobile phone is not strictly online research, the use of the smartphone (a mobile phone with access to the Internet), the netbook (a small laptop computer with Internet access) or a tablet (a flat hand-held computer with Internet access) offer us the possibility to invite people to answer questionnaires via the Internet on a mobile basis.

Also there are limited ways also of using ordinary mobile phones (i.e., phones that are not smartphones) to send short questions that can be turned into a series of interactive text messages that can resemble a questionnaire. Therefore, even with simple mobile devices, some sort of market research using questions and answers is possible.

It is clear—and this issue is also addressed by the ESOMAR guidelines for mobile-phone-based research—that interviews via a smartphone, tablet and so on pose a number of problems that are different from those where computer-accessed Internet surveys are involved.[6]

First, it is of great importance to keep in mind that not all mobile phone users can be reached by online research. An Internet account is necessary and the user must be experienced in accessing it. Second, the screen size available on smartphones (even the newest larger sizes) is not suited for all possible kinds of questions. And finally, the duration of the research encounter is also a decisive factor, as respondents may find it difficult to stay online on a mobile device for as long as may be the case with a laptop or other keyboard computer, and probably not longer than a few minutes. Therefore, interviews confined to a very few questions with simple choice answers work better than anything longer or more complex when one has respondents using a hand-held mobile device.

However, mobile phone research has certain major advantages. It allows certain applications not possible with online research through a home computer. For example, research can be done at the same time that respondents are actually doing something else that may be of interest to a client—shopping, real-time media use (watching TV, listening to the radio, reading a paper, magazine or book, etc.).

Another advantage and potential source of rich data is the fact that participants with smartphones can use them to take pictures of what they are reading, advertisements that they are seeing and the street where they are and more. In consumer research, for another example, they can photograph the contents of their fridge to send to a research agency asking questions about consumption of groceries. Younger people already and no doubt people of older age very soon will be experienced enough in operating their mobile devices that they will certainly become a well-functioning target group. Autocorrect features, now available with many types of smartphones, assist owners in answering open-ended questions more readily. Thus, mobile research via smartphone is likely to continue to be a growing market research activity. It has been used in some less developed regions and countries. For example, in 2008, the development communication arm of the BBC, BBC Media Action, when researching opinions about government services in Sierra Leone, got respondents using their mobile phones to photograph and send examples of things they came across that illustrated both good and bad examples of government services.[7]

Technologies to help us carry out online quantitative research through mobile phones are developing rapidly. With the help of mobile applications, participants can post messages and pictures while they are out of home. Nowadays also geo-location (the automatic recording of a respondent's geographical location by his/her cell phone) is a valuable facility for several kinds of quantitative research.

The introduction of 4G (the fourth generation of cell phone mobile communications standards which enables mobile ultra-broadband Internet access) started in South Korea in 2006 and in Europe in 2009 and is making further progress around the world. It facilitates the use of the smartphone for real-time observation via live video. It may also introduce other possibilities and also make it easier to use more complex question formats than are possible with previous devices.

It is advisable to find out by special screening interviews which panel members are most suited to be invited for mobile online research. One possibility is to offer special apps for smartphone-based online research. Another method is to employ the Quick Response (QR) Code method to lead smartphone users to an online survey project.

QR code for the English Wikipedia Mobile main page

QR codes are becoming popular and are increasingly seen. QR codes can be published on billboards, in newspapers or magazines. By scanning a code with a smartphone, the user has direct access to a website, a micro page (i.e., a button leading to a company page) or a Facebook fan page—without typing anything.[8]

QR codes can be used to access train timetables, TV and radio schedules and a lot more. Their potential in market research is beginning to be exploited.

Recently, MMRA, the Mobile Marketing Research Association, was established in 2011 to be a 'global trade association dedicated to the promotion and development of professional standards and ethics for conducting marketing research on mobile devices'. On their website, more information about mobile research is available.[9]

5.3 Other Forms of Quantitative Online Research

It is of course possible to carry out online research without having ready-formed panels. And indeed these methods were used from the beginning of the Internet as a medium in the 1990s. Surveys can be conducted using addresses supplied by the client. In 2003, OCHA, the UN Office for the

Coordination of Humanitarian Affairs, commissioned a study of the way in which their news agency, Integrated Regional Information Networks (IRIN), dedicated to the collection and distribution of news and information about vulnerable, underdeveloped and unstable regions of Africa, Central Asia and the Balkans, was working. Among the many methods used in this evaluation was a questionnaire sent by email to all 18,000 subscribers to the IRIN online news service. It was also provided as a 'pop-up' on the IRIN website—http://www.irinnews.org/. There were 1,891 responses to the emailed questionnaire—10.5 per cent—a little disappointing perhaps. But at this time, most of the subscribers (the service was free but to get the daily news digests, you had to provide IRIN headquarters in Nairobi an email address) were news media, development and emergency relief agencies, government departments and interested individuals in the regions that IRIN operated in, at that time mainly Africa. At that time, Internet connections were often very slow, unreliable, expensive (many users relied on Internet cafes) or otherwise difficult. Replying to a questionnaire was not a priority, however worthy the cause, for many users. This experience showed, however, that the method worked well, provided useful and actionable results and was inexpensive and quick. The questionnaire on the website produced only 91 responses. This seems to be a common phenomenon; questionnaires directly targeted at relevant people will get a better response usually than pop-ups on a website that will appear to users either at random or at certain intervals between 'hits'.[10]

5.4 Subscriber (Readership/Editors) Studies

Another way of conducting online surveys without the help of an address pool is to cooperate with a print medium which is interested in the ways its regular readers use the medium and their opinions of it. In this case, a sample is drawn at random from a list of subscribers. In cases when not all email addresses are known, the institute would have to call subscribers asking for cooperation or screen its pool for readers. For general insight, only medium-size samples are required. Should the paper/magazine want to contrast the opinions of its readers with those of its editors, the journalists' email addresses must also be provided. Response rates will be higher with readers however. The exercise can be done once—in order to find out about reading habits and the general acceptance (likes and dislikes) of the printed product. Or it can also be done in the form of periodical detailed monitoring or tracking or reader activity and opinion. Also, some magazines use this arrangement for 'title page tests' in order to find out with which front page photo or headline will work best with its readers. Another application is testing the efficiency of ads ('copy tests').

5.5 Online Survey Software

There are now a very comprehensive and varied number of software packages available from the Internet, some of them free that help you create and send out online questionnaires. The most well-known is probably the SurveyMonkey® www.surveymonkey.com

There are several guides to what is available with good advice how to use them.[11]

5.6 Online Quantitative Research for Traditional Media

We end this section with a brief look at the thus far rather limited use of online methods to measure audiences for TV, radio and print.

TV

The many varied functions of television (information, entertainment, education and advertising) and its different forms of reception (live, time-shift, online, mobile) offer a great number of opportunities and challenges for practical Web-based audience research. In much of the world today, TV audience measurement is still largely done using people meters. However, it is being challenged now to include the measurement of Web TV or the viewing of TV on personal handheld devices, including smartphones and tablets.

This challenge is being met and it is likely that most users of TV audience measurement data—management, programme directors, TV advertising sales departments, media agencies and advertisers will continue to rely primarily on the data delivered daily by TV meter measurement (ratings, market shares, GRPs, appreciation scores and other metrics). Online methods will be used to add to what the people meter systems already provide, but we are not likely to see online research methods displace the people meter systems, albeit suitably amended to cope with new ways of viewing TV, at least in the foreseeable future. If all televisions eventually become connected to the Internet *and* if all terrestrial, satellite and cable transmission of TV signals ends, it would be a different matter. This seems very unlikely. But then, where we are now would have seemed even more unlikely when the first edition of this book was published little more than two decades ago.

However, online research still has a role today in quantitative research for TV. Online surveys can be used on an ad hoc basis for particular projects. But as these are chiefly to obtain audience response, opinion and the like they are covered in Chapter 8.

Radio

As explained earlier, radio audiences are usually measured in three ways—through the use of diaries, face-to-face or telephone surveys asking about yesterday listening, and by personal meters that record what the person is listening to.

For the diary and the aided recall method, much depends on the listeners' memory. The two methods are usually restricted to quarter hour by quarter hour time recording and rarely get any more detailed than that. It is rather different to the TV people meter system which records activity in a way less prone to human error and also in much more detail so far as time is concerned, down to seconds in fact. But as noted earlier, the radio meter is very unlikely to be a successful means of radio audience measurement because of the drawbacks mentioned.

But can online methods add anything to the existing methods? In the Netherlands, the JIC for radio research, Nationaal Luister Onderzoek (NLO) has a system run by Intomart GfK for national radio audience measurement which uses a diary, online or on paper. This panel consists of 7,500 listeners who record their daily radio consumption in 15-minute blocks. In addition to this, 325 members of the panel wear one of the passive radio meters described earlier. This is the kind that is built into a watch and which records short snatches of whatever is being listened to. In this way, the two technologies come together to 'offer the Dutch radio market minute-by-minute information on radio audiences for the first time.' Additionally, it was announced in 2014 that a smartphone e-diary for young members of the panel is being introduced to provide a more complete picture of their radio habits.[12] In the UK, RAJAR, the JIC for radio measurement has introduced online diaries that 52 per cent of the UK panel now uses.[13] It is of course of great advantage to have research done this way. It substantially reduces costs (of postage, data entry and the online advantages of error minimisation and logic).

Print

As with both TV and radio, online quantitative research is used for the measurement of print readership in rather limited ways, mainly to supplement existing methods. One good example is this one from Austria. The main readership measurement tool in use continues to be a national survey ('Media Analysis') using a large sample and daily face-to-face interviews.

Since 2006, there has been a special online print readership survey for print media that can prove a circulation of at least 20,000 printed copies. The survey provides a chance for all those publications to be measured which cannot take part in Media Analysis, the big national media survey, for different reasons (cost, regulations, etc.).

This survey is carried out online and uses the methodology referred to earlier—the recent reading or RR mode. The last two issues of each publication are presented onscreen and this helps to increase the ratings achieved by less well-known titles, the recent readership of which may easily be forgotten by many respondents. The online questionnaire used contains numerous questions regarding personal interests, leisure activities and lifestyles.

In the above mentioned example, 41 publications were included in the questionnaire, most of them free sheets. The survey normally runs over the first half of every year and has a sample 5,000 selected to be representative of people between 14 and 65 years of age. The sample is drawn from an online pool maintained by the agency. Results are published in a small brochure; a data set is available for analysis.[14]

There are many more ways in which online methods can be used in media research, but in this chapter we concentrate on audience measurement. First there is the new approach that comes with online technology— passive measurement using the very technology on which the Internet is based and we find that in the following chapter on Passive Measurement. The many other ways that online methods are used are found in later chapters on Qualitative Research and on Audience Opinion and Response.

Internet

Obviously online methods can be used in quantitative research about the Internet. However, as research using the Internet to measure or assess the use of the Internet by users falls into two main categories—passive measurement and mainly qualitative research techniques and outcomes—these topics are left to the appropriate chapters.

Notes and References

1. YouGov was founded in 2000 in the UK. It was the first successful attempt to use the Internet for quantitative research. Its UK panel has 400,000 members. It claims to have a further 2 million panellists in 11 countries, but this hardly justifies the title it gives it—a 'global panel'! http://yougov.co.uk
2. ESOMAR, *Global Market Research* (2014), pp. 122–123 and passim.
3. It is very probable that respondents in many more developed countries refuse to take part in face-to-face or telephone surveys because they are asked too often or even more likely that what purport to be surveys are in fact marketing exercises and lead on to attempts to sell insurance, double glazing or other goods and services. This is often called 'sugging' which comes from the acronym 'SUG'—Selling Under Guise—meaning trying to sell goods and services under the guise of market research. Professional market and opinion researchers detest sugging for obvious reasons. Sugging has not yet infected less developed markets. When it does, it will probably push up refusal rates for legitimate research.
4. Some examples are www.nebu.com/, www.confirmit.com, www.markettools.com, www.micropanel.com/ and many more. Google 'panel management software' to find what is available.
5. http://www.esomar.org/publications-store/codes-guidelines.php (accessed 16 September 2015).
6. Ibid.
7. BBC Media Action former research director Gerry Power.
8. For further information about QR codes go to http://en.wikipedia.org/wiki/QR_code (accessed 27 August 2015).
9. http://www.mmra-global.org/ (accessed 16 September 2015).
10. Sharon Rusu and Graham Mytton, *IRIN Evaluation* (New York: OCHA, 2003). Available online at https://docs.unocha.org/sites/dms/Documents/IRIN_Evaluation_FINAL_version.pdf (accessed 16 September 2015).
11. Rodney A. Reynolds, Robert Woods, Jason D. Baker (eds.), *Handbook of Research on Electronic Surveys and Measurements* (Hershey, PA: Idea Group Reference, 2007); Vivek Bhaskaran and Jennifer LeClaire, *Online Surveys for Dummies* (Hoboken: Wiley, 2011).
   As far as Internet software is concerned aside from Survey Monkey www.surveymonkey.com, there are others including www.surveygizmo.com, www.keysurvey.co.uk, www.smartsurvey.co.uk, www.esurveyspro.com, and many more (accessed 16 September 2015).
12. GfK Press Service Hilversum.
13. Correspondence with Lindsay Ferrigan of RAJAR, 23 March 2015.
14. http://www.tmc.at/studien/cawi-print.html (accessed 16 September 2015).

Chapter 6

Internet Audience Measurement: Passive Methods and Technologies

6.1 Introduction

This chapter is about Internet audience measurement. Mostly it involves measuring the audiences of 'online media' in a 'passive way', that is, without asking any questions of respondents, but with metering technologies using inbuilt digital technology.

Why is this important? Obviously it is because our consumption of online media has exploded over the last three decades. An illustrative metric that demonstrates this is the evolution of IP addresses. Wikipedia defines an IP address as 'a numerical label assigned to each device (e.g., computer, printer) participating in a computer network that uses the Internet Protocol for communication'.[1] Remember that it was only in the early 1980s that first IP address ever was assigned. In February 2011, the last remaining bit of the available IPv4 (IP Version 4) addresses was released, thereby exhausting the pool of 4,294.967,296 (2^{32}) addresses in IP protocol v4. The new IPv6 (IP Version 6) has 2 to the power 128, or about 3,403 × 10 to the power 38 addresses. This ought to be sufficient for the coming decades.

This chapter is not about IP addresses. It is about people and how they engage with the online media they use. Advertisers, publishers and e-businesses are investing a lot of money to reach their audiences and consumers online. But how effective are they in reaching these? Who did they reach and for how long? Were users engaged? And did the messages have impact?

One would think that the Internet makes everything measurable. That is certainly true! Every piece of activity on the Internet leaves exact and recordable evidence. So the above questions should be easy to answer. And yet, the opposite is true. The problem is that there are so many metrics available to us that one does not really know which one is 'true'. Besides that, things are changing so rapidly on the Internet that even if you have the truth, you do not know exactly 'when' it was true, nor for how long. And finally, the landscape is enormously complex, so one needs to understand exactly what one is measuring and what are the biases and interferences.

This chapter is about the distinction between 'old and new' and what makes modern Internet audience measurement different from traditional audience measurement. We explore this by the following topics: in the second section, we discuss the most common metrics in Internet audience measurement. In the third section, we take a close look at how the metrics are obtained, that is, the technologies used. The fourth section deals with the commercially available tools. In the fifth section, we discuss what is different when working with these types of data mostly 'Big Data'. Last, we will look at some text analysis software.

Our challenge is to explain the basics of the methods and the pros and cons of each of them in a comprehensive way, but without going too deeply into the technologies. With our simple explanations, we do not mean to overlook the sophistications of any existing and new technologies, but readers interested in the technicalities can find more from the plethora of documentation on the topic readily available on the Internet, for example, the famous Lumascapes.[2]

Stated versus Actual Behaviour

We saw earlier in the description of people meters used for measuring television viewing that in research, we often come across differences between what people say they do and what they actually do. The Internet allows us to measure what can be measured, while traditional questionnaire surveys continue to be used for what cannot be measured by technology, such as opinions. Some measurement companies claim to measure Internet audiences, but after asking one or two more questions, it appears that they are measuring not by metering, but by surveying. So you have got to be aware of the measurement techniques that are being used, and what can and what cannot be measured. That is what this chapter is about.

Metering, also referred to as passive metering, is defined as a tool (using software or hardware) that registers (passively) certain behaviours of the individual. So the collection of the 'actual' data is passive (no questions are asked). The fact that the participants whose behaviour is monitored have had questions put to them before their online activity is measured—such as 'are you willing to participate in this type of research?" or "what is your age?'—does not make the method an 'active' method. In active (survey or interview) methods, questions are asked with the purpose of actually gathering data about somebody's behaviour.

Measuring actual behaviour has several advantages over measuring what people say about their own behaviour. Metering data are almost real time, while survey methods can take weeks or months of fieldwork. Data from surveys using questionnaires, however administered, depend on memory, which can be faulty. Moreover, online behaviour is complex and multifaceted and passive methods measure behaviour in the kind of detail and with a level of accuracy that is impossible from memory alone. Some online phenomena (like the amount of ad-impressions or the duration of viewing a preroll[3]) can be measured more accurately than with traditional methods (if it can actually be measured at all by these methods). Data collection by metering is usually significantly more cost-effective and less cumbersome for the respondent. Moreover, in recent years, there is evidence according to Nobel Prize winner Kahneman that participants usually are in a so-called system 2 mode when they are surveyed, which makes their answers more rational. System 2 thinking is slow, effortful, infrequent, logical, calculating and conscious. If you catch respondents within a few minutes of doing something, their answers are more straightforwardly produced by system thinking 1: fast, automatic, frequent, emotional, stereotypic and subconscious.[4]

6.2 Metrics

Owned, Paid and Earned Media

You might want to measure the use of media that you own, like your own website or your mobile app. You might want to measure the usage of media which you pay for, like your online advertising campaigns. You might lastly want to measure the share you have on social media, often referred to as 'earned media'.[5] The starting point is to decide which medium or which media you want to measure.

Owned media are all the online media that you directly own. These are for example, your website, your mobile site, mobile apps, blogs, your Twitter account and Facebook page. Paid (also known as bought) media are the media you use to leverage your owned media, such as paid search, advertisements and sponsorships. Online advertising contains a range of possible formats that will surely grow and get more and more creative in the future: display, rich media, prerolls, homepage takeovers, advertorials, and so on. Earned online media are also known as 'when the customer becomes the channel'. Buzz, word of mouth, anything that is said about your brand in online (social) media.

The next thing you need to decide is what metric you want to have measured exactly? Reach, buzz or audience? And do you need a metric or do you need a currency? Let us dive into these subjects now.

Website Metrics

The most important reach metric is the number of unique visitors (UVs) your media have reached. UVs differ from visits in that if you visit a certain website twice, you will be counted as two visits but you remain one UV. Immediately you see here that, related to the metric of a UV, is the definition of the time span in which those consecutive visits have to take place. UVs can be calculated on a daily, weekly or monthly basis. MAU is a well-known abbreviation meaning Monthly Active Users and is the most commonly used metric. The difference between DAU (Daily Active Users) and MAU is an interesting measure of how frequently the site is visited. Has the site become part of daily use? With Google and Facebook, for example, the differences between daily and monthly measures are very small. It means that most users over a month are very likely to be daily or nearly daily users.

Other key metrics are 'page views', 'visits' and 'duration'. These are measures of engagement with the site. The number of page views is exactly what it says: the number of Web pages visited to a specified website (also called main domain). A visit is a series of page views within in one website (main domain) visited by the same participant. Between each page view, there is a period of no more than 30 minutes; otherwise, it is defined as inactivity. Duration answers the question: how long was the visitor looking at a certain page, or how long his/her visit took? A range of metrics is available derived from the key ones above, such as the number of page views per visit, the number of visits per UV, and so on.

The IAB (the Interactive Advertising Bureau) maintains a good set of definitions on the most important metrics for websites and also for advertising.[6] Always be aware of definitions; it makes a lot of difference if a website visit is defined within a period of 30 minutes or 15 minutes, or whether the UVs are daily or monthly.

With reach metrics, one can obtain a good picture about the 'traffic' on ones owned media. Most owned media are equipped with Web-analytics tools, such as Google Analytics or Omniture (now Adobe). These produce the required reach data on the domains that you own and that you have activated. In a separate paragraph on Web analytics, we explain which tools there are and exactly how these work.

If you are interested in the amount of traffic on your site as a 'percentage of the total traffic' (in a country), you need measurement of the activity of the total population in order to calculate this. For example, if your site had one million UVs last month, then your reach in terms of MAU is one million. If you want to calculate your market share (or relative reach), you need to know how many users were active online last month in your total country (or population). Suppose that was 10 million, then your relative reach was 10 per cent.

Bigger online measurement companies like comScore, Nielsen or Compete, usually provide population numbers, usually based on a panel combined with a weighting and projection algorithm. Sometimes these population metrics are even adopted as the official currency.[7]

The concept of reach and page views is also applicable for online advertising, but then page views are called impressions. This is simply because the visitor can look at one page that contains several ad-impressions. Additional parameters in advertising are visibility (the percentage of a display ad that has been displayed to the visitor) and duration (the percentage of the preroll that has been viewed by the visitor).

A special metric is 'bounce rate'. A 'bounce' is when a visitor sees only one page of a site, a one-page visit. The visitor does not enter the site because he/she came there by accident or coincidence, or because it is his/her starting page (e.g., google.com or microsoft.com) and he/she immediately browses to another page. A high bounce rate is also an indication of high-affiliate mail activity. Those are email campaigns that try to seduce the reader to click on an ad or a link. Sometimes, people are even paid for to click on those links.[8] When the visitor has reached the destination site and he/she sees it is not of interest for him/her, he/she bounces! So the bounce rate is the amount of one-page visits as a percentage of total visits.

Another special metric is CTR (Click Through Rate) defined as the total amount of clicks on an online ad (banner or preroll) divided by the total amount of impressions. The average CTR has decreased over the years to less than one per cent. One should not conclude, however, that campaigns have more than 99 per cent waste these days, because it could also be that it was not a transaction campaign but a branding campaign. In other words, the objective is to raise awareness rather than specifically to gain sales.

Reach data on your owned social media accounts and your paid media are also available, usually provided by the platforms on which these are served, such as the way Twitter provides the numbers of followers, and Facebook the number of likes and fans. Google search provides for unique searches. Advertising networks provide for impressions and sometimes also uniques (UVs).

Overlap

One individual is able to consume different kinds of media, on several devices, and more and more so at the same time. Using your tablet when watching TV or reading a paper with music from your smartphone, we all do these media activities at least sometimes and the practice may well increase as the technologies make it possible. For publishers that have a strong presence through different channels, it is crucial to know the relative importance of each medium and the 'overlap' between those channels.

Let us take an imaginative example of a news site called yournews.net. Suppose they have a website with 10 million unique monthly visitors, half the country's Internet population (of 20 million online monthly uniques). They also have a successful app for smartphones and tablets with 10 million unique monthly visitors. If yournews.net wants to know its total reach in that country, it cannot just add 10 + 10 = 20 million, suggesting that it has 100 per cent reach in that country. This would only be the case if the overlap between the website visitors and the mobile app users = 0 per cent. On the other hand, if the overlap is 100 per cent, the total reach our yournews.net would be 10 million, being 50 per cent of the total population. In reality, it will be between 50 per cent and 100 per cent, depending on the 'overlap': the number of visitors that are visiting yournews.net both on the website as via the app, on a monthly basis.

Audience Metrics

All reach data derived from the technology on which the Internet relies give quantitative data on the traffic. But they do not tell you anything about 'who' you are reaching. Yet, each company having any marketing strategy at all has a target segment they want to reach with their online media. Most reach measurement techniques are so-called server-side, that is to say that the traffic is measured at the Web server or the ad server, and they cannot measure who is visiting a site or seeing an ad. So-called user-side audience metering (which sits at the other end of the online activity—the user's devices) is usually panel based and offers the possibility to measure the background characteristics of the audience in terms of basic socio-demographics (age, gender, income, education, region and sometimes other) and also more advanced data such as brand preference, household composition, psychographic segment, and so on. For a further explanation on user-side metering and server-side metering, we refer to the specific section on this topic—in Section 6.3 Technologies.

'Waste' is a term used a lot in advertising. It is a special measure that says how many impressions did not reach the target group. Although never measured accurately, it is believed that only 25 per cent of online campaigns are served to people within the specified target group (e.g., males between 20 and 45), thus creating 75 per cent waste.

Social Media Metrics

Measuring social media (or earned media, that is to say, media where your brand, product or service are mentioned but you do not pay for this) is usually done with a range of so-called 'buzz' metrics. The first is the number of followers (equivalent to UVs) and—when measured over time—the audience growth rate. The second is their engagement, measured by the amount of updates, posts or tweets per unit of time. The visitor frequency rate, also known as the number of return visits, is a measure of how effective the acquisition strategy has been. Are these all one-time visitors, just trying the product, or do they come back often?

Sentiment analysis is used to indicate the sentiment of the posts or tweets, being positive, negative or neutral. Of all tweets, typically one-quarter contains a brand or product name (the rest is about more trivial subjects, like the weather), and of that, only one quarter has a positive or negative sentiment. This means that only a quarter of a quarter—1/16th (6 per cent)—of all tweets are relevant for audience measurement purposes. The rest are about the weather or similar matters unrelated to a brand, product or service, or express no sentiment.

Multi-device Media Consumption

Advertisers, publishers and media agencies use owned, paid for and earned media to relate to their audience across all their online devices. One can measure several metrics on each device, or each channel but that does not give any insight into how these channels combine to engage with the user. For example, a famous TV show might generate tweets and visits on a branded mobile app on tablets (a second or third screen). The best measurement solution is to have all data from a whole lot of single individuals, the so-called 'single source'. The same person whose social media use you seek to measure is the same person whose website visits and mobile apps usage are of similar interest to you. The best place to measure all this media consumption is at the level of individual participants, simultaneously on all his devices (multi-device) and all the person's activities (multi-activity). Technically, this is very challenging, but some companies are showing great capabilities here.[9]

Since, as we noted earlier, less than one per cent of online advertising leads to a click through (meaning it leads to a possible purchase transaction), the rest must be about indirect (or delayed) effects, such as an uplift or increase in site visits, app usage, search behaviour and social media posting in the days or weeks 'after' somebody has seen a campaign. This has to be done at a single source level. Some user-side techniques even measure any consecutive online purchases a person has made, which means that purchases can even be attributed to specific online campaigns. This can be very valuable data for media buyers.

These days, it is most common to source audience measurement data from different sources or databases and to then try to fuse them. Data fusion is a statistical method that integrates two or more databases that come from different sets of individuals, by matching up these individuals on common variables or 'hooks', such as demographics, lifestyle and media usage and product preferences. While scientifically a very sophisticated technique, it nonetheless proves to be very difficult to produce accurate and useable multi-device data.

Currencies

The data described above can be obtained by in-house software solutions or via third-party data providers like comScore, Nielsen, and so on. In-house software solutions do not go beyond the media that you own, so it's hard to compare the performance of your site to that of your competitors. Third party data providers may well have that opportunity if they have made deals with other players in the industry to exchange data, or if they are user based.

As a publisher, you will obviously be interested in the reach you have in the total population; what share of the total Internet population was consuming your media at a certain point in time. How many people were reached exactly, and in which audience segments? The reason for this interest is that publishers create attention from the audience and sell this attention to advertisers. So the better you are in creating attention among the right segments, the more valuable any specific advertisement on that page was.

Some countries in the world have adopted online 'currencies'. These are the official and independent standards for the online reach and audience data of the country's websites, just as in the same way there are currencies for radio, TV and press audiences. The currencies for online media consumption do not have to be always exactly right, but they are the industry-accepted standards by which advertising exposure is being valued.

There are different systems for how to select, manage and monitor a currency. In countries like the US, any company is allowed to sell currencies, as long as they are accredited by the Media Rating Council. In other countries, there is a system of one single currency that is officially endorsed by a JIC, usually the existing representatives from the advertisers, publishers and media agencies, as is the case in most European countries for radio, TV and the press.

These currencies for traditional media have been around for several decades. Currencies for the Internet prove to be quite difficult because of the rapidly changing character of the medium. It usually takes more than a year before a JIC has set its standards for online data and has commissioned the research. Then, the method chosen to collect these data must also be a proven method. This means that once the currency data are available, they are produced by technologies and methods that may be some years old, which is a long time in the Internet era. On the other hand, everybody seems to know that online currencies are not the whole truth, they are an attempt to create a practical measure of media use, comparable to currencies that already exist for other media and which are a standard endorsed and accepted by the industry.

6.3 Technologies

Topology

The best way to understand the Internet measurement is to divide it into three sections: the server side, the user side and the network side. The flow of bits from the user to a site starts with the person, using a device, the device having an operating system on which a browser is running. All this is user-centric. When the user starts the browser, it makes a connection to the Internet. When the user types a certain site into the browser bar, the browser starts looking at this destination site and the corresponding Web server. This process is all network-centric. The user has a connection with the Internet; this connection is provided by an Internet Service Provider (ISP). Within milliseconds, the browser connects to the server of the destination site and the browser displays the requested Web page. In the meantime, ad servers may inject ads into the advertisement spaces on that particular page. The actions of the Web server and the ad servers are all server centric.

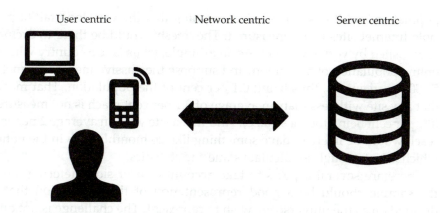

User centric   Network centric   Server centric

In this section, we explore how these technologies work and we discuss the advantages and disadvantages of each.

User-centric Metering

User-centric metering[10] is obviously the closest we can get in the digital sphere to measuring what an individual online user actually does. We are looking here at individual people and what they actually do when they are online. This is especially so when it concerns personal devices such as smartphones, and less so when concerning a household computer. (This is because the latter is more likely than the former to have more than one user.) The technique requires installing a meter on the device of the user or a plug in within the browser software of the device. This is not possible for a total population, but for a specific sample of the population, a so-called passive metering panel. Participants are asked for socio-demographic details and in this way an accurate assessment of 'audience metrics' is obtained. In order to enhance the panel data to population data, the data are filtered, weighted and 'projected'.[11]

Besides being highly accurate when it concerns audience characteristics, the big advantage of user-side metering over server side is that it does not require the participation of advertisers or of publishers: there is no need to place a tag or beacon on the site or in an ad to make it measurable. User-side metering requires only the permission of the user. From that moment onwards, their total online behaviour can be measured.

The drawbacks of user-side metering are all related to the fact that it is a panel-type method: the panel needs to be given incentives, it needs to be recruited using hybrid methods in order to minimise biases, it needs to be managed in a way that makes it a representative of the total online population and it has a mesh size, meaning that the very long tail of possible Internet sites is not measured. The 'mesh' would be there to exclude sites visited by very few users. As an example, let us take a country with an online population of 50 million, and suppose the passive metering panel is 50,000 participants, thus being 0.1 per cent of the population. That means that any site with less than an average of 0.1 per cent reach is not measured (0.1 per cent being the mesh size). And that a site with an average 2 per cent reach would be likely to have something like 20 monthly UVs in the panel, which is just enough to calculate some site statistics.

There are several aspects to take account of user-side metering. First, the sample should be a good representation of the population that is decided on as the universe we wish to represent. The challenge is not only managing the composition of the panel, but also accurately determining the composition of the population of rapidly changing Internet audiences. The second aspect is that one needs to be aware of the fact that several different people may use any device being metered in a household. Finally, when initiating the panel, one should try to get as many devices in the household activated as possible, attached to one individual (single-source metering). International measurements standards (from the IAB) also emphasise the need for clear definitions in user-side metering: is it measuring unique browsers, unique devices or UVs?

User-side techniques are usually fast in data reporting (near-time or real-time). User meters can contain some intelligence, such as intercept surveys (a pop-up survey as soon as a participant visits a specific site or measuring the actual visibility of a display ad, and so on).

Meanwhile new kinds of meters with the software to go with them are being developed that can do different tasks at the same time: for example, a mobile app that measures the mobile phone usage and at the same time takes samples of audio to check if you are watching TV or listening to radio.[12] This is done by matching the audio sample with a database of sound samples from the available radio and TV sources, using a technique called ACR (automatic content recognition).

Server-side Metering and Cookies

Among all the methods discussed here, server-side metering—also called site-based metering—is the most established one. It initially began by analysing the website log files and became more sophisticated by the use of cookies. A log file is a file containing a list of actions that have occurred. Web servers, for example, maintain lists from every request that is made to the server. When analysing log files, one can obtain a good picture of how often visitors are coming to a site, how they navigate through it, and so on. When cookies are used together with these log files, Web masters can even get more detailed information about the individuals.

A cookie is a piece of data stored by a server or website on the device of the user (within the browser), and then subsequently sent back to the same server or website by the browser. So the websites keep a track of their users by putting a simple piece of code on the browser of the user, that piece of code collecting what the person is doing on that particular website. Functional cookies were designed as a mechanism for websites to remember things that a browser had done there in the past, which can include having clicked particular buttons, logging in or having read pages on that site previously. Later on there came statistical cookies, used to calculate site statistics. Then, also came third-party tracking cookies, commonly used as a way to collect long-term records of individuals' browsing histories over 'different participating' websites. These third-party cookies build up intelligence about the individual, which can be used for advertising or e-commerce purposes: the server reads the cookie and displays the content (a promotion or an ad) that is thought to be most attractive to this individual.[13] The European Directive on (online) Privacy allows only the use of third-party cookies when they are collected with the 'informed consent' of the individual.

By design, server-side metering is good at metering 'all actions' of all visitors performed on a site during a certain time period. On first sight, that looks attractive for the calculation of reach metrics, especially when compared to the panel-based user-side metering. However, there are several aspects to take into account.

The main problem with server-side metering is the cookie-duplication phenomenon. In short, cookies overestimate the amount of unique users. It is not uncommon for any Web-analytics tool to report that there were more UVs to a certain website than that country's entire Internet population. The point is that cookies are not measuring people, but they are measuring 'unique browsers'. Cookies do not distinguish real people from Internet robots. Every new browser gets a new cookie. So if a person uses both Chrome and Firefox, he counts as two separate actors. If he also uses a tablet and a laptop, this counts as two more. He is also counted as a new person every time he deletes his cookies (which is on average done about 2.5 times a month). By inviting you to login to Google on all the devices you use, Google is able to de-duplicate your visits and in this way solve the double count issue. But, in general, it can be said that cookies overestimate the amount of unique users.

The other obvious drawback of server-side metering is that by design, it does not measure audience metrics. Because the individual is not involved in this technique, it is hard to know the socio-demographics or any other background variables of interest about the actual user. Some techniques try to solve this by deriving background variables based on what people key in, or on statistical algorithms based on their behaviour. Currently, our research shows that the best possible cookie-based audience metrics are still on average 50 per cent off-spec, meaning that in 50 per cent of the cases, basic socio-demographics like age and gender are not predicted well.

Large metering companies like comScore and Compete have advanced techniques to overcome these problems. Fundamentally, it comes back to using 'panels' with different sorts of cookie recognition that are used to 'link' the different data sources together. De-duplication and linkage typically takes a week or two of data analysis, which means that these statistics cannot be real time but have a delay of a few weeks.

Whereas user-side metering requires only the participation of the user, third party cookies require participation from a range of different media channels. Tags need to be implemented by each medium to ensure the browser-cookies record a certain action or impression. Some companies, like Google and Facebook, limit their participation to these third-party cookie programmes, leading to black holes in the data.

Network-centric Metering

The Internet, being a worldwide public network of computers, connects servers with the devices. The route between the two systems can also be measured. This is the so-called network-centric measurement. It differs from the previous two types of measurements because it is not targeted towards specific nodes in the Internet, but to the network that is in between. It is usually the ISP which has access to all these data (including wireless providers and mobile operators) and which also needs them to manage the network capacity. Network-centric metering deals with analysing the headers of the IP packets that are sent through the Internet. The purposes are network visibility, traffic optimisation and policy enforcement. One technique is called aggregate traffic measurement.

Deep packet inspection (commonly known as DPI), is the most sophisticated technique and gives the ISP access to the contents of the IP packets sent through the Internet. DPI runs on network routers and is the real-time measurement of enormous amounts of bits. It can only be applied by network ISPs. This technique is mainly used as spyware for governmental purposes. In some countries, law forbids the use of DPI. It is hardly used for research purposes because it would require the ISP to inform the total subscriber base about them inspecting the contents of all traffic that passes their network.

Hybrid Methods

With the many current and on-going technological developments on the Internet, new techniques will arise. An example is a 'smart cookie' technique used nowadays for advertising tracking. First, a huge panel is realised. This 'panel' is not the classical market research panel; it is a low engagement panel existing only on a database containing the IP addresses and some socio-demographics of the users. Participants in this panel only need to give their approval and their background information once, after which they are not invited to install meters or to participate in surveys. So a huge database containing the right information also suffices. These techniques are usually commercialised by online advertising tools and several advanced panel companies.

For each campaign, a tag needs to be placed in the code of each banner, more specifically, in each banner or website combination. For example, if the campaign contains nine different creatives (advertisements) that will be shown on eight different sites, 72 tags (9×8) need to be placed. The tags are programmed in such a way that every creative item presented to a known IP address (from the database) is registered. In this way, the number of impressions can be measured and the audience characteristics also.

A prerequisite for this technique is that a database with IP addresses and socio-demographics is available (and obtained with the right permission), and that all tags are placed in the right way by all parties involved (this is very difficult; usually at least a dozen tags do not work properly). This technique measures only if the ad has been shown or exposed, not any indirect effects of the ad on the behaviour of those exposed (like a higher search volume or a higher online engagement with the brand).

Online Privacy and Data Ownership

The concept we discuss here can easily be made into a separate book. Legislators, authorities, public opinion leaders and consumer groups are becoming ever more concerned about the way that the data we have been discussing in this section have been obtained. Were the consumers aware that their digital activities were being monitored? Did they give informed permission for this to be done? The whole issue is very widely debated, especially in Europe, and relates to the interpretation of a suitable definition of what are personally identifiable data and of who owns different kinds of online data.

One of the causes or progenitors of this on-going debate is the difference between the practices relating to privacy in the United States and in Europe. In Europe, it is a matter of 'privacy by design'. Privacy is a fundamental right and an obligation for any technique measuring the Internet. In the US, privacy follows the opt-out principle: it is a right that can be obtained 'when asked for'. Despite this fundamental difference, both sides of the Atlantic seem to converge on the same point of view. This is that there is the obligation to obtain 'informed consent'. 'Informed' does not mean a 49-page EULA (End-user Licence Agreement), but an understandable piece of information describing what data are collected, for what purpose and who is going to use them. 'Consent' usually means 'double opt-in': 'Yes I want to participate in this type of research' and 'Yes, I give permission after having understood what it exactly is.'

The strict European legislation makes a distinction between functional cookies (the cookies used for measuring website traffic, for improving the website performance) and third-party cookies (those used to collect data on your surfing behaviour in order to serve specific advertisements). The underlying development that drives this discussion is the hybrid models that companies like Facebook and Google use. On the one hand, they offer an unrivalled user experience: the largest social network in the world, and the fast search engine and browser. At the back end of these platforms, the advertisers come in. Google and Facebook collect data on each individual and they then sell these data plus access to these individuals to advertisers. With these revenues, they improve their consumer proposition, increase their market share and thereby increase their advertising revenues.

On the other hand, more and more individuals become aware of the increasing value of this knowledge and detailed intelligence of their digital footprint. In 2003,[14] based on the social exchange theory, it was estimated that, given the right conditions, people are willing to exchange 'privacy' information against a value of $15. In 2006,[15] the European Union (EU) calculated that the value of open data in Europe (i.e., releasing all government information for free) would be €27 billion. That is €55 per European citizen, with a valuation of around $100 billion, the value that Facebook held in 2012 is roughly $120[16] (€90) per active member. So the footprint of an individual seems to increase in value every year. One could, therefore, ask: who actually owns these data? Is it the individual who produces a digital footprint by being online? Or is it the technology that records this and makes the footprints visible? Or is it both?

Cookies or Persons?

As a summary of this section, let us take a look at the following chart. Clearly, there is a trade-off between cookie-based data on the one side and user-side metering on the other side. Cookie-based data are easily available on all the visitors to a certain site or domain and they are inexpensive. But they are also inaccurate and with sparse content. Data available from user-side metering, which are highly accurate, are extremely rich data on the behaviour of individuals across all their online devices and all their online activities. But they are also more expensive, elaborate to set up and are sample based, thus requiring weighting and projection techniques. In the first case, you measure cookies; in the latter case, you measure people. In the coming years, companies will surely try to get closer to the sweet spot (the upper right-hand corner): rich and accurate data about large parts of the Internet population.

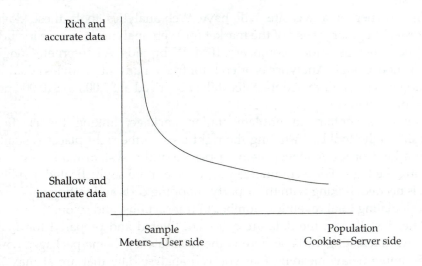

6.4 Tools and Vendors

Now that we understand the metrics and the technology that produce these metrics, it is good to see what tools are commercially available to work with these data. There are simply four categories: Web analytics, social media monitoring, advertising tracking and behavioural metering. We discuss each of those categories in this section, explaining what they are and what they are used for. The end of this section is devoted to (new) quality standards applicable in this area of data collection.

Web Analytics

Web analytics (also known as automatic Web traffic measurement) are defined as the measurement, collection, analysis and reporting of Internet data for purposes of understanding and optimising the usage of one's own website.[17] As we know, Web traffic can be measured with the help of log files recorded on the Web server. A hit is generated when any file is served. A page itself is considered to be a file, but images are also files, thus a page with five images could generate six hits (the five images and the page itself). A page view is generated when a visitor requests any page within the site. A visit is the uninterrupted use of a series of website pages. In this way, quite precise measurement is possible about contact and length of contact of a device (personal computer, laptop, smartphone, tablet, and so on) with a Web page and its content. Thus, precise comparison of websites regarding the number of hits, unique users and visits, as well as the duration of visits is possible.

Any owner of a website will have Web-analytics tools these days. Forrester's regular scans[18] of the market for Web-analytics software include suppliers such as Adobe, comScore, IBM, Webtrends, AT Internet, Google and Yahoo. Google Analytics is offered for free for any site with less than 10 million hits per month. Adobe Sitecatalyst is priced at $5,000 to $10,000 per year for a small site.

The tools contain an implementation package, linking the existing website to the tool by installing the right tags on the right places (usually with a kind of tag manager, being a person and a system managing and placing the tags). For e-commerce purposes, a more sophisticated installation is needed, linking with third-party shopping carts and setting variables for calculating total revenues, number of transactions, and so on.

After installation, the data are collected, filtered and prepared for analysis. An interesting variable here is the data latency. Some packages have a 15-minute delay; meaning that you can analyse data that are at max 15 minutes old. Some (cheaper) tools have a 24-hour delay in the data, meaning that today you work with the data of yesterday. In a quick changing Internet landscape that may be a bit slow. Storing of the data is another important aspect, because of the analysis of (historic) back-data that is sometimes required. Some tools also offer integration with social media monitoring here.

Finally, all tools have an online dashboard on-screen for reporting and analysis, with a default structure, a customisable part, and mostly with export and sharing and distribution functions. An interesting feature is campaign attribution, where you can upload your media scheme and analyse the effect of the campaign on your Web traffic. Most dashboards contain nice visualisation tools, several ways to deep-dive into the data and funnel/conversion analyses.

Web analytics are a universal and crucial tool for any site owner. The data apply only to the sites you own, and yet the integration with other data sources may enlarge the scope. The technology is server-centric, so the main problem here is that hits, page views and visits are generated by devices and not by persons, even though there is a person doing the clicking. Log file analyses can, therefore, not considered to be a reliable guide to the actual number of human visitors. And what is more, and this is of great importance in media research, especially when it comes not only to meeting the needs of advertisers but also of those engaged in providing worthwhile and effective public services in communications. The demographic nature of the visitors to a site as well the actual location where access takes place (at home, at work, at school, etc.) remain unknown.

Social Media Monitoring

Social media monitoring is about listening to what your audience is saying about you on social media. It is about analysing the data and finally, it is about creating insights that will improve your social media strategy or even your overall marketing strategy. Social media for our purposes here include blogs, wikis, micro-blogs, social-networking sites, video/photo sharing websites, forums, message boards and user-generated content in general. Most tools used are already connected to a range of social media, either by using 'crawlers' or by an API.[19] Crawlers are Web robots that crawl Web pages—pretending to be a human being—and that scrape information from those websites. They go beyond your own social media; they monitor everything that is posted on the different channels. The quality, quantity and speed of the data exchanged strongly determine the price of the social media monitoring tool. For example, the Twitter fire hose is a real-time connection with all the public data of Twitter; it contains 100 per cent of the Twitter data, in real time. The tools process the data from social media to a range of typical social buzz metrics. Some also calculate the impact of a post. Obviously, the more outspoken a tweet is, posted by a highly influential person, followed by many followers and re-tweeted many times, the more impact this tweet has.

A critical part of data processing is the so-called sentiment analysis. Special algorithms are developed to automatically determine the sentiment of a mention on social media—positive, negative or neutral. The family name of these algorithms is NLP—natural language processing. Practice teaches us that coding by hand is generally still necessary because these professional text analysis programmes cannot do the whole job reliably. They can also be quite expensive. However, there are a number of free or very inexpensive programmes that can help to gain a first impression of the content and meaning of a text. One way of proceeding is to make lists of positive and negative words and phrases to look for. This may seem straightforward but take care with this. Sometimes what may seem to be a negative sentiment may in a certain context be positive. The obvious case or example is the word 'wicked'. In the context of a blog by young people, it is probably most often used as something positive. The word 'cool' is usually a positive one, but it can also be negative in some contexts. There are likely to be several similar examples and more will emerge in conversations and other forms of human communication. The best social media monitoring tools contain a part of automatic processing and leave the 'difficult' social mentions to be analysed by humans. It is easy to evaluate the quality of the sentiment analysis feature in any tool: just browse through the categorised (positive) tweets and check if there is any tweet that is negative and thus is categorised wrongly.

After the data collection and processing, the social media tools break down into two categories, depending on the purpose of the tool. One category is aimed at audience analysis and insight generation, the other category is aimed at customer service. For some companies, Twitter has grown to a full-fledged customer service channel and is an integral part of their contact centre. The customer service tools can be very sophisticated and integrated with the existing customer relationship management (CRM) software.[20]

Social media monitoring as an audience measurement tool, for example, for measuring share of buzz, is available in a range of tools. Some of them are free, some of them are expensive.[21] When you are looking for a tool, it is good to try a couple of free ones and then choose the one that suits your needs best. The cheap tools are not an alternative to enterprise-level tools[22]; the latter offer a much higher variety of services and in-depth analysis. They also offer richer and faster data and more accurate sentiment analysis.

Advertising Effectiveness

The easy way to measure online advertising effectiveness is to use your Web-analytics tool, determine the baseline (the number and length of the visits before the campaign) and check any effects on the baseline after the campaign. A bit more sophistication can be introduced when using a specific landing page for this campaign, and then the traffic derived from it can be measured directly. The ad network will also bring its own data to the table: the amount of impressions and the amount of clicks.

Tagging ads is another way of measuring ad effectiveness (see section on hybrid techniques). Companies like comScore, Compete and Nielsen provide the campaign data based on these techniques. To date, indirect (or delayed) effects of advertising are not offered as a separate software tool. They might become available in the future. Behavioural metering tools though are a rich and very powerful source of indirect advertising effects, yet the data need some processing in order to derive the real effects of advertising on real individuals (on singe source level), across all their devices and all their activities.

Behavioural Metering

Behavioural meters are pieces of software (tracking applications) that are placed on the device or devices of the user. Depending on their capabilities, these meters register browsing (urls), searching, ad-exposure, video and music consumption, on one or more devices. These data are also referred to as clickstream data. Some of these meters act at the level of the operating system, some at the level of the browser. If it is browser specific, one might miss out on parts of the individual's online behaviour when he/she uses a different browser.[23] Usually these meters cache the online activity and send it back to a central server without disturbing the performance of the devices and with minimal battery depletion. Some meters have advanced functionalities like intercept surveys (pop-up surveys) and GPS tracking.

Behavioural meters are on the user-side. Companies like Nielsen, Compete and comScore use these user-side meters as an integral part of their metering technologies to create their data products. Other companies, like Wakoopa, Symphony AM and Reality Mine, offer these behavioural meters white-labelled (meaning that the technology is fully branded to the requirements of the client) so that they can be used to track and analyse proprietary panels, such as a readership panel of a big publisher or a survey panel from a large market research agency. Traditionally, there were companies that specialised in PC meters and ones that specialised in mobile meters. Only Symphony AM and Wakoopa have cross-device meters, measuring single individuals across multiple devices. Both are also independent companies (i.e., not belong to a big research group). With the acquisition of Arbitron,

Nielsen has also bought the mobile-metering technology of the Finnish firm Zokem. GfK has acquired Nurago in an early stage, which was specialising in PC metering. TNS has strategic links with the PC meters of Compete and the mobile meters of Reality Mine.

When working with an independent vendor of metering software, you will need to recruit, manage and incentivise the panel yourself. Once the meters are installed, you will either get the raw data files directly or you will get access to a nice dashboard displayable on your computer screen by which you can analyse and digest these big data. The collected datasets find their applications in four different areas: competitive analysis and benchmarking, advertising effectiveness, customer journey research and audience research/market segmentation. In all of these cases, considerable data analysis is required to obtain the desired insights.

Quality Standards

When working with an external vendor, one needs to check if they have the same standards of quality as you have. This is especially relevant in the domain of passive metering because most of the technologies and vendors come from outside of the research industry. Some of them are start-up companies that ended up doing audience research. Traditional suppliers of market research, like panel companies, survey software companies and telephone data collection centres, are all spin-offs from research firms, they come out of the research industry so they know the industry 'rules' because of their origin.

There is no world-wide International Organization for Standardization (ISO) standard yet for this passive and digital analytics area. The Dutch market research association, the MOA—as one of the first associations of its kind in the world—has defined this quality standard[24] and has started to audit and accredit companies that are active in this area. Since one of the authors of this book has been involved in setting up these standards, it may be worthwhile to review the most important points here, from first hand.

In summary, there are seven points that your software vendor needs to clarify when you work with its data:

1. What are the known biases in its data? 'If the vendor knows that its sample has for example an overrepresentation of younger people, it needs to inform you about this.'
2. What sources are included/excluded? 'Your vendor needs to inform you if certain sources are not included in its data, such as for example

https traffic in behavioural meters, or certain social media in social media monitoring.'

3. Were there any (accidental) black-outs in the data collection? 'Your vendor needs to inform you whenever there was a temporary black-out in the data collection, for example, when the Twitter API was out of order and data were (possibly) lost, or when the passive meters were not functioning well because of a serious outage on a cloud computing facility.'

4. What are the controls they have on the continuity of the data inflow? 'Your vendor needs to inform you about the way it monitors the continuity of the data inflow. Suppose Google launches a new version of Chrome (which they do quite often) and suppose one of the meters stops functioning, how and how fast is this signalled?'

5. What are their policies on storage and destruction of data and reports? 'Your vendor needs to inform you what is done when you complete a project. What is being done with your analyses? What is being done with your data records and your log files? How long are they being stored? How are they destroyed?'

6. Are there any data-fusion assumptions (e.g., on socio-demographics)? 'Your vendor needs to inform you what assumptions he has made in presenting the data. For example, if a tweet has been given a high impact, how exactly is that impact calculated? And if, say, 35 per cent of the tweets on a specific subject come from men, how do they know these are really men? Has it been asked, or is it a sophisticated guess-timate?'

7. What are the recruitment and incentive schemes (if applicable)? 'Your vendor needs to inform you how the panel has been recruited, by which method and with what incentive scheme. Using different methods decreases possible biases, and a neutral incentive (like money) is better than a specific incentive (like a ticket to a football match, or the chance to win a special freezer for your Heineken beer!).'

6.5 Working with the Data

So far, in this chapter, we have discussed the metrics that describe audience behaviour on the Internet. We have looked at the technologies that produce these 'passive' data and the commercially available tools that enable you to work with these data. Some of the tools have dashboards that immediately give you the data you need. In some cases, you need to do some processing yourself to come up with the required answers.

This section deals with the latter case. What happens when you start working with these—so called big—data? The section breaks down into several topics. One is about the new rules that apply to working with big passive data, also containing some with methodological reflections. Then we discuss what software tools are available for your data processing, like statistical tools and text analysis tools.

New Working Principles for the Internet Era

The Internet makes everything measurable. While more and more data become available, producing audience measurement ratings for online media become more and more difficult. Why is that? Well, the simple answer is the more methods you have, the more data you have. And if you change the method, you change the data. So the more sources, the more differences there are, the more effort is needed to get all these data to converge into one (acceptable) number that represents something like the reality. But there are more fundamental differences between today's online media arena and the traditional measurement of radio, television and print media consumption.

One very obvious characteristic of today's online behavioural patterns is that they change rapidly. Uptake of new technology is today much faster than it was a few decades ago. Just when the researcher has established and validated a new methodological framework, the world has changed and the validity of this model becomes questionable. Statistics and methodologies are usually introduced as a kind of Holy Grail, but that is merely because we do not really understand what they are saying. So we tend to think that their algorithms improve the quality of the outcomes. In reality, they introduce uncertainty in the data and decrease the effectiveness of the measurements. So the following principle applies here: 'In a world that changes rapidly, assumptions are dangerous, so make as few as possible!'

The second issue that relates to this rapidly changing environment is that researchers do not have the time to accurately establish the 'universe'. The universe is the definition of the total online population based on several variables like age and gender. That definition is needed to weight and adjust any sample-based measurement. In the past, the universe may fluctuate somewhat, but for market research purposes, it was generally accepted to use a so-called 'Golden Standard', which was renewed every year. If we look, for example, at the currently available golden standard for online media in the Netherlands, it is based on measurements that are about a year old, resulting in an underestimation of smartphone and tablet penetration of more than 50 per cent. The principle that applies here is: 'use golden standards (on media usage) only if they pass the logic test'.

Another significant distinction with traditional media research is that virtually all data on online media use are obtained by 'passive metering' instead of surveys. So there is no interference by the respondents who are being monitored, the data come in automatically. Also, you will get data that you have not asked for. And they also come from multiple sources. It is as if the data say: 'when we are passive, you have to become more active'. Every data source is another representation of the reality. So you, as a researcher, need to make up your own picture of reality by the 'triangulation' of different sources. You need to use Bayesian statistical thinking. Bayesian statistics are described as a field of statistics in which the evidence about the true state of the world is expressed in terms of degrees of belief or, more specifically, Bayesian probabilities. So here is our third principle: 'When data come from everywhere, accuracy comes from you.'

Heisenberg, a famous physicist, once stated there is always a basic level of uncertainty that is buried in the relationship between time and properties (in this case of elementary particles). When the properties are exactly known, then the time and place are uncertain. And if the time and place are exactly known, then the properties are uncertain. This principle applies too in our world of online media measurement. It goes like this: it is impossible to know 'exactly' what the total online activity of a whole country was, say yesterday at 'exactly' 4.45 PM. If you want to exactly know the total online activity of a whole country, it will be an average over several months (if not more). If you want to know what happened on the Internet yesterday 'exactly' at 4.45 PM, you will be able to say that for only a small part of the population.

Since behavioural patterns can change overnight, one needs to have data on these patterns on a daily level, if not on an hourly level, real time or at least near time. These time constraints go at the expense of the representativeness of the measurement, which brings us to the principle of 'workable accuracy: better be fast and about right than slow and exactly wrong'.

Our last and final principle has to do with a phenomenon that is strikingly present online: the effect of heavy users. The page views and visit duration of a certain website are usually non-random distributed: there are always some extreme users that form a long tail in the distribution. So besides averages, you also need to have a coefficient to describe the inequality among values of a frequency distribution of page views or visit duration on a certain website or app. Our final principle is: 'Don't throw data (outliers) away, they are part of the observation, just be warned that the outcomes may be volatile.'

Statistical Error

So when we say, 'the accuracy comes from you', you will need some background on statistics. Here we go.

The basic metrics in online audience measurement are the number of people that are reached (reach); the frequency and duration of the page views and the frequency and duration of ad impressions. User-side online audience measurement estimates reach, frequencies and duration in the population by measuring it in a sample. The precision of a metric is described in terms of error. The total error is the difference between the metric in the sample and in the population.[25] Errors occur for different reasons. One reason is that not all members in the population can be measured[26]; these errors are sampling errors. Large sample sizes help to reduce sampling errors.[27] Coverage errors occur because of differences in the composition between the population and the sample. Furthermore, errors occur when not all participants cooperate in the research; this type of error is non-response error. Non-response can be caused by missing at random, partly missing at random or not missing at random. When non-response is not missing at random, the respondents and the non-respondents differ systematically.[28] And if the non-response is dependent on the variable of interest, it can lead to biased results. There are no corrections for non-response not missing at random and it can be detected only if the sampling frame is known.[29]

To be able to draw conclusions about the population, the sample needs to be a reflection of the population or universe that we are interested in. The ability to make inferences about the chosen universe or population rests on the assumption that it is possible to draw or create a representative sample of it.[30] But it is difficult to define the Internet population, because of its dynamic nature.[31] There is no sampling frame of the total Internet population; therefore, the desired probabilities of inclusion or exclusion cannot be computed.[32]

Online access panels are a primary source of data for marketing research. Online access panels are recruited using non-probability or self-selective recruitment methods. By adopting non-probability sampling methods, the probabilities of being in the sample are unknown. A major part of online access panels cover only a small part of the population and the estimates possibly suffer from non-coverage errors or self-selection bias.[33] It is hard to determine the quality of online panels, and there are no real guidelines or rules for the construction of an online access panel.

Panel members have some things in common that make them to some degree different from the rest of the population. They like to complete questionnaires and they use the Internet frequently.[34] 'Professional' panel members are panel members who like to participate in multiple panels, they are oriented towards the rewards on offer and they may even change their user demographics so as to be able to participate in more research.[35] Professional panel members are overrepresented in online access panels compared to the share of professional panel members in the population. Additionally, professional panel members frequently visit free-ware or coupon sites.[36] Vonk, van Ossenbruggen and Willems[37] compared 19 online panels in the Netherlands. They found that the panel members on an average participate in 2.73 panels.

Weighting Adjustment

A possible solution to correct for some biases can be weighting adjustment. Weighting techniques correct for differences between the sample and the population through auxiliary variables (covariates). The covariates are measured in the sample and in the population, and the distribution of the covariates in the sample and in the population is compared. The sample is selective if the distribution of the covariates in the sample and the population differs.[38]

Two weighting techniques are used frequently in online measurements: propensity score adjustment and iterative proportional fitting (IPF). Propensity score adjustment compares the sample with the population and it estimates group membership based on the distribution of covariates in the sample and the population.[39] The propensity score is the probability of being in the sample or in the population.[40] IPF (also known as RIM weighting or raking) is an iterative method that corrects a table of data cells first performed in one dimension and then in another until convergence is reached. IPF is designed only to correct the marginal distributions.[41]

In audience measurement, it is a common practice to use these techniques because they reduce biases. For the weighting adjustment to be able to work, it is crucial to identify the relevant covariates: a) all relevant covariates have to be included in the model. If not all, relevant covariates are included in the analysis, this results in a hidden bias; b) the covariates should be dependent on the variable of interest as sample and the population on the variable of interest.

Weighting techniques are used to correct for biases, but it is not always tested whether this succeeds. They are often applied either way because it is thought that it does not hurt to try. Yet, the weights introduce error and this reduces the reliability of the metrics. Therefore, weighting should always be applied with caution and wherever possible, assumptions should be checked.

Practical Guidelines

After this scientific section on statistics, we need some practical tips when working with big passive data sets. The four V's apply for big data: volume, velocity, variety and veracity. Our definition is: you get 'a lot' more than the data you have asked for, so you need to find the interesting bits. This requires a new skill called synthesis. Where analysis starts with a piece of interesting data and digs deeper and deeper, synthesis is about finding interesting patterns in an enormous file of data, most of which you will not use. Synthesis requires blending in other data sources to test your assumptions (including free data sources like Google Trends), and it also requires your common sense. Synthesis is a skill that consultants typically have, while researchers are better analysts. The market research company Brainjuicer produced what we believe to be an excellent paper on this topic. It also won at least one award and is accessible on the Internet for free.[42]

We have five recommendations when working with these big passive data:

1. Start anywhere, go anywhere: Don't focus too much on the research objective, you might overlook new and interesting patterns. Just start.[43]
2. Start small: When you start working with the data, your mind will not be available to process all the information. You will suffer a light form of 'infobesitas'.[44] So you need to help your brain by filtering out data that are more meaningful. You better start small. If you do clickstream analysis, for example, why not start with the clickstream of one person, to understand his customer journey? This one journey alone will probably contain sufficient observations and will raise sufficient questions to continue your research on your total sample.
3. Test and kill: As soon as step 2 has generated sufficient hypotheses, just start checking them one by one. If they do not hold, kill them. If they hold, you may have found something interesting.
4. Combine methods: The most powerful research set-up is mostly when passive is combined with active. So once you have found interesting patterns in passive data, you may use a pop-up survey just to check if your assumptions are right. Or if you find a few people with highly interesting online behaviour, you might want to invite them for a focus group.

5. Team above tools: You will get the best results when other people form your team look at the data too. Take a technological point of view, an industry point of view, a client's point of view and a researcher's point of view. That combination is far more powerful than any research tool.

Statistical Software

Most tools that were described earlier have a dashboard to make the required analysis and possibly to cut out the interesting pieces of data. Once you have found such an interesting part of the data set, you can choose to export it and start analysing it in further detail with the programmes that you are accustomed to using (SPSS, Excel, and so on). In case you have a data set that is too big to be handled by SPSS or Excel, there are special big-data-packages available for this volume of data. An example is Tableau.[45] Google is also offering capabilities in this area. These are typically enterprise packages that need to be implemented and that require training. There are also more dedicated packages available. On Wikipedia,[46] a comprehensive list can be found of open source statistical packages and proprietary statistical packages. You may expect that these statistical packages become smarter and more powerful every year. Statwing[47] is an example of this. You can import your data easily, and Statwing starts generating statistical relevant relationships between the variables you choose. Depending on the type of variable, Statwing automatically chooses the best corresponding statistical method. It generates conclusions by itself, it has a solid statistical justification and advanced graphics.

6.6 Text Analysis Software

Word Clouds

A word cloud generator is to be used to analyse quickly a text 'corpus': for example, answers to open- ended questions (verbatims) or search terms.[48] Any other text can be converted into a colourful 'cloud' that displays the words in sizes according to the frequency of their occurrence. Two examples of word cloud software are:

1. Wordle: Using this programme, all one has to do is to paste the chosen text to be analysed into the box on http://wordle.net. Wordle also

accepts texts from Web pages or blogs. It is possible to restrict the number of words displayed, convert all words to lower case, and to select a specific layout and colouring. The so-called 'Advanced' feature of Wordle http://www.wordle.net/advanced makes it possible to create word clouds in which the colours are not coincidental but are predefined. Thus, for example, word frequencies can be indicated by using different colours for different frequencies instead of only size as an indicator. This feature can also be used to express 'sentiment', that is, to present positive, negative and neutral opinions by specific colours.

2. Tocloud: This free programme http://www.tocloud.com/ also creates word clouds. They are not as flashy but can contain the number of occurrences (word frequency). So it can be used for a first look at a text corpus to find out which words dominate it. The following example is an analysis of the US constitution. The words 'United', 'States' and 'State' were excluded and the number of words was restricted to 100.

US Constitution

President(34) Congress(29) House(23) law(23) Section(22) Office(19) Senate(17) person(16) Representatives(16) time(16) Constitution(14) Cases(12) Years(12) Power(12) thereof(12) Number(11) Laws(11) thirds(9) Consent(9) Legislature(9) Votes(9) Members(8) provide(8) Vice(8) Manner(8) vice president(8) Officers(8) Year(8) public(8) Senators(8) Article(8) executive(7) supreme(7) Electors(7) Citizens(7) Duties(7) Authority(7) Treason(7) Case(7) Bill(7) Union(6) Money(6) Persons(6) chuse(6) Court(6) elected(6) Service(6) chosen(6) coin(5) Houses(5) Jurisdiction(5) Majority(5) Impeachment(5) receive(5) supreme court(5) respective(5) vote(5) day(5) vacancies(5) enter(5) foreign(5) Term(5) establish(5) Rules(5) ten(5) Government(5) public ministers(4) subject(4) Party(4) Trust(4) War(4) Legislatures(4) Powers(4) proper(4) Militia(4) ministers(4) direct(4) Representative(4) Trial(4) Page(4) Places(4) Senator(4) holding(4) vested(4) Ambassadors(4) Officer(4) present(4) Journal(4) bound(4) new(4) grant(4) post(4) inferior(4) Citizen(4) Proceedings(4) Imposts(4) —to(4) judicial(4) equal(4) Times(4)

Further Text Analysis Software

Text Analyser is a free online tool that offers frequency count, percentages and occurrence of phrases (2–8 words). It is fast, simple and can read Cyrillic and other alphabets. http://www.online-utility.org/text/analyzer.jsp—The software may be familiar to many readers as it is often used in teaching institutions to detect plagiarism in student's essays. Another tool is AntConc 3.2.2.1w.[49] This programme is another free, academic online tool. It offers frequency count/wordlist, one-click concordance, multi-language.

Download it from: http://www.antlab.sci.waseda.ac.jp/antconc_index.html

Concordance Programmes

While frequency counts give you a first impression of the main ideas contained in a text corpus, concordance opens the way to a better understanding of context. Simple Concordance[50] is a programme that allows you to see key words in their contextual environment ('concordance' is here called 'Kwic' = 'Key words in context'). This helps to distinguish between its use in positive and negative context.

Coding Programmes

Sophisticated data analysis and coding software is available from different firms, mostly at considerable cost.

1. Weft QDA
    It is an easy-to-use, free and open-source tool for the analysis of textual data such as interview transcripts, field notes and other documents. Unfortunately, this software has not been maintained or updated since it was issued in April 2006. But you can download it from: http://www.pressure.to/qda/

2. Transana
    It is software for professional researchers who want to analyse digital video or audio data. Transana allows analysing and managing data in very sophisticated ways. With it, you can transcribe videos, identify analytically interesting clips, assign keywords to clips, arrange and rearrange clips, create complex collections of interrelated clips, explore relationships between applied key words and share your analysis with colleagues. Download from: http://www.transana.org

3. MAXQDA
    It is a qualitative data analysis software—also called QDA software—which supports performing qualitative data or content analysis by helping to systematically evaluate and interpret textual data. MAXQDA 10 is the newest member of the MAX software family. The first version of MAXQDA was released in 1989, which makes it a pioneer in the field of qualitative data analysis. Download from: http://www.maxqda.com/

4. Atlas.ti
    It is a commercial coding programme available at http://www.atlasti.com/

5. NVivo 9

   It is software that helps you to work with unstructured information like documents, surveys, audio, video and pictures so that you can ultimately make better decisions. Download from: http://www.qsrinternational.com/products_nvivo.aspx

6. QDA Miner

   It is an easy-to-use mixed methods qualitative data analysis software package for coding, annotating, retrieving and analysing small and large collections of documents and images. QDA Miner qualitative data analysis software may be used to code interview or focus-group transcripts, legal documents, journal articles, even entire books, as well as drawing, pictures, paintings and other types of visual documents. Download from: http://www.provalisresearch.com/QDAMiner/QDAMinerDesc.html

Web Mining

By Web mining, we mean the use of certain analysis techniques to discover patterns from texts on the Web. Web mining can be divided into three different methods—Web usage mining, Web content mining and Web structure mining. Web content mining is a three-stage process. First, one has to find out which sources to work on: search engines are employed for this purpose to browse the Web in order to select appropriate sites, blogs, communities, and so on. The second step is to extract text automatically. Finally, data analysis procedures are used to classify and code the copy gained. Software to support analysis was mentioned above.

In order to arrive at meaningful results with reasonable effort, special programmes have been developed (NLP, computational linguistics, and so on). Mainly, they help finding about emotions and polarities. So far, it has not been established if Web mining is a product that can be sold at a reasonable price with regard to the high programme-based and manual effort involved.

6.7 Sentiment Analysis: Filtering the Web for Feelings

Sentiment analysis or opinion mining intends to identify and extract subjective information in source materials such as answers to open-ended questions, transcripts of bulletin boards, content of Weblogs, 'buzz', and so on. Sentiment analysis aims to determine the attitude of a speaker or a writer with regard to some topic or the overall contextual polarity of a document. The attitude may be his or her judgement, effective state or the intended emotional communication.

A basic task in sentiment analysis is classifying the 'polarity' of a given text—whether the expressed opinion in a document is 'positive, negative, or neutral. Beyond polarity sentiment classification' looks at emotional states such as 'angry, sad and happy'.

Social media contain an enormous amount of user-generated content. This produces the need for an automatic evaluation of emotions transported via tweets, comments and blog entries. For companies, organisations and individuals, it is interesting to see not only who has published related content where and when on Facebook, Twitter and many other social sites, but also whether such content contains criticism or praise, positive or negative comments. Sentiment analysis is an attempt to search the Web for moods and emotions of the user. This technology filters the Web for key words: they are based on analyses of polarity, subjectivity or of the types of chosen words. With the help of complicated algorithms, at least a tendency can be given about the emotions that are expressed by a particular text. Most sentiment analyses are 'built in' the social media monitoring tools. Below are some tools that you can use yourself on your own data sets:

1. Tweetfeel
   It is a free analysis tool for Twitter (http://www.tweetfeel.com/index.php). The general sentiment of any key word contained in a tweet is evaluated. Tweetfeel orients itself primarily on unique words like 'love', 'hate' or 'better' and, therefore, analyses only English language tweets.
2. Context Sense
   It is a tool that analyses any site in terms of their overall polarity (http://www.wingify.com/contextsense/). The result is output as a percentage from 0 (negative) and 1 (positive). This service is also only applicable to English pages.
3. Rank Speed
   With the search engine 'RankSpeed', it is possible to extend search terms with additional emotion-laden adjectives. Thus, Rank Speed can look for smartphones that are 'excellent', 'easy' or 'cool'. The software analyses the statements made on blogs and Twitter, allowing also conventional Web search as well as product search. About the quality of search results, one can indeed have one's doubts, but Speed Rank is nevertheless an inspiring foretaste of what might become possible with further development of sentiment analysis.

The prerequisite for a useful and accurate analysis of emotions is an extensive database of words and language including different abbreviations, slang and the constantly changing youth slang. Moreover, intelligent semantic technology is necessary to understand the overall context. This will have to include the ability to identify negations (e.g., 'not at all satisfactory') and distinguish between completely different fields of meaning (e.g., Apple computer vs. apple pie).

Notes and References

1. http://en.wikipedia.org/wiki/IP_address
2. This is one of the famous Lumascapes, produced by the UK-based media and technology consultancy LUMA Partners. Also see http://www.lumapartners.com/resource-center/lumascapes-2/
3. A preroll is an online commercial that is displayed before viewing; for example, a YouTube video.
4. Daniel Kahneman, *Thinking, Fast and Slow* (New York: Farrar, Straus and Giroux, 2011).
5. The term is used in advertising and public relations to refer to publicity gained through promotional efforts other than advertising. It is a significant factor when looking at social media and companies make considerable efforts to 'earn' their place on these platforms.
6. http://www.iab.net/
7. We will come across this use of the word 'currency' later in Chapter 8 on Data Analysis. Currency here and generally in media research refers to the standards or measures by which media use is measured and the word is used to reflect the fact that these are measures that are accepted by all—media owners, advertisers and agencies alike.
8. These so-called click farms are an example of internet-fraud.
9. www.wakoopa.com
10. Also known as passive metering, behavioural tracking and clickstream monitoring.
11. The selection of panel members can be done in ways similar to that described in the previous chapter where the use of the Internet as a measurement tool was discussed and where we saw the development of Internet panels for quantitative research.
12. Elsewhere we will refer to the use of this technique as a way in which radio listening has been measured in some cases in recent years.
13. More on the topic of behavioural tracking, see a great video from *Wall Street Journal* http://live.wsj.com/video/how-advertisers-use-internet-cookies-to-track-you/92E525EB-9E4A-4399-817D-8C4E6EF68F93.html#!92E525EB-9E4A-4399-817D-8C4E6EF68F93
14. http://129.3.20.41/eps/io/papers/0304/0304001.pdf
15. http://ec.europa.eu/information_society/policy/psi/docs/pdfs/mepsir/executive_summary.pdf
16. http://dealbook.nytimes.com/2012/02/01/tracking-facebooks-valuation
17. http://en.wikipedia.org/wiki/Web_analytics
18. http://www.forrester.com/The+Forrester+Wave+Web+Analytics+Q4+2011/fulltext/-/E-RES59453 Forrester is a research company that specialises in online research intelligence.
19. API stands for application programming interface and it allows different software programmes to interact with each other and exchange data automatically, without the need for manual exports and imports.
20. See for example, the tool Radian 6 at http://www.salesforcemarketingcloud.com/
21. A useful list can be found on http://wiki.kenburbary.com/.

22. Such as www.Brandwatch.com.

23. Remember there are many different browsers available—Mozilla Firefox, Safari, Microsoft Internet Explorer, Google Chrome and others. It is not unusual for people to use different browsers for different purposes.

24. See http://www.moaweb.nl/kwaliteitsnormen/Kwaliteitsnorm%20Digital%20analytics/view.

25. J. Bethlehem, 'Representativity of Web Surveys—An Illusion?', in *Access Panels and Online Research, Panacea or Pitfall? Proceedings of the DANS Symposium, Amsterdam. DANS Symposium Publications 4*, eds. I. Stoop and M. Wittenberg (Amsterdam: Aksant Academic Publishers, 2006), pp. 19–44.

26. M.P. Couper, Web Surveys: A Review of Issues and Approaches, *Public Opinion Quarterly* 64 (2000): 464–494.

27. I. Stoop, 'Access Panels and Online Surveys: Mystifications and Misunderstandings', in *Access Panels and Online Research, Panacea or Pitfall? Proceedings of the DANS Symposium, Amsterdam. DANS Symposium Publications 4*, eds. I. Stoop and M. Wittenberg (Amsterdam: Aksant Academic Publishers, 2006), pp. 5–17.

28. R.J.A. Little and D.B. Rubin, *Statistical Analysis with Missing Data* (New York: Wiley, 1987).

29. J. Bethlehem. 'Selection Bias in Web Surveys'. *International Statistical Review* 78 (2010): 161–188.

30. S.J. Best, B.Krueger, C. Hubbard, and A. Smith, 'An Assessment of the Generalizability of Internet Surveys', *Social Science Computer Review*, 19 (2001): 131–145.

31. D.J. Hand, 'Sampling', in *Advising on Research Methods: A Consultant's Companion*, eds. H.J. Adèr and G.J. Mellenbergh (Huizen: Johannes van Kessel Publishing, 2008), 83–104.

32. Stoop, Access Panels and Online Surveys, pp. 5–17.

33. G.J.L.M. Lensveldt Mulders, R.Lugtig, and J. Hox, 'Assembling an Access Panel: A Study of Initial Nonresponse and Self selection Bias', in *Access Panels and Online Research, Panacea or Pitfall? Proceedings of the DANS Symposium, Amsterdam. DANS Symposium Publications 4*, eds. I. Stoop and M. Wittenberg (Amsterdam: Aksant Academic Publishers, 2006).

34. T. Vonk, R. van Ossenbrug gen, and P. Willems, 'A Comparison Study across 19 Online Panels (NOPVO 2006)', in *Access Panels and Online Research, Panacea or Pitfall? Proceedings of the DANS Symposium, Amsterdam. DANS Symposium Publications 4*, eds. I. Stoop and M. Wittenberg (Amsterdam: Aksant Academic Publishers, 2006), pp. 53–76.

35. L. Meurs, R. van Ossenbruggen, and L. Nekkers, 'Rotte Appels?' in *Ontwikkelingen in het marktonderzoek: Jaarboek MarktOnderzoekAssociatie*, eds. A.E. Bronner, et al., 2009. (Haarlem: SpaarenHout, 2009), 34.

36. W.A. Cook and R.C. Pettit, 'comScore Media Metrix U.S. Methodology: An ARF Research Review'. Available online at thearf org aux assets.s3.amazonaws.com/downloads/research/ comScore RReview.pdf (accessed 20 March 2012).

37. Vonk, van Ossenbruggen and Willems, A Comparison Study across 19 Online Panels (NOPVO 2006), pp. 53–76.

38. Bethlehem, Representativity of Web Surveys, pp. 19–44.

39. ⸻, Selection Bias in Web Surveys, pp. 161–188.

40. P.R. Rosenbaum and D.B. Rubin, 'The Central Role of the Propensity Score in Observational Studies for Causal Effects', *Biometrika* 70 (1983): 41–55. And P.R. Rosenbaum and D.B. Rubin, 'Reducing Bias in Observational Studies Using Subclassification on the Propensity Score', *Journal of the American Statistical Association*, 79 (1984): 516–524.

41. F. Pukelsheim and B. Simeone, On the Iterative Proportional Fitting Procedure: Structure of Accumulation Points and L1 error analysis. Available online at opus.bibliothek.uni augsburg. de/volltexte/2009/1368/pdf/mpreprint_09_005 retrieved (20 March 2012).

42. http://media.brainjuicer.com/media/files/ESOMAR_Congress_2012_Research_in_a_ World_Without_Questions_1.pdf

43. This shows how a research objective can influence your brain: http://www.theinvisiblegorilla. com/gorilla_experiment.html

44. Information obesity of information overload.

45. http://www.tableausoftware.com/

46. http://en.wikipedia.org/wiki/List_of_statistical_packages

47. www.statwing.com You can download a simpler version free of charge. More complex packages incur a monthly fee.

48. NB. It is normal to exclude conjunctions (and, but, then, etc.) prepositions (to, by, with, from, etc.) and other words that have a function within a sentence but no individual or separate meaning. Unless of course you want to do an analysis of these words!

49. Download it from: http://www.antlab.sci.waseda.ac.jp/antconc_index.html

50. Download from: http://www.textworld.eu/

Chapter 7

Qualitative Research

We are now going to look at a rather different kind of research. Whereas in quantitative research, we have been dealing mostly with precise facts that can be described with clear titles, counted in numbers, converted into percentages, ratios and the like, in qualitative research, we are trying to 'discover' or 'understand' human attributes, attitudes and behaviour in a more exploratory or interpretative way. Numbers cannot describe everything. Even less so can they 'explain' anything. Human behaviour and everything else that can be said about people cannot be fully encapsulated in or understood from numbers and percentages. Although the latter are valuable and often necessary to give an overall picture of some aspects of human life, they can never provide the whole picture of it. As good researchers, we need to embrace other methods in order to give this broader, more comprehensive view.

Qualitative research was first developed within the study and discipline of psychology and later in the more general field of social sciences, especially social anthropology. But in recent years, it has found its fullest development in the field of commercial market research. The success of qualitative methods in market research has in turn influenced social scientists in the academic world to make a greater use of the method.[1] They have found in qualitative research a very useful way of understanding human behaviour. Focus groups are a good way of exploring how media messages are interpreted.[2] We know from many studies that people are influenced not just by media messages but, perhaps more, by the intervening influence of other people. Qualitative research can bring out these influences more clearly than is the case with quantitative methods. This is partly because quantitative research tends to focus on individual behaviour within a household or family, whereas qualitative research conducted using group discussions or focus groups puts the respondents into a social setting in which the personal influences that operate in the day-to-day and familiar social settings are reproduced and can be observed.

No method, qualitative or quantitative, is superior to the other, although it is often true that researchers enjoy being involved more in one than the other. This sometimes leads to a rivalry between practitioners of the two broad research disciplines. But each method is used for different purposes and has different outcomes.

Qualitative research is often able to add depth, perspective, colour and understanding to the 'dry' data and figures from quantitative research. This is why we find that very often qualitative and quantitative research projects are done in conjunction with each other as part of the same project. The one set of methods can often complement the other. Results from quantitative research can often be understood better when combined with qualitative research. Conversely, the findings of qualitative research can be given a broader social perspective by quantitative research conducted at the same time. And, as we hope to demonstrate, the use of qualitative research is an excellent way to ensure before you set out on a quantitative project that you are making your research culturally appropriate and sensitive.

Qualitative research can also be used as a prelude to quantitative research by exploring those issues and motivations that are most relevant in the choices people make when using the media. Comments and opinions discovered through qualitative research can be tested in a systematic quantitative way to discover which of them receive general support and agreement and what the strength of that agreement may be.

There are three main qualitative research methods—'focus groups', 'in-depth interviews' and 'participant observation'. Sometimes focus groups are referred to as 'group discussions'.

The techniques of qualitative research are not very easy to describe. Whereas questionnaire design and sampling both have procedures to be followed that are relatively straightforward and can be itemised, the same is not so true for qualitative research. The main difference is implied in the word itself. 'Qualitative' denotes interpretative and exploratory activities, rather than factually descriptive ones. In qualitative research, we are not usually involved in precisely defined terms or in accurate measures of human behaviour or attitudes.

In qualitative research, we normally use only a relatively small number of people. Structured questionnaires are not used and the results are not normally open to any kind of statistical analysis. Qualitative research usually cannot prove or disprove anything in the way that quantitative research may be able to. But used effectively and appropriately, qualitative research may be the only way we can really understand peoples' motivations, attitudes and behaviour. There are good disciplines and professional methods in qualitative research, which, if followed, can ensure that qualitative research is both reliable and valid. How are qualitative data different and how do we handle them? What relevance do they have for audience and other media research?

7.1 Focus Groups, Sometimes Known as Group Discussions

The most common form of qualitative research is the focus group. People are selected and invited to meet together with a trained moderator to discuss some aspect of, in our case, media use. The same techniques are used in product and advertising research.

A focus group is a kind of group interview. But unlike the face-to-face interview, a focus group is not a structured dialogue between an interviewer and a respondent, with the latter's answers carefully recorded. What happens, and this is what gives focus groups their great strength for research, is interaction within the group. The interaction is always based on topics supplied by the researcher or 'moderator' whose important role we will describe shortly. This interaction produces information and insights into the behaviour and attitudes of people that would not be likely to emerge from a straight one to one interview.

The first task in any research project is the definition of the problem or issue to be addressed—the intended 'focus' of the discussion within the group. Unlike much quantitative research, which is often repeated in order to watch changes in behaviour over time, qualitative research is almost always carried out 'ad hoc'—that is to say, each project is a separately constructed activity, starting more or less fresh each time.

Those who need the results and those carrying out the research need to agree the objectives and expected outcome. The members of the research team need to make sure that they obtain clear information about what is expected of them. Very often, those who are seeking answers through research have not worked out in any great detail what needs to be investigated. For example, radio producers involved in creating programmes for, let us say, the entertainment and enjoyment of youth, may have found out from audience measurement surveys that their programmes are not popular and do not attract large or appreciative audiences. They want to do something about this but do not understand what is wrong nor have much idea how to find out. Qualitative research, conducted among the target group, could give them pointers to what could be done. It could help them to see what potential listeners think of the programmes, how they compare them to what else is available to watch or listen to, and it could set all this in the context of the listeners' daily lives. But the commissioners of the research—in this case the producers of the unsuccessful programmes—may have little idea of how the research is to be done, nor even of what has to be investigated. The professional researcher will work with them to develop an understanding of the problem from the broadcasters' point of view, and then to turn this into a carefully constructed research plan.

A research proposal like this will be turned into a research brief, agreed by both commissioner and researcher, before the research can begin. The research brief will usually contain three crucial elements.

1. 'Background' to the research—in this case, the problem about the poor performance of certain programmes. What is known about the programmes and their present audience—the broader broadcasting context?
2. 'Objectives' of the research—in this case almost certainly to discover why the programmes are not popular and to give guidance on ways of improving or changing what is being produced.
3. 'Research Method' to be used to achieve these objectives.

Two things then need to be agreed. A 'discussion guide' is drawn up. This translates the research objectives into subjects to be covered during focus groups (if that is the chosen method). The discussion guide, like the questionnaire used in quantitative research, needs to be written by those who are actually going to do the research. The usual practice is for the discussion guide to begin with general matters before gradually narrowing the discussion down to the particular. A discussion guide will always begin with subjects that help the participants to relax, gain confidence and develop relationships and understanding within the group. One would not start the discussion on these programmes with a question like 'why don't you like these programmes?'

The second thing to be decided is the kinds of people and how many of them are to be invited to take part. Normally, groups need to be matched quite deliberately and carefully. It is unusual for people of different sexes to be included in the same group. It is also usually inappropriate for people of widely different ages, social classes, wealth or education to be included in the same group. Knowledge and experience of the subject being researched is also important. It is not a good idea to mix experience with inexperience, for the former will overwhelm the latter. What we usually look for are people who will relate well together by having some experiences and backgrounds in common. We might be investigating the way farmers in a particular area use the media. We would probably seek to select groups of farmers who have broadly similar backgrounds. We might want to select farmers of similar wealth or similar amounts of land, or be engaged in similar kinds of farming. The success of a group lies in the group dynamics that develop in the conversation led by the trained moderator. If the differences between the members of the group are too great, these differences are likely to make conversation difficult.

You can see already that in order to cover all possible combinations of demographic and other relevant characteristics, one might need many groups. If, for example, we divided people into the two sexes and, let us say, three age groups, we would have six groups:

	Age		
	15 to 24	*25 to 40*	*41 and over*
Male	1	1	1
Female	1	1	1

Then, if we divided by class, education and wealth (usually these are to some extent inter-related) and made three categories of these, we would have 18 groups. Further, three-way categorisation, by experience or knowledge of the matter being researched, for example, would give us 54 and so on. What is more, usually we would want to have more than one group in each category to avoid the chance of drawing conclusions from only one.

In practice, this degree of subdivision of groups is unnecessary. The subject matter and the resources available for the research determine the choice of groups and their categories. One very commonly used way of organising groups is to divide them by whether or not they use the product or service being researched. If, for example, you were investigating attitudes towards radio as a medium for learning about health, it could be a productive method to divide groups according to whether or not they used radio in this way.

Recruiting for focus groups is done in various ways. Young mothers might be sampled through their attendance at mother and baby clinics. Farmers could be recruited by visiting them at a selection of farms. Radio listeners and television viewers are often recruited through quantitative surveys. A question, usually asked at the end, asks the respondent if he or she would be prepared to take part in further research. They would be told what it would entail and where the focus group would be held. Not everyone on the survey would be asked; the interviewer would have a list of the qualifications required for taking part in the focus group. It could be that listeners to a particular radio station were being sought, or people of a certain age group, occupation or social class, or any combination of these or others. The name, address and telephone number (if they have one) are noted and the person is contacted later with instructions and directions about where to go and when.

The moderator plays a crucial role and it is worth spending a little time looking in some detail at the moderator's function. There are dangers inherent in group moderation. Remember that you want to bring out genuine and real relationships and attitudes that arise in the group. But the presence of the moderator, an outsider in effect, can, if you are not very careful, introduce a false element. The situation is somewhat unnatural. Participant observation, which will be described later, overcomes this to a great extent but takes very much more time. All qualitative research is to some extent an intrusion into normal social interactions. Experienced moderators learn how to reduce the influence they inevitably introduce.

One important thing in focus groups is the seating arrangement. Rather than sitting around a square business table, participants should be seated in a semicircle. This facilitates conversation, enhances a feeling of equality and produces a better record on videotape.

The moderator is trained to lead the discussion, beginning with a general discussion before moving on to the particular. It is important to involve everyone present. The moderator has a discussion guide which may include a series of questions. This is not a rigid framework but is designed to keep the discussion going along the desired lines and is a reminder to the moderator of the purpose of the research. A good moderator plays a low key role. He or she should not express opinions but seek to ensure that the attitudes and opinions of everyone present are heard. A good moderator certainly asks questions, but these should normally reduce in number and frequency as the discussion proceeds. A good moderator should not only avoid expressing opinions; he or she must avoid showing any negative reaction to anything anyone in the group says. Positive reactions are OK, provided that they are to encourage further contributions and interchange. No opinions are 'right' or 'wrong' even if the moderator thinks so. People in groups often admit to practices that are unwise or foolish. The point is not to put them right but to allow these things to be expressed and discussed. It is, of course, all right for other members of the group to disapprove of or disagree with what others have said.

Moderators should look out for opportunities to promote further discussion on items that come up and which seem relevant to the topic. Sometimes what is said may not be the whole story; moreover, what seems to be apparent may not be what is actually being said. The following questions are typical of the kinds of things a moderator might say in a focus group:

'What do others think about that?'

'Tell us a bit more about that?'

'X, do you agree with what Y has just said? Have you had the same experience?'

'X said earlier how much she enjoys Radio One's morning show. Does anyone else feel the same?'

'What do others enjoy in the mornings on the radio?'

The moderator will normally seek to get the group as a whole to express and discuss experiences and opinions. The plan should be to get each group member to participate and interact with each other rather than just with the moderator. The moderator is there to ensure that the discussion continues to be about the subject being researched, to ensure that all the areas for discussion have been covered, to stop any one person from dominating the event and to encourage the less vocal participants to have their views heard.

Sometimes the discussion will flag; the moderator's task is to get it going again along the right lines. The most successful groups are usually those that develop a natural dynamic of their own, when all the member participate and talk between themselves, interacting freely and without much prompting or guidance from the moderator. When groups work really well, ideas, opinions and attitudes emerge, which would be far less likely to do so in formal interviews using a structured questionnaire. The moderator needs to be well prepared, having anticipated possible problems that might emerge. He or she should know the discussion guide very well and not need to refer to it often, if at all. The moderator also needs to listen very carefully at all times to the discussion as it proceeds and be ready to be very flexible, not always sticking rigidly to the plan implied or laid out by the discussion guide. The focus group must not degenerate into a sterile series of questions and answers between moderator and group members. The whole point is to get a free discussion going which develops its own momentum and dynamic. A good group is often the one that goes on for much longer than the time allocated because everyone enjoys the occasion and there is a creative and interesting interchange of ideas and experiences.

Focus groups are always recorded, either on audiotape or increasingly these days on videotape. This frees the moderator from the need to take any notes and it provides an accurate and thorough record of what happened and what was said.

Although the discussion is completely captured by the recording device, sometimes it is a good idea to have an assistant making short notes about the proceedings. Not all that happens is going to be always captured on a video recording.

Participants should always be told that they are to be recorded, but confidentiality must be assured. The moderator must tell everyone that the tapes will be used for no other purpose than the analysis and reporting of what was said. The identity of individuals in the group should not be recorded in any report and group members need also to be reassured on this point.[3]

The moderator's skill is to enable the group, brought together for a short time, to coalesce into a body of people that will trust each other, argue, agree or disagree, explore each other's backgrounds and contributions and illustrate by what they say some important aspects of the topic under review. You will not get to this point immediately. There are several stages to go through. First of all the moderator has to help the group to form, to relate to each other and to develop trust. Then the topic can gradually be introduced and discussed. When this has been fully aired, the group can be encouraged to become more creative. It is at this stage that some of the projective and other techniques described later can be introduced. At the end of the time, the moderator needs to attempt to bring things to a satisfactory conclusion, summing up what has been said and confirming if there is agreement or otherwise. Moderators should always give everyone a chance to say anything that they feel still needs to be said.

Qualitative research often uncovers things that no face-to-face structured questionnaire would. A good moderator can shift the discussion in any direction and this can lead to the discovery of information that can be wholly unpredicted and unexpected. Questionnaires, by their very nature, measure ranges of expected behaviour and attitude. But they cannot deal with the more subtle and hidden meanings in human response and behaviour, which can be very important in media research. Very often people do not know their own attitudes and motivations, or they know them only superficially. A person may express a mild opinion in favour of something in response to a question, while in conversation in a group, he or she may make it clear that the views held are very strong ones.

Qualitative research is most commonly used in media research to:

1. Discover behaviour and attitude ranges that can be tested quantitatively.
2. Define areas for systematic research on a larger scale.
3. Eliminate irrelevant areas from larger scale quantitative research that follows.
4. Illustrate or expand what has been discovered in a quantitative survey.
5. Provide insights into the way existing services and programmes are used.
6. Provide a richer range of responses to particular press, radio or television content than is provided by the questionnaire methods so far described.
7. Provide information about the acceptance of key figures in a production or programme.
8. Provide ideas for communicators and planners.

Group discussions usually involve between 6 and 10 people in each group. Too large a group can lead to some members losing interest or to the development of subgroups within the group. The number 8 seems to be ideal in the most current practice. The discussion usually takes between one and a half and three hours. The same group can be reconvened to carry on a discussion or, more often in audience research, to listen to or watch programmes. Reconvened groups can help you to gauge perceptions and attitudes and discover how these change over time. In media research, reconvened groups can be very useful for considering new programmes or content and then later to plot attitudes and responses when these innovations are developed and introduced.

Sometimes group discussions can last longer than two or three hours if the subject matter really does require some in-depth discussion. The point to make about groups is that the 'rules' are only guidelines and can be modified according to requirements. There can be a lot of interaction within a relatively short space of time and a lot of data can be generated for analysis.

Various techniques can be used in qualitative research to stimulate better response. There are many of these and many ways of leading discussions and conducting in-depth interviews.

Focus groups and in-depth interviews often use creative techniques to reveal aspects of human behaviour and attitude that do not become so apparent through normal conversation. Many of these can be described as 'projective techniques' because they require the participants to project their imagination on to a concept, product, service or situation. Here are some examples of techniques quite commonly used.

1. Role play: Respondents may be asked to act out their perceptions becoming actors in a make-believe enactment of something related to the subject of the research. For example, you might ask respondents to act out the roles of radio or television producers. This might give you some revealing information about how their place and role is regarded. When a group is going well and the respondents have learned enough about each other to feel confidence and trust, role play can work very well.

2. Photo sorting: Respondents are given a pile of photographs and asked to select those that they might associate with the product or service being researched. This is sometimes used, for example, to understand a brand's image. You might ask people to find all the photographs that seemed to go along with a particular brand of soap as against those which seemed to go with another. You can do this with radio programmes or networks and can learn a lot about the perceived image and status of each of them.

3. Collages: Respondents can be asked to create collages—pictures made up of bits of coloured paper, cuttings from magazines and other visual material of different texture and appearance—in order to express or depict what they feel about a product or service. They might be asked to depict the ideal or something as it is now.

4. Personification: 'If this radio station were a person what would he or she be like?' Respondents are asked to stretch their imaginative capacities to imagine some extraordinary things. Often they enjoy this and come up with perceptive observations. Some qualitative research using focus groups was carried out for the BBC World Service in Egypt in 1986. Participants were asked this question about the BBC and other stations they listened to.

There were many similarities in the depictions. The BBC was seen as:

'A serious, truthful person

A good spokesman

A strong personality

A person with "etiquette"

A classic man with a moustache

Like Margaret Thatcher, a woman of strong personality

Solid as Mokattam Mountain

Snobbish

Stand-offish'

Nearly all the personifications of the BBC were masculine. The BBC is seen as reliable and trustworthy, doing things 'properly' but rather stiff, formal and not very friendly.[4]

By contrast, Radio Monte Carlo, another international radio station popular in Egypt and elsewhere in the Middle East, had a quite different image:

'A nice attractive lady with a lot of make-up

A young man, wearing an open shirt, a gold chain and driving a BMW.

Monte Carlo is a good person—a priest, a wise teacher—cheerful and entertaining.

A cheerful, intelligent young girl, lively and entertaining'

The association of priest and teacher with cheerfulness and entertainment is not one that is familiar to all cultures, but it is not necessarily at odds with the other images. This list is a reminder that it is very important that qualitative data are interpreted objectively but by someone who has some knowledge of local cultural reference points and conventions.

5. Attribution: In this exercise, participants are asked to attribute a number of objects to the topic in question:

   'Imagine this product would be a car, an animal, a lake or river, a drink, a food etc. which kind of ... would fit or go well with the product?' 'If you would give it a coat of arms, what would it consist of?'

6. Picture or scene completion: Respondents are given a picture to complete or provide a caption to. You might ask respondents to write in what they imagine a television viewer to be saying to a non-viewer after seeing a certain programme. You might ask respondents to imagine that the picture is of someone from a particular radio station and ask him or her to use coloured crayons to give an impression of the kinds of clothes they wear. We have seen these and other ideas for picture completion working very well. You might think that people would be embarrassed by being asked to behave a bit like a child, to draw or colour pictures when such a thing is something they may not be accustomed to doing. In our experience and that of many colleagues, it is something that after a little diffidence most people enjoy doing.

7. Word association: Respondents are asked what words come to their minds when a product or service is mentioned. This can be tried out using the names of radio or TV stations, newspapers and magazines, presenters and personalities, and so on.

8. Product and service mapping: There are various ways of mapping or positioning a product. One approach is to ask respondents 'What kind of person uses this product?' The image of a product or service can be illustrated by discussion of this question. The lifestyle, class, social status and many other attributes of the user of a radio, TV station, newspaper or magazine, 'as perceived by others' can tell you a lot, not about the real customers but about how people perceive different media and their users. These perceptions influence people's choices. Consider how people might ask themselves, 'If I associate in my mind that radio station with that kind of person does that attract me to the station or repel me? Is that the kind of person I am or want to be?' Perhaps nobody ever asks that question in that clear conscious explicit way, but there seems little doubt that this is one consideration which influences the choice of radio station as it influences the choice of many other products and services.

9. Sentence completion:

   'The perfect radio station for me would be one which . . . . .'
   'The kind of broadcaster I like to listen to is one who . . . . .'
   'If you want to know what is really going on in this area you need to . . .'

The answers to these can be the starting point for a further exploration of these subjects. Like the other projective techniques, they can be a very good way of unlocking ideas and opinions.

10. Obituaries: 'Imagine this radio/TV/newspaper were to die and you had to write an obituary. What would you say about it?' 'What were the strengths and weaknesses?' 'What will you remember it for?' 'What do you think that radio/TV/newspaper would like to be remembered for?' These and similar questions can bring out some of the main qualities as perceived by users.

This list of projective techniques is not exhaustive. New ideas can and do emerge and you may think of new ideas that could be tried out to reveal people's inner thoughts and views.

Examples of Focus Groups Used in Audience Research

Qualitative research using focus groups is used quite extensively in audience research in the process of developing new programme ideas and services or of modifying or transforming the existing one. An example will help illustrate this.

In 1982, a new science series, QED, was launched on BBC television. The target was a mass audience not a well-informed, technically educated one. It presented a series of programmes, each one of which was on a different scientific or technical subject. The aim was to do this in an appealing and easily understood way.

Research was needed to find out, among other things, how well the programmes were understood, how viewers had categorised the programmes and their satisfaction with, interest in and enjoyment of the programmes. If the researchers had provided the programme makers with numerical figures or percentages showing that most had enjoyed and understood the programmes, no doubt the producers would have been pleased, but their understanding of audience response would have been little improved. Instead, it was decided that in order to understand better the audience's values and attitudes, qualitative research would be used. Producers wanted detailed in-depth reactions from viewers. So, it was decided to convene six groups each of eight viewers of QED. The groups were to discuss programmes about science in general and QED in particular. At each group, a recent edition of the programme was played about halfway through the session.

The groups were kept fairly informal. They were conducted in the homes of the moderators. Respondents who were invited to take part were allowed, indeed encouraged, to talk freely and among themselves about the subject of TV programmes on science. None of those involved knew beforehand what the subject of discussion would be. Selection was straightforward; six groups of eight each were recruited from the general public. Those recruited had to be people who had watched QED programmes. The usual method of doing this is to have what is known as a recruitment question on a survey questionnaire. In this case, during the course of a regular face-to-face interview in which general questions about TV viewing were being asked, the respondent would be asked if he or she was a regular viewer of the QED series. If the answer was in the affirmative, the respondent would be asked if he or she were prepared to take part in further research at a future date. If the person is willing, name and address details are taken down and the person is recontacted later.

The discussions showed that the issues identified as important by the viewers were broadly similar to those of the producers. Viewers did categorise the programme in the area of 'science for the layman' intended by the programme makers. The research underlined the importance of presentation in helping the understanding of otherwise complex subjects. Respondents were quite enthusiastic about an informative series that was nonetheless entertaining and not heavy-handed or dull. Some criticisms emerged, however, and they did so sufficiently across the groups to convince one that this was probably a reliable reflection of more widely held views. Most of the criticisms grew from the series' own success and popularity. Its viewers expected more than the programmes were able to provide. For example, there was some criticism of the structure, some viewers complaining about the lack of logical flow of the subject matter.[5]

Although most selected group members could understand the programmes, they did not always feel they had learned very much. They wanted simplicity, but this should not mean a lack of content. Interestingly, when viewers felt they were able to learn something, enjoyment was greatly increased.

What did the producers do with the research? They were pleased to discover that the audience welcomed and appreciated the programme idea, that the level of content was about right and that the variety in style in the programme was not an obstacle.

As a result of the criticisms, however, certain changes were made. The narrative structure was improved. Producers tried to avoid inconclusive or muddling subjects and they tried to ensure that programmes contain more 'nuggets' of information. The series, which had little identity of its own, for the viewers to remember, was, after the research, given a stronger identity with its own presenter, more use of programme logos and use of the title QED.

Quite often, qualitative research through group discussions can show that audience and producer definitions of what a programme is about can differ considerably. This may not matter, but it can be an eye opener to a producer. This is actually one of the greatest strengths of qualitative research, appreciated and understood by creative people—writers, producers, performers and similar communicators—in ways that quantitative research rarely can be.

In-depth Interviews

The second main form of qualitative research often used is the in-depth individual interview. These are sometimes referred to in short as 'depths'. The intention and broad purpose is broadly similar to other forms of qualitative research, which is to 'reveal' or 'understand' rather than to measure or describe. In-depth interviews are characterised by being open-ended, flexible, respondent-centred and designed to use respondent creativity and imagination. Like focus groups, they are also used to attempt to go beyond those things which are on the surface.

Although in-depth interviews are often discussed and described alongside focus groups, they are quite different in many important respects. There is no social interaction except between interviewer and respondent. The emphasis is on the individual. This is the crucial point of choice between the two methods. When one wants to probe highly individual, personal reactions and behaviour, in-depth interviews are appropriate. There are a few other reasons why we might use the method, which we shall come to later.

In-depth interviews can provide quite detailed and rich data on individual behaviour and attitudes. In the field of media research, they can be appropriate in a number of areas. In many cultures, radio listening has become very much an individual rather than a family-based or group activity. The new medium of the Internet is, by its very nature, almost entirely an activity for an individual operating alone, except of course when interacting with other users online. In a field where so little may be known about how people use this new medium, a series of in-depth interviews with users of the Internet would be a very good way of beginning a research project designed to show how the new medium is used.

Another major use of in-depth interviews is when you want individual creativity rather than group work. Some of the projective and imaginative techniques described earlier can also work well when done with individuals working on their own.

There are a number of other reasons why we might want to use in-depth interviews rather than focus groups. For example, certain sensitive or controversial issues may be difficult for some people to discuss with others in a group. If you were investigating attitudes towards aspects of sexual behaviour or its depiction on television, group discussions might not be possible in view of the diffidence that many people might display when asked to discuss such matters in a group. This will vary greatly between cultures and sometimes within those cultures.

In-depth interviews also may be used when selecting focus group participants is especially difficult. The population might be very scattered. The people you are looking for may not be easy to find. It may take a lot of effort to find enough people to form a group, especially one that can come together on a specific date and time in a specific location. You might wish to explore rural school teachers' use of radio. By their nature, rural professionals are thinly scattered. It might take a long time and be very difficult to arrange a focus group of rural teachers, remembering that ideally focus group members should not know each other.

There are also some people who, because of the nature of their job, will rarely or never be able to take part in group discussions. Senior civil servants, managing directors of large companies and other senior executives, politicians and other high status people may be of interest in media research. But their involvement in qualitative research may be possible only through in-depth interviews.

Questions used in in-depth interviews are not derived from a structured, pre-formed questionnaire. An interview guide will be prepared, and there will be at least some prepared questions to start with, but the interviewer always needs to be alert and flexible and watch out for things that the respondent says which will need further elaboration and 'ad hoc' questions. The following examples, all taken from transcripts of in-depth interviews that we have seen, give an idea of the kinds of questions that are asked. You can see that all of them could not have been thought of beforehand.

'What did you feel like on that occasion?

Why did that make you feel that way?

Did you discuss your reactions with anybody else? How did they react?

Are there other occasions when similar things have happened?

What was your experience with this product/programme/service etc.?'

Remember to probe anything that might lead you on to deeper understandings of how the media are used and thought of by the respondent. Watch for hidden assumptions and unspoken, underlying beliefs.

Participant Observation

Participant observation means what it appears to mean, which is always helpful. The researcher, to varying degrees, participates in an activity, a social group, lives with a family or families, joins a club or some other social formation in order to observe and understand it and the people involved. The focus group is an event of social interaction that we hope will replicate something of the cultural and social realities of the real world. But it is a somewhat unnatural event. Can we always be sure that people are like that in real-life situations? There may be some aspects of life, especially in the family situation, which are not revealed in focus groups. Participant observation is a less unnatural procedure much used in ethnographic and anthropological research, far less so in commercial market research, although it is not unknown. The technique can help us to see real-life situations with a high degree of clarity.

The main differences between focus groups and participant observation lie in the degree of control the researcher has and in the time it takes to do. In a focus group, although the moderator tries to avoid too much intervention, he or she is still in control. Participant observation by its very nature involves much less control, often none at all. The researcher sees people on their home ground behaving as they do normally. For it to work, it is essential not to even try to control events. The advantages are in being able to see the real-life social interaction and behaviour. More openness and less control may enable you to see what might otherwise not be known.

In focus groups, you rely almost entirely on people's verbal and body language. You might also give participants tasks to perform but these are always to some extent artificial. You are left with the question: 'Is this how they would behave in real life?' Participant observation enables you to find out. You have the chance to observe a whole range of behaviour and social interaction. People communicate within a focus group because that is what they are asked to do and what is expected of them. In participant observation, they do what they normally do in everyday life, because that is what it is—normal everyday life.

Participant observation is not often used in commercial media or market research, largely because of the time and expense involved. One example where it is used is the so-called 'shop-along' where a researcher accompanies a person during his or her shopping activities. In media research, there is much of relevance and importance that could be gained through this method. Most media consumption in most societies takes place in the home. A BBC researcher running an audience research survey in Morocco was staying in a rural village home. He reported that a male member of the household came home while he was there, took a key out of his pocket, unlocked a cupboard and took out a radio set and went off to another room to listen. Later, he returned the set to the cupboard, locked the door and left the house. Is this, a typical behaviour or something peculiar to this household? We do not know, but the episode reminded us that the mere existence of a radio set in a home does not guarantee that everyone has equal access to it. It might be among factors that could explain why many survey results from around the world show a higher reported level of access to radio by men than women, whereas the figures for each sex should be nearly the same, unless there are a significantly large number of male-only or female-only households. These are common in many developed societies, but the differences in access to radio and television by sex tend to be found mainly in less developed societies where single person or single sex households are much less common. The probability is that many women when asked the question 'Do you have a radio or television where you live?' answer that they do not, even though there may be a set or sets because they personally do not normally have access or control. Understanding these subtleties of real domestic life does matter a lot and can help us understand quantitative data better.

Participant observation can be a way of seeing and recording who turns the radio or television on, who chooses or switches the channels and at what time or times of the day different people in the household do this. If there are newspapers, magazines and other reading material in the home, where are they, who picks them up, when and for how long do household members read them? And what sections do they read? If there is a computer or computers in the house, who uses them, what for and how often? These and other observations collected in a number of homes give you an idea of the ways in which media are used in that society and these can give you a guide on how to structure and word any questionnaire you subsequently use in a survey.

Arthur Asa Berger in his excellent book for college students on media research suggests the use of participant observation for studying that very modern phenomenon, video game players who frequent amusement arcades. Here are the users of a contemporary and new medium with its own subculture. Participant observation is very suitable, he suggests, in eliciting information that might be otherwise very difficult to obtain. Berger suggests that the participant observer note such things as the location of the arcade, where the players come from, their sex, age, apparent lifestyle, apparent class and status, ritualised behaviour, interaction with each other and conversations. He suggests that the researcher should also carry out some short interviews to supplement these observations to complete the picture.[6]

The practice of participant observation requires the researcher to have a good discipline of how he or she is going to record the observations. Practice is needed to avoid writing things down in full view of everyone being observed. People can become uneasy at this kind of behaviour. It is best to write notes at the end of the day or at periods when you are alone. Sometimes it is possible to use recording equipment, either audio or video, but you need to be aware that the presence of cameras and recorders can make people self-conscious and perform differently. Photos can assist memory and illustrate some aspects of life, but again great care needs to be taken not to either offend custom or affect actual behaviour.

There are a number of difficulties with participant observation, quite apart from the long time it takes to obtain data from many households or other situations. How, for example, do you know what behaviour is significant? How do you record what is going on without this affecting the behaviour you are there to record? Experience and sensitivity are required and like all qualitative methods, it is a learning process in which you can expect to improve techniques and discoveries over time.

7.2 Reliability and Validity in Qualitative Research

One might suppose that qualitative research, in the way we have described it here, is difficult to define in precise procedures, is therefore vague and must be either unreliable or not valid or both. It is true that there appears to be less precision in qualitative than in quantitative studies. But this should not imply a lack of objectivity or distance from truth. It should also not imply a lack of precision, procedural discipline, professionalism and attention to detail. We are dealing here with a different way of investigating and describing reality.

There are ways of testing both the reliability and the validity of qualitative research. Remember that the reliability of a method (questionnaire, sample, focus group, and so on) is the degree of consistency whereby the same results would be produced by different researchers using the same method. Does the method we employ give the same data when used by someone else? If so, the method can be said to be reliable. But remember also that something may be reliable but wrong. We then need to be sure that the method is valid. Validity is the degree to which what we find through research corresponds to reality. Does the method we employ get to the truth of the matter, or at least something very like it?

We do not have the space here to address the complex question of proving validity or reliability. However, there are relatively simple procedures that can maximise the confidence you have in qualitative procedures. The raw data—recordings, notes, transcripts and results of any written or visual tasks collected from a series of focus groups—can be given to analysts separately to analyse and report. A new moderator's conduct of focus groups can be monitored by more experienced ones and any deviation from objectivity can be corrected through training. Validity can be tested through other research.

We need to remember that one of the great strengths of qualitative research is that it helps us to discover or uncover aspects of behaviour that otherwise might not be apparent. But the method does not tell us how widespread some kind of behaviour or set of attitudes is. We do not get numbers from qualitative research. What qualitative research may do is help us create hypotheses that can be tested quantitatively.

The key to best practice in qualitative research is 'objectivity'. The researcher needs to develop a critical discipline that will minimise subjective judgements and interpretations. To help this process, it is a good practice to carry out regular exercises in what is referred to as 'inter-rater' reliability. The following exercise is derived from one suggested by Silverman in his excellent book on this subject.[7]

Sometimes when doing qualitative research, you will get a consistent story or set of data. But you may find that it is invalid. Kirk and Miller in their short book on reliability and validity in qualitative research tell the story of doing research into the social and cultural place of coca in Peru. Coca being the source of the illegal drug cocaine was a difficult subject to research but the writers found that there seemed to be no problem in obtaining good responses. The results of their enquiries were consistent and seemed reliable. But they soon found out that they were wrong. Their respondents had not been telling the truth. They had suspicions because the results were too perfect. They knew that something was wrong. They introduced the topic of coca in a different way revealing a very different story under the surface.[8]

7.3 Analysis and Reporting Qualitative Research

Analysing qualitative research is not a precise, numerical process. The task is to take all the data—video or audiotapes, transcripts, notes and any written or pictorial work done by the interviewees—and try to make sense of it and produce a summary that will attempt to answer the issues posed in the particular research brief. The process involves a thorough review of all the material, structuring it in a relevant and ordered way, identifying those things that are of greater importance and drawing significant conclusions. The qualitative researcher should also keep in mind at all times the purpose of the research and ensure that where possible, the report should answer what the user or commissioner expects of it.

There is often a lot of work to do. Tapes need to be transcribed or at the very least summarised and the significant quotes collected. In the meantime, there is computer software available to assist the researcher in producing transcripts from sound or video recordings.

The researcher should look for what findings there are in common between the various focus groups, and where there are differences. Some of this analysis can go on while the project is proceeding. Good qualitative research is usually a dynamic process involving the continuous testing and modification of hypotheses.

One way to organise the data is to create a matrix on which to sort the various things to come out of each of the groups. This could have the sample characteristics on one axis and the topics on the other. This is a good way to see an emerging picture with clear comparisons between the different groups.

The qualitative researcher requires certain professional skills to assist in this process. A qualification in psychology is a good basis for qualitative research. So also is the knowledge of anthropology and sociology. It is unusual to find someone who has all the skills and knowledge that might be required. This is why agencies that specialise in qualitative research usually employ people with a range of these and other skills. As we noted in the previous section on reliability and validity it is good practice to have more than one person doing the analysis and comparing their findings and conclusions.

A final point about qualitative research within the field of audience research is that creative people like it. Qualitative research is much more highly valued by producers, writers, journalists and artists working in the media than quantitative research. They value the insights that qualitative research can give into motivations and individual response to media content. When qualitative research is used to develop ideas and draws on the creativity of people either individually or in groups, it can also be of great value and stimulation to creative people.

7.4 Qualitative Online Research

The Internet has not only revolutionised quantitative research—which can now be conducted more efficiently, faster, and cheaper than by conventional methods—but it also has brought new opportunities for qualitative research. This may be surprising on the face of it because qualitative research as described thus far depends so much on personal face-to-face contact.

Side by side with the development of the World Wide Web, other technical innovations have been spreading at great speed: mail has become email;

the fixed line telephone tends to be replaced by the cell phone or 'mobile', and in many parts of the world has by-passed the fixed line. Smartphones and tablets are taking over from desktops and laptops, and the hard disk is being replaced by solid-state storage media. 'Cloud' storage, that is storage in a Web space provided by Internet companies, is growing. Meanwhile, e-readers like Amazon's *Kindle* are revolutionising the book market and book reading. From early childhood onwards, people are confronted with a multitude of possibilities and challenges of information technology. Even older age groups and less educated segments of the population are becoming Internet users. These changes have had major impacts on all kinds of human interactions and activities, and it is hard or impossible to think of any that have not been profoundly changed.

The Internet has brought about far-reaching changes in the use of media. We now have online newspapers, Web radio and Web TV. The Internet is having a huge impact on our shopping habits and our use of services. This is true mostly of course in the advanced developed countries, but it is becoming true in less developed ones also. One major example of change in those countries is in banking and moving money. Online technology, especially through the mobile phone, is transforming the way people in large parts of Africa and Asia move their money, pay for goods and services and send money within their home countries as well as internationally.

Technical innovation is fundamentally changing interpersonal communication and social behaviour. With the Internet slowly reaching out into those segments which were, to start with, poorly served by new media, things are beginning to change. Older people, the less well off and even the less educated and the illiterate are being reached by new media, although there are of course still some limitations. But digital media are becoming a reality for most human groups. This means that sooner or later nearly all segments of all populations will have become familiar with keyboard, mouse, phone keys, touch screens, headphones and all the rest of the paraphernalia of digital life in the 21st century and thus be able to be respondents in online research including qualitative research.

One consequence of this is that the new, so-called social media, all of them relying on online access, are spreading out into all age groups and in ever more countries and regions. Facebook, Twitter, YouTube and LinkedIn are global businesses in this field, but there are many others which have regional, linguistic or cultural relevance and strength and provide strong competition.

Qualitative research benefits from these developments and there are many ways in which online technology can be used to do qualitative research. It is possible today to invite people to take part in online focus groups or group discussions which, although they are not the same as the equivalent groups held where everyone is able to meet and speak face to face, can nonetheless provide good data at very much lower costs and in a shorter time. Online technologies have also brought in some new qualitative methods and these include online bulletin boards, online diaries and the posting of messages on social networks and the subsequent analysis of these for research purposes.

Online technologies have also opened up new opportunities for people with training in psychology to probe deeply into the motives and habits of consumers—regardless of age or region. Online qualitative research is faster to complete and can be done at lower costs than conventional qualitative research.

Online ethnography allows researchers to observe via Webcam or mobile device what people own, how they live, shop and consume in the home and elsewhere. Of course, these activities require the informed consent of the respondent. We will talk about this point in a later section.

Not all topics lend themselves to online qualitative.[9] There will always be room for person-to-person research in groups or individually. Sometimes the topics in question or may require hands-on action (smelling, tasting, handling, drawing or doing)—or because of the sheer importance of a personal appearance before the specialist researcher or when actions and reactions in the presence of other people is an important component in the research.

Defining Online Qualitative

For our practical purposes, qualitative research is defined as research resulting in text-defined data rather than data that are analysed numerically. In-depth interviews, focus groups or group discussions, participant observation and similar methods previously described are the 'traditional' and familiar methods used in qualitative research. As we shall see, the new online methods do in some ways attempt to recreate these methods, albeit reinvented and changed as necessary, using online tools. But online technology also allows some new methods to emerge and be used to good effect.

Online projects, like traditional qualitative projects, can range very widely in the numbers of people involved. They reach from small samples as, for example, in one-to-one interviews and online focus groups to bulletin boards and online diaries with up to 30 respondents. They comprise Delphi studies with, for example, 50 experts and semi-qualitative projects with up to 200 representative interviews.

One-to-one Research

There are applications in which qualitative interviews are best conducted on a one-to-one basis. This ensures in-depth exploration in which various stimuli or psychological tests can be used and in which rich text can be gained. Care should be taken about the software used. Basically, any up-to-date chat programme can be used to engage an individual respondent to 'talk' with him/her about a specific topic.

Graphs used in this chapter are to be understood merely as examples constructed with open source programmes.

Online Focus Groups

An online focus group is an opportunity to assemble a group of usually six to eight persons to conduct a live discussion via the Web. Most up-to-date software will include a whiteboard. A whiteboard is a separate area on the screen on which the moderator can display objects or links to other sites. The participants can enter text or use the whiteboard for drawing. Other focus group programmes may also provide for the use of voice and Webcam.

A modern chat programme allows the inclusion of images, video and sound.

If demonstration objects (or stimuli) are to be presented on a whiteboard, the set-up can be seen online if you search for the software available at the 'Groupboard' website at http://groupboard.com. The website offers some material and examples free of charge but more advanced features need to be paid for.

A more refined application would be to use a state-of-the-art 'Web conferencing tool'. Such software enables dialogue in real-time via Webcam. The conversation is recorded in the form of a video file and can be replayed later for analysis. In this case, no written text will be available. However, body language can be included into the analysis—at least in the form of facial and vocal expression.

There are a number of programmes available for Webcam communication. These include 'Adobe Connect for Web Meetings', 'Webex' and 'Teamviewer'.

The requirement to be able to draw on an online whiteboard requires that participants have 'Java' software enabled in their browsers. This must be mentioned in the invitation email. In some cases, it will be necessary to provide this or other software when required to the participant.

Working with online focus groups introduces us to some new problems and difficulties. One of the most common objections to online research using this method is that respondents' body language cannot be observed. This means not only that the moderator cannot see what people are showing by their facial expressions, demeanour, movement, and so on, but this also applies to the participants. Something of the social immediacy of a real live group is lost. However, Web cameras can be used. But there are technical restrictions. The maximum number of participants' faces to be displayed simultaneously on one screen is limited to a maximum of eight. This same problem also arises in the case of 'screen-sharing'. By this is meant the possibility for participants to follow the screen actions of other remote persons.

Despite some limitations, practice has shown that the results of online focus group discussions are not very different from those gained in conventional group discussions. And there are several advantages. One major one is that it is possible to conduct a discussion among persons living in any place in the world. Of course, you do have to remember time zones. You cannot expect participation by people who are usually asleep or perhaps at work at the times chosen for the activity.

As with quantitative research online, incentives have to be given and because of the greater effort and time involved, they have to be larger and/ or more attractive than for quantitative online research. In this respect, as in many others, practices will vary from project to project and also between countries and in different areas of research, but experience will show best what works.

As with conventional groups, it is always a good practice to over-recruit because practical experience shows that some of those invited do not actually turn up or else are not willing or able to give their time when it comes to the actual event.

Members of online focus groups sometimes use nicknames instead of their real names to maintain anonymity. Often thumbnail photographs of participants can be shown with their postings rather in the same way as Facebook. Participants must be familiar with computers and what they can do and be used for. Participants usually need to be able to think and type quickly because an online discussion normally runs at quite a fast pace. Everybody is allowed to enter text at the same time, and this does remind us that this is not like normal conversation whereby people need to wait until other have finished speaking, show politeness and use other social skills that we learn from each other for normal conversation to take place. Online conversations are different and of course develop their own social conventions and norms. But do remember that we are dealing with a different kind of human interaction here.

One of the drawbacks of the online focus group method is that generally speaking, those who might be described as 'heavy' Internet users can have an advantage over others. On the other hand, these kinds of people—early adopters and younger, upmarket segments of the population—may be of special interest to those engaged in research into media use. What they do today can be a way of seeing how others will follow in the future.

As with conventional focus group recruitment, the selection of people from the target groups you have decided upon for the particular project needs, of course, special attention and must be carefully planned.

The moderator must be very quick on the uptake. He/she must have a carefully prepared discussion guide at hand with the questions, topics and uploads (images, videos, links, and so on) earmarked for being discussed in the short period of time available. Normally, running an online focus group will require that the moderator is aided by a technical assistant who posts the topics, stimuli and links. The assistant welcomes visitors, discourages latecomers from entering the chat room or invites additional participants, if need be, while the moderator keeps the discussion going. The moderator can ban participants who violate the rules set for the discussion. Above all, he/she must encourage shy or reticent participants to speak up.

Usually, an online focus group runs for 60 to 90 minutes. With regard to the limited time, lengthy introduction and welcoming passages must be kept to the minimum required for politeness and enabling participants to relax and get ready. For an online group to be effective, every minute counts—otherwise the resulting copy (or video file) will be rather thin. Participants must be instructed about typing ('disregard spelling mistakes', 'keep your sentences short', and so on) and 'netiquette'. This word emerged in the early days of the Internet and refers to the social codes of acceptable behaviour on the Internet or network etiquette. It prescribes what proper behaviour is and what is not. For example, to use capital letters is equivalent to shouting and should be avoided.

The text produced and the processes triggered in an online focus group are recorded on the server so that a precise transcript including images can be downloaded immediately after the discussion. Modern chat programmes enable the moderator to tag statements in order to distinguish between positive, negative and neutral opinions.

Online Bulletin Boards

The online bulletin board is an Internet facility where a person can go and post a message about something. Other visitors to that site can view this message and can either post another message or reply to any of the messages already on the board. As more messages are put on the board, a 'thread' is formed. A free and easy to administer bulletin board service is MyBB: http://mybb.com.

Recruitment can be carried out in the same way as for traditional focus groups. But instead of inviting people to a central location at a specific date and time, people are invited to a website. Respondents must agree to visit the site a specified number of times. It could be, for example, four times or more during a period of one week to 10 days.

This is the major difference between online bulletin boards and focus groups. Whereas the latter involves everyone at the same time participating for an hour to 90 minutes, a bulletin board involves people over a much longer period and they are not involved on a continuous basis but when it is convenient. The respondents can visit the site when they can and want to. Normally, every day in the morning, a new topic is introduced or reference is made to prior discussion themes.

Emails are used for recruitment and they will carry a link to the bulletin or discussion board, a password and instructions. Email is also used for sending out reminders ('don't forget to visit the online discussion today'). Initial recruitment should provide for about double the number of participants needed to take part during the entire period.

It is important that respondents are committed to the task, otherwise there is an obvious risk that people will forget to visit the site. To help ensure that respondents are active and responsive you need to make sure that incentives are given and reminders are sent. Many of the rules and restrictions mentioned above in the section on online focus groups pertain also to the online bulletin board. The decisive difference, however, is the fact that the bulletin board method is more relaxed and flexible in giving the participants time to choose themselves when to take part.

The moderator posts topics or questions on the board using a special signature to distinguish him/her from the other participants who reply to the moderator's messages but can also reply to any other respondents' postings. In this way, a discussion 'thread' is created. Care should be taken by the moderator that the discussion is more than just question and answer. This is helped by stimuli like pictures, charts or other graphical items. Interesting topics will guarantee active participation.

The moderator should create an open, comfortable environment that allows participants to realise they are communicating with a real person in real time. Moderators can truly get to know many of their participants, depending on the length of the board.

Along with providing a personal touch with the moderator, prolonged online research allows participants to glimpse into their fellow members' lives. They start to naturally interact with each other, sharing their opinions and personal stories. Many participants express regrets when projects are over.

Sometimes it is advisable to ask participants to do some homework in advance and send it electronically prior to the group. This can help with setting up the discussion guide. There is an added benefit here: people who send their homework ahead of time are more likely to show up.

Like in online focus groups, there is the possibility to let the commissioner/client (from any place in the world) visit the site and follow the discussion as an observer—unseen by the participants but able to interact with the moderator. Many clients nowadays like the possibility to observe qualitative research projects themselves. With traditional group discussions, this is usually done from behind a one-way mirror. The participants can be seen by the client but they cannot see him/her. When it comes to online qualitative projects, similar facilities can be provided both with groups and bulletin boards. Also it is possible for the client to communicate with the moderator without the participants knowing.

Modern bulletin board software provides for the inclusion of all kinds of multimedia (images, videos, sound and links). With the help of a whiteboard, respondents are confronted with images of products, maps, graphs and other optical stimuli. They may be asked to comment in writing or drawing. Respondents can be asked to create collages, videos or photo journals, metaphors and more. Other projective methods are storytelling, sentence completion and letter writing.

Some bulletin board computer programmes enable 'sentiment tagging'. This means the possibility for respondents to mark objects on the whiteboard and add text to express likes or dislikes. These markers can eventually be condensed into a visual display showing what participants did, or analysed via the transcript. Another possibility is to enable the moderator to tag opinions uttered by respondents with his/her own remarks. These tags/remarks will eventually facilitate the final text analysis.

One of the big advantages of the online bulletin board, which can be described as an 'asynchronous' or as a not-at-the-same-time discussion—is the rich volume of copy generated (sometimes more than a hundred pages) from the postings and the analysis of them. Postings can be viewed in the transcript in their original form which means that in this phase of the analysis, individual statements can be identified. Respondents can be pre-grouped in segments (young–old, female–male or by their level of usage of the product or service being researched, and so on.) in order to analyse their posts accordingly. Some programmes even provide basic instruments for text analysis such as word frequency counting software or programmes producing 'word clouds'. Online bulletin board software can also usefully include a chat feature for occasional real-time conversation between respondents and moderator.

Because online bulletin boards are a relatively new method in qualitative research, there is still some hesitancy about using them. There are some very obvious advantages which make bulletin boards worthwhile and it can be a good idea to demonstrate the usefulness of the method in a pilot project with colleagues and associates. Wherever applicable, offers for qualitative research should include the online bulletin board option because it can be superior to other qualitative online methods due to its speed, the amount of useful data generated and its cost-efficiency.

There are some other advantages in online bulletin boards that need to be considered. Online bulletin boards are well suited for brainstorming exercises of all kinds. And they can operate across different time zones without difficulty, whereas this is not so easy with online discussion or focus groups. The participants can be geographically dispersed. Respondents do not have to travel to a central location; instead they can take part in the discussion from any Internet-connected PC or hand-held device. Respondents do not have to reserve a specific hour to participate; instead they can take part whenever it is convenient for them. Therefore, target groups that find it inconvenient to take part in a traditional focus group or even an online one may be more willing to take part in an online bulletin board. It is also possible to handle a relatively large number of respondents per session—up to 25 or so. Bulletin boards provide anonymity to the respondents through the use of nicknames. People tend to use a detailed and more colourful language when participating in bulletin boards, which results in a more qualitative flavour compared to online focus groups where the discussion is always pressed for time. The time factor is also a benefit inasmuch as respondents can think for a while before giving an answer. This makes it possible to ask more complex questions than otherwise would be the case when a quick answer is required.

Also, with an online bulletin board, there is no limitation on how much a participant can say in each of their responses, so every participant can have equal space or time to explain their viewpoints. They do not have to negotiate sharing time with others in a designated response window. The moderator does not need to act in real time and can, therefore, take his/her time to reflect and revise the guidelines or even consult with the client before asking follow-up questions or launching new topics on the board.

As in all online research, topics which are normally not at all easy to talk about openly and face-to-face (alcohol, taxation, sex and health problems) can be more readily discussed in bulletin boards.

However, there are some disadvantages with the method. It is not possible to get really spontaneous reactions from respondents. There is a lack of non-verbal input from respondents, unless Webcams are used. There is no possibility to test taste, smell and handling of products (unless samples are delivered to the homes). It is not possible to have respondents do what can be called 'get up and move' exercises where they get out of their seats and interact with stimulus, pick things up, physically sort them, and so on, which helps to keep respondents engaged. Traditional psychologists might dislike the 'high-tech-feeling' and, therefore, reject the method. This may also be true for persons normally willing to fill in questionnaires. Sometimes the output of a bulletin board (or several) can be so large that analysis becomes too time-consuming.

Online discussion software is constantly developing. Some of the providers offer not only whiteboards but also a chat feature and various possibilities for the participants to highlight specific aspects of a product or take part in polls as well as text analytics. Check out these leading software providers:

Dub-Ideastream: http://www.dubstudios.com/

ThinkingShed: http://www.thethinkingshed.co.uk/features.php

Qualboard (20 | 20 Research): http://qualboard.com

VisionsLive: http://www.visionslive.com/

Online Diaries/Blogs

Most users of the Internet will be familiar with the word 'blog'. It comes from the two words 'Web log', and it refers to any kind of regular Web-based narrative on any topic by individual Internet users. A blog is a personal journal published on the Web, consisting of more or less regular entries or 'posts'. These entries are typically displayed in reverse chronological order so that the most recent post appears on top. Such activity can be used as another qualitative research tool deliberately used for the purpose, as well of course as the fact that existing blogs can themselves be analysed for research purposes. In contrast to online focus groups and bulletin boards, an online diary, Web log or blog is kept on an individual basis and for a much longer period of time, sometimes for months.

The purpose of an online diary as an instrument of market, media or social research is to record occurrences on a daily basis in digital form. Typical applications are diaries to record radio and/or other media use, or blogs to collect experiences of the users of a particular product or service. The technique has been successfully used in the field of health.

If someone is recruited to complete a regular blog for research purposes, he/she must be prepared to enter the required data on a regular, possibly daily basis. Incentives, therefore, must be attractive enough to ensure that this happens and to prevent respondent fatigue and drop out.

Market Research Online Communities (MROCs)

Web 2.0, the so-called social Web, is characterised by the existence of many types of user groups, forums, informal and formal communities and, especially, commercially oriented social networks such as Facebook, LinkedIn, Xing and Google+. There are a very large number of social networks available. Go to Wikipedia and you will find a comprehensive list of current social networks. http://en.wikipedia.org/wiki/List_of_social_networking_websites

Internet-based communities like these social media enable quick information sharing and collaboration among their participants. The software used for communication may include the possibility to conduct short polls—mainly informal one-question surveys with instant display of results. For the purpose of professional market research, there are two different options:

The most obvious and immediate way is to use the existing social networks by becoming a member and attempting to conduct discussions, polls or surveys among the other members. In some ways, this resembles acting as a participant observer. As a member of a community, it is possible to initiate conversations about specific subjects, conduct polls or at least share and record the 'buzz' (Web lingo for online communication, for example, between customers or consumers of specific products for the exchange of opinions, criticism and recommendations). But such activities must not be confused with 'Web mining' by which is meant the digital method of locating conversations on blogs or in forums (by means of search engines) and extracting text and images from these by means of special software (robots, spiders).

But one can also create a specifically designed-for-purpose MROC with the intention of using it for tracking the distribution of a product or a service or monitoring communications or advertising campaigns. Participants can be recruited from a sufficiently large online pool or from address lists provided by the body commissioning the research. Participants must be willing and able to integrate themselves into a community to exchange opinions and actively engage with and comment on topics. Moderators must be experienced in community activity and be able to use the special Web vernacular.

Depending on the product/service, short-term MROCs can be used for qualitative purposes. For example, they could be created in order to comment on and discuss a particular range of media content, or perhaps an advertising campaign, a new TV series or other product or service. But is using these online methods of attaching to or specially creating online communities an appropriate instrument of professional market research? Side-by side studies have shown that reactions by members of online communities do not differ substantially from those of online panels—except for the special interests shared by the members. It is self-evident that, for example, the members of a motorists' forum initiated by a specific car maker will be emotionally closer to their sponsor's product than the general public. But as with any research, target groups must be considered carefully. What do you want to achieve? If it is to know your own customers or users better, rather than the wider public, it may well be a very useful and convenient research approach.

Meta research into studies of communities suggest that community members remain candid and honest over time—despite many months of ongoing participation where they form relationships with one another and the sponsoring company.

However, doubts remain about the use of online communities for research. Practical experience with research in or by communities is still quite scarce and there are still doubts that the effort necessary for recruiting and maintaining a functioning community can be calculated such as to cover the costs so that at the end, the outcome will justify the money and time spent.

Website Usability Research

Testing the Performance of a Website ('Usability Check')

There are several different approaches to testing the performance of a website and determining the demographic structure of its visitors. One good way of establishing the quality of a website is to discuss it personally with users while they access the site to be tested. One can do this using a questionnaire administered by an interviewer with the respondent actually using the website in question.

A quicker and less expensive way is to make the website a topic for a focus group session. This can be done offline in the conventional way or by means of an online group. In order to find out about the performance of a website with a topical character (e.g., a news media site), the use of an online bulletin board can work very effectively. Naturally, such tests not only can comprise one website, but may include one or more competing sites for comparison. And, as with many other applications of qualitative research, it is possible to corroborate findings by a subsequent quantitative survey.

Accompanied Surfing (Qualitative Web test)

The most intensive qualitative approach to discover the usability/performance of a website is to subject it to a so-called 'safari' by a number of respondents. Respondents are being invited to test a website in a one-to-one situation. With a qualified interviewer present, the respondent is asked to visit a site and go through its pages like a typical user. While the respondent explores the site, he/she is asked to speak aloud about his/her experience and observations.

This method is called 'think aloud'. It enables the researcher, not only to observe what the test person is doing, but also to listen and pick up the spoken word via microphone and recording device.

The mouse movements on the screen are recorded. There are a number of programmes which do this, for example, Screencorder.

http://www.matchware.com/ge/products/screencorder/default.htm

It is also possible to use a video camera to record the facial expressions of the test person. The exact number of test persons required to produce a detailed report on the usability of a specific website depends on the level of detail needed. As a minimum, six carefully selected persons (users and/or potential users of the site) should be taken to gain a first insight. Reliable results can be achieved by interviewing 12 to 24 persons in this manner.

The actual website-using experience should be followed by administering a paper-and-pencil questionnaire to record the demographic data of the respondent and to ask the test person to rate the most important aspects of the site dimensions on a standardised scale. Experience can show that sometimes—often to the great surprise of Webmasters, screen designers and site owners—accompanied surfing as described here can reveal problems in the design of a site that nobody had thought of.

A conventional focus group can also be used to discuss the usability/ performance of a site as well as including one or two competing sites within the same study. In this case, either a screenshot of the site(s) is displayed on a big screen for all participants to see or—by means of a live connection to the Internet —the website proper is being displayed. This has the big advantage that the group can in fact 'surf' that site in their own way and time.

To optimise discussion, respondents should be seated at small coffee tables in a semicircle facing a screen where the moderator's assistant shows the sites/pages to be discussed. After the discussion, the respondents are asked to fill in paper-and-pencil questionnaires to rate the standard dimensions of the site(s) and enter their personal demographic data.

The specific situation of a focus group is different from other methods. In contrast to accompanied surfing, the discussion of a website in a group of 8–12 persons is not as intensive with regard to personal experience. After all, the surfing process must be simulated by the moderator's assistant. On the other hand, the discussion in a group can be quite creative: new ideas may spring up; views by one person can be supplemented or corrected by somebody else, and so on.

The results of a group discussion about a website may be somewhat more superficial than those achieved by accompanied surfing, but this approach is faster and less expensive.

Testing a Website with an Online Focus Group or Bulletin Board

It may well be that testing something that exists only on the Internet is best done using the same medium. We are then doing the research in the same setting. Testing the usability and performance of a website in a qualitative way may best be done by means of an online focus group or an online bulletin board.

All up-to-date online discussion boards are equipped with a whiteboard on which a screenshot of the website to be tested can be shown to the participants. But it is also possible to open the site to be tested in a second window so as to discuss it in a 'live' setting. The members of an online focus group— usually not more than eight persons—must be recruited from the target group of the site to be tested (users or potential users). The same applies for recruiting members of an online bulletin board where the number of participants can be considerably higher.

Eye Tracking

Eye tracking has long been known and is often used as a method to study the visual attention of individuals. There are several different techniques to detect and track the movements of eyes. A number of companies offer analyses of websites, emails and other stimuli presented on a computer screen by following the movement of the respondent's eyes. The results of such research are displayed in 'gaze plots' (graphs depicting vision paths), 'heat maps' on which red colour indicates the spots with highest attention and 'focus maps' in which the most visited parts of the object tested are shown as white areas on black background.

The most commonly used non-intrusive eye tracking technique is 'Pupil Centre Corneal Reflection (PCCR)'. Its basic concept is to use a light source to illuminate the eye causing highly visible reflections and a camera to capture an image of the eye showing these reflections. The image captured by the camera is then used to identify the reflection of the light source on the cornea (glint) and in the pupil. Thereby a vector formed by the angle between the cornea and pupil reflections can be calculated—the direction of this vector, combined with other geometrical features of the reflections, will then be used to calculate the gaze direction.

One supplier that provides research services in this area is 'Tobii'. What Tobii does resembles the conventional form of accompanied surfing (see earlier) with the respondents thinking aloud in front of a specially equipped laptop. This method which can be performed in a laboratory or also using mobile gear in a client's location is described on Tobii's website at http://www.tobii.com/eye-tracking-research/global/library/white-papers/tobii-eye-tracking-white-paper. Another company, Eyequant (http://eyequant.com) offers to analyse websites directly on the Web.

Eyequant says that they achieve over 90 per cent predictive accuracy when compared to a real eye-tracking study with more than 30 human subjects. Results are considered a representative for the first five seconds of a new visitor's viewing behaviour.

The method used is by special software that can simulate human attention by analysing and comparing the 'strength' of different segments of a Web page.

'Note': Eyequant offers the first test of a website free of charge. For examples of what this software can do, go to http://www.eyequant.com/

Readers will find new examples of what can be done in online qualitative research by regular surfing and searching.

Notes and References

1. David L. Morgan, *Focus Groups as Qualitative Research* (Thousand Oaks, London and New Delhi: SAGE Publications, 1997), pp 1–13.
2. P. Lunt and S. Livingstone, 'Rethinking Focus Groups in Media and Communication', *Journal of Communication* no. 46 (1996): 79–98.
3. There are codes of conduct to which all professional market researchers subscribe. ESOMAR's *International Code of Marketing and Social Research Practice* is probably the most widely used and is obtainable by post from ESOMAR, J.J. Viottastraat 29, 1071 JP Amsterdam, The Netherlands. It is also available on the Internet at http://www.esomar.nl/codes_1.html. There is a list of this and other guidelines in the bibliography.
4. 'The BBC in Egypt: Social Context and Station Image', BBC World Service, International Broadcasting Audience Research, 1986. The remarkable thing about this and other similar studies in many parts of the world is that the BBC World Service has a very similar image and reputation virtually everywhere—reliable but with a tendency to being a bit dull or old-fashioned. It is something that the BBC World Service is making great efforts to change—maintaining the reliability but at the same time trying to appear more interesting, lively and friendly.
5. Anne Laking and Mick Rhodes, 'Q.E.D: Research for a Second Series', *Annual Review of BBC Broadcasting Research Findings* 9 (1983): 118–120.
6. Arthur Asa Berger, *Media Research Techniques* (Thousand Oaks, London and New Delhi: SAGE Publications, 1998), p. 107.
7. David Silverman, *Interpreting Qualitative Data* (Thousand Oaks, London and New Delhi: SAGE Publications, 1993), p. 147.
8. Jerome Kirk and Marc L. Miller, *Reliability and Validity in Qualitative Research* (Thousand Oaks, London and New Delhi: SAGE Publications, 1986).
9. In the market research profession, this is shortened to 'online qual', just as the equivalent in quantitative research becomes 'online quant'.

Chapter 8

Audience Opinion and Reaction

In an important way, this section is about kinds of hybrid research methods that are used to understand and sometimes measure audience opinion and reaction, especially to radio and television, but the methods can and are used more widely than only for these two media. Some of the audience measurement methods we looked at in Chapters 3 to 5 allow for some research into opinion and reactions. And of course, some of the qualitative methods described in the last chapter are also used. In this chapter, we bring together both qualitative and quantitative approaches and look at practical ways in which audience opinion and reaction is measured and understood. Questions can be asked on telephone and face-to-face surveys as well as in self-completion diaries, but what is obtained through these methods has limitations. People meter systems can also capture some audience reaction and response, also by its nature very limited in depth.

There are limitations on what can be achieved through these regular vehicles, and you do not want to clutter a measurement instrument with too much on a discrete topic or topics. In order to obtain detailed audience opinion and reaction, we usually need to design specific research vehicles for the purpose.

8.1 Panels

Panels are one of the earliest methods used to obtain regular data on audience opinion. It is intriguing to note that panels now play a very big part in media research in new areas and activities as the new online media grow and as online research is developed to meet the challenges of this growth. We have seen the use of panels in Chapter 6 in passive online measurement and also in Chapters 4 and 5 where we see the use of panels in both traditional and new forms of measurement research.

Panels go back a long way. In the early days of market research, postal panels were created in some countries. Respondents were chosen in different parts of a country to agree to take part in regular surveys by answering self-completion questionnaires on selected topics. In many cases, such panels were created to represent the adult population of the country. Panels played a major role in the development of representative market and opinion research in Canada. Given that very large country's widely scattered population, random probability surveys using addresses that needed to be visited by an interviewer would be very expensive and time consuming. Although the latter method was used in more easily accessible major urban and suburban areas, it was less easy to cover more remote areas. Postal panels provided better coverage and continued to be used until the Internet and email replaced the postal mail as a method of delivery and collection.

For the collection of TV and radio programme reaction and opinion, whether on a regular or ad hoc basis, listeners and viewers can be selected and invited to help by being members of a panel. Members are asked to give regular feedback on selected programmes, networks or services. The panel never meets; the word is used to refer to a group of people who may have little else in common other than they are chosen to carry out a specific function or several tasks over a given period of time.

One of the several advantages of panels is that they enable behaviour and opinion to be measured or assessed for various programmes over time among the same people. This is not normally possible with face-to-face interviews.

One of the first uses of the panel approach in audience research was in the BBC when listeners to 'variety' (light entertainment) programmes were sought to give regular feedback on this kind of radio programme. The means of recruitment was to invite listeners to volunteer. A series of appeals was made via the press and on radio programmes. The announcements or appeals explained that volunteers would be asked to complete some relatively straightforward tasks that would not take a lot of time. It was explained that completing these tasks would help the BBC to give a better service to listeners.

The response astonished and rather overwhelmed the BBC. Almost 47,000 listeners sent letters offering themselves as volunteer panel members. It was decided to enrol only 2,000. But how should they be selected?

Those who had volunteered were not even the cross section of the population. Their demographic composition did not match that of the population as a whole. There were more men than women. They were younger than the population as a whole and they had a slight middle-class bias. The southeast, generally more prosperous and close to London, was over-represented.

The BBC attempted to reduce this bias, making the sample of 2,000 a representative as it could of the population as a whole. They were enrolled for a 12-week period. Each week they received by post, a list of the forthcoming week's light entertainment programmes—usually about 35 of them. Panel members were asked to report which of them they listened to and whether they had listened to all or part of each of the programmes.

The main purpose of this exercise, before the establishment of regular audience measurement, was to find out what was listened to, for how long and by what kinds of people. Later, all this could be better supplied by a fully representative survey. As was soon discovered, the nature of volunteers makes them untypical of the audience as a whole. A volunteer panel like this was an unsatisfactory basis for 'inferring the absolute quantity of the general public's listening programme by programme'. However, this method can be a reasonably reliable guide to the relative popularity of different programmes.[1]

We have mentioned this early experiment to show that inexpensive and simple methods can be used for research when representative surveys are impractical or cannot be carried out regularly. They can be used between surveys to plot the relative popularity of different programmes and the demographic nature of the different audiences for them. If selected to be representative of the whole population, panels can also be used for quantitative measurement. They are more usually used nowadays for the assessment of opinions and reactions in audience research. To obtain the most representative results, it is best to select a panel according to criteria set by the nature of what is being sought, and to be fully in control of the selection. However, volunteer panels may still be used because they do have certain advantages.

It is best to illustrate how panels may be selected by an example. Let us suppose, we need a panel to provide us with regular feedback and reaction to a network that specialises in cultural and arts programmes. We want to obtain a representative panel of the audience. But what constitutes the audience? Someone who normally listens or watches the channel in question every day is obviously a member of the audience in which we are interested. But what of the person who watches or listens very occasionally? He or she is also a part of the audience.

It is not a good idea to encourage panel members to do any duty listening or viewing.[2] We want them to behave normally and we should ask them to report on or react to the programmes they encounter as a result of their normal viewing or listening behaviour. You may find that a panel member has nothing to report in the period of his or her membership of the panel. That has to be accepted as a reflection of the reality we are attempting to measure and understand. However, we may decide to eliminate the occasional audience member, concentrating instead on those with a greater degree of commitment and interest.

Practically speaking, your panel may have to consist of those who listen or view programmes on a fairly regular basis. Instead of recruiting people as volunteers, a procedure which requires them to volunteer or 'self-select', it is possible to find a more representative sample and avoid the bias of self-selection, through face-to-face interviews. During the course of quantitative research, a respondent who, from his or her answers, fits the description required for the panel being recruited can be invited to become a member.

One disadvantage of this approach is that it can take a long time to find a panel for minority programmes. Another is that having selected a panel, you may find that their viewing, listening or reading habits provide insufficient data for analysis. For example, you may invite 1,000 people to be panel members and send them all the weekly or fortnightly questionnaires asking for reactions to programmes or articles listed. But response to any one of these may be only 10 or 20 people—too few cases for analysis.

You can, of course, guard against this by greatly increasing the size of the panel so as to ensure that even for minority programmes, you would probably get a sufficient response. But this can be very expensive in time and labour. Maintaining panels involves continual work, updating addresses, sending out reminders and generally keeping records in good order. The larger the panel, the more work there is to do.

For more than 40 years, listener reactions to programmes on the BBC were collected via a volunteer general listening panel. Three thousand panel members aged 12 and over were recruited by broadcast appeals for volunteers on the three, later four national radio networks. A panel made up from listeners who responded was then selected to be the representative of each network's audience in terms of age, social class, sex and geographical region. The panel members, who served for two years, each received a weekly booklet with questions about programmes in the radio network they listened to most. The system succeeded in supplying regular reaction to programmes. But how representative were these? Were volunteers different in some way from those who did not volunteer?

Inevitably, what was really a self-selected sample was different in being more articulate and biased towards the middle class, despite all attempts to correct this. Listeners to the more serious kinds of programmes dominated the panel. The system was replaced in 1984 by panels based on a controlled recruitment method. The Daily Survey provided an excellent source for this. Light listeners—those who listened to less than 10 hours of radio in a week—were excluded. It meant excluding one in three of all listeners to the BBC, but it was the only practical way to proceed. Infrequent listeners would hardly maintain interest in the task if they found themselves regularly returning blank questionnaires. Excluding them undoubtedly reduces the representative nature of the panel, but it was noted that the infrequent listeners accounted for only 10 per cent of listening to the networks in question.

The new panel was selected to represent the radio audience as a whole, structured by class, sex, age, social class and geographical distribution. It was grouped into nine categories according to the listening habits of the individuals. The groups represented listeners to any of the then four national BBC networks or combinations of networks. However, there was a problem about the arts and culture network, *Radio 3*. In the sample recruited for the panel, few had listened to any Radio 3 programmes in the previous week and many were only infrequent users. With Radio 3 and other networks like it, it is necessary to over-recruit in order to secure enough data for analysis. And so it was that the Radio 3 panel was boosted by appeals in the traditional manner for volunteers whose replies were used only for the analysis of response to Radio 3 programmes.[3]

Panels can be used effectively even when many listeners are illiterate. If what is needed is informed, considered feedback from literate listeners and viewers, panels can be very useful, provided that it is remembered that they do not represent the opinions of illiterates. It is a good idea to give a modest incentive to members of a listening or viewing panel. Members of the Ghana Broadcasting Corporation's listening panels in Ghana used to have a free subscription to the now defunct *Radio and TV Times*. Later, they got a free TV licence and, if they had rediffusion radio (an early form of cable or wired radio), they paid no hire fee. These were acceptable policies in what was then a broadcasting monopoly, but when there is competition, it would be methodologically safer to use incentives unrelated to the broadcast services in any way.

You might wish to have another kind of panel, one which is not a representative of listeners as a whole, but only of those you particularly wish to reach. For example, you might have a radio programme or a series of programmes for mothers with children. Others not in your primary target group might also be in the audience. Almost all kinds of radio and television programme are regularly consumed by people for whom they may not be primarily intended. You may well decide that in your research, you wish just to concentrate on your primary target audience. That may well be an appropriate and efficient approach. In this case, you would need to devise an alternative way of recruitment. Do you have or can you devise a suitable sampling frame from which to recruit?

8.2 Appreciation Indices

Producers, programme makers and planners need to know not only who listens or watches and how many, but also what they think of the programmes and to have some measure of the level of overall appreciation of them. And they may need to obtain information or feedback in a more systematic way and one in which response can be compared over a period of time. We have seen various ways in which opinions can be measured.

Appreciation Indices or AIs are a commonly used method in some countries. They have strengths and weaknesses.

Audience size is a useful guide to overall performance of a particular network or programme on that network. But it will never give you the whole story. We also need to take account of audience appreciation as a measure of a programme's achievement. People may listen or view a programme merely because it was on at a time when they usually listen or view. We may want to know what they really think of it.

A programme may attract a low audience but be appreciated very much by those who did watch or listen. This might well be thought to be a satisfactory and worthwhile achievement, especially within public service rather than commercial broadcasting. Sometimes a programme with a small audience and a high AI may attract new listeners or viewers. The enthusiastic minority may talk about the programme and others may hear about it and try it out, like what they see or hear and become regular listeners. Sometimes high AIs can be predictors of audience growth for the programme in question.

This is how AIs are achieved. They are often used in the kinds of diaries described earlier. Listeners or viewers are asked for their reaction and response to the named programmes. Often only a selection of programmes will be asked about; sometimes the viewer or listener is asked to give a view on all programmes encountered.

On the BBC Daily Survey, which was used to measure radio audiences, all respondents aged 12 and over were asked to complete a booklet called 'What You Think of What You Watch'. In it were listed various TV programmes over the next five days. They were asked not to do any special viewing but to answer questions only about their normal viewing.

Most of the questionnaire concerned AIs. Each respondent was asked to rate each programme they watched themselves on a six-point scale from 'extremely interesting and/or enjoyable' to 'not at all interesting and/or enjoyable'.

For every television programme, the percentage of viewers who recorded each level of appreciation is calculated. From these is then calculated the AI as a percentage. The following could be the results from such an exercise:

Extremely interesting and/or enjoyable	6	5	4	3	2	1	Not at all interesting and/or enjoyable
	28%	29%	26%	8%	6%	3%	

The AI is the mean of these calculated as a percentage. The score of 1 is eliminated. In effect, we are giving the judgement 'Not at all interesting or enjoyable', the score of 0. We are left with five scores of appreciation of different levels. Assigning scores to each from 5 to 1 and dividing the sum by 500 makes the calculation.[4] This is how it is done:

$$\frac{(28 \times 5) + (29 \times 4) + (26 \times 3) + (8 \times 2) + (6 \times 1)}{500} = 71$$

We divide by 500 in order to obtain a score related to the scale 0 to 100. If everyone had given the top rating of 6—'extremely interesting and/or enjoyable'—to which we assign the score of 5, the calculation would give us a score of 100.

$$\frac{100 \times 5}{500} = 100$$

If everyone, equally unlikely, had given a bottom rating of 1—'not at all interesting and/or enjoyable'—to which we assign the score of 0, the result of our calculation would be a score of 0.

We say that the programme in the above example has an AI of 71, a typical result. These AIs are not absolute measures. Their value is in comparability between programmes of a similar type, or of the same programmes in a series. Experience shows what AIs a drama programme will normally achieve. One can then see if a particular programme achieves a higher or lower than normal AI.

For radio, a similar method can be used. In Britain, a five-point scale ranging from 'very well worth hearing' down to 'not worth hearing' has been used. The number of points in the scale can be higher or lower but experience shows that five- or six-point scales work well.

Indices can also be provided on specific opinions about a programme. For example, a radio service may have featured an interview with a leading politician, perhaps the Prime Minister. A specific question or set of questions can be asked.

	Agree Strongly	Agree Somewhat	Neither Agree nor Disagree	Disagree Somewhat	Disagree Strongly
X was a good interviewer	5	4	3	2	1
X was too deferential—he did not ask really searching questions	5	4	3	2	1
The Prime Minister dealt with the questions convincingly	5	4	3	2	1
The Prime Minister had difficulty in answering some of the questions	5	4	3	2	1

(Continued)

(Continued)

	Agree Strongly	Agree Somewhat	Neither Agree nor Disagree	Disagree Somewhat	Disagree Strongly
I learned a lot from this interview	5	4	3	2	1
I found the interview unconvincing	5	4	3	2	1

Individual scores and overall indices for each aspect can be given. The decision on how to report results may depend on how the results emerge. The issue with all research reporting is how to make complexity simple. Instead of a set of figures, it may be sufficient to report in words what the average of opinions in each category was—most listeners found it interesting, most found X a good interviewer, although a substantial minority thought he was too deferential, and so on.

8.3 Other Measures

Audience researchers often seek to devise new ways of measuring the way people view or listen to programmes, especially in response to the concerns of programme makers. In the Netherlands, the public broadcaster NOS has used a different way of looking beyond ratings, share and appreciation. Do these really tell us all we want to know? NOS researchers came up with a way of measuring two other important factors about radio listening behaviour, 'attention' and 'group or individual listening'.

On their regular diary measurement for radio, NOS used to ask respondents to say where they listen, whether in the car, at work or at home, and to grade their enjoyment of programmes on a scale from 1 to 10. They later selected some of the diary participants to complete a further diary on which they were asked to record two other matters. Were they listening with attention or not? Were they listening alone or in company? Also, in addition to the usual list of stations, an additional 'station' was added to the diary charts—the respondents' own record, cassette or CD player. The results were of considerable interest and importance.

Attention to programmes varied at different times of the day and at different parts of the week. It was highest in the early morning and late evening and lowest during the day between 10.00 AM and 4.00 PM. Listening alone or with others also varies in a similar way. There is a greater tendency to listen alone in the early morning and late evening. Older people also tend to listen more on their own.

There were also great differences between stations. For example, the popular music stations with the highest shares, Radio 3 and *Sky Radio*, have the lowest attention scores among the major stations. The news station, *Radio 1*, has a lower share but enjoys a high score for attention among its listeners. It is also more likely than other major stations to be listened to alone. Some minority interest stations with a low share have the highest scores both for appreciation and attention, and among the lowest for listening in the company of others. It seems very obvious that NOS have discovered two very important measures that must surely be a factor in the respective impact and importance of these stations.

In a similar way, postal diaries used to do research into the reception of Radio Österreich 1 (an Austrian station offering both classical music and information) not only contained a six-point appreciation scale but always also the dichotomous variable 'listened attentively' or 'did not listen with attention'.

The measure of attention has important implications for the use of popular communications media as educational and developmental tools.[5]

8.4 Use of Online Methods to Test Audience Reaction, Response and Opinion

Much of the above is to look at the past. The new research possibilities provided by online research have transformed this area of media research. Whereas there are limitations on the use of online methods to measure audiences, the new technology has provided many useful tools for research into audience reaction, response and opinion. Some of these tools are new; others provide enhancements of mainly face-to-face interview methods previously employed. Online methods can be used on an ad hoc basis for particular projects. Some are outlined here.

Bulletin Boards

Due to the fact that bulletin boards may last for a week or longer, it is possible to use them for tracking the introduction of, for example, a new daily soap. In case of a longer monitoring period, online diaries can be used. Pretesting TV programmes can also be performed online. If there is sufficient time and funds before the actual screening of a programme, perhaps the best approach is to deliver DVDs to respondent's homes and asking them to view the test programmes and comment on a bulletin board. Another possibility is to upload test material to YouTube—if confidentiality is not at stake, or else to a website with special access to respondents being arranged. There are many examples that can be seen by putting the phrase 'Bulletin boards' into a search engine.

Online Ad Hoc Surveys

Of course there is always the possibility to ask a larger sample of respondents to view a specific TV programme live. In this case, respondents are asked to fill in an online questionnaire immediately after viewing. Usually, respondents cooperate well with this kind of research task as they enjoy it and like being asked about TV which plays a big part in their lives.

Another possibility is to conduct a survey with a questionnaire presenting either a storyboard of a TV programme or a summary short video of around 3 minutes. With the spread of the smartphone, online research can now be used to ask panellists in real time about their media use at that moment and have them rate the perceived quality of the medium just being used. This, however, needs relatively large samples and is not as easy in practice as it might seem in theory. It is also regarded by many as annoyingly intrusive, while others might enjoy being asked. The problem with this is that a bias is introduced—those who are irritated at the intrusion may be rather different from those who willingly accept the intervention.

Online projects with their capacity to include image, sound and video samples offer ideal technologies for TV research of the kind that assists with programme making. Only a few examples can be included here.

Here are some practical examples of some simple TV programme research using online methods:

Programme Genre Research

The illustrations given ahead are examples of possible online questionnaires and results of such surveys. They are based on the actual experience with a public-service TV station. For a commercial TV station, other genres may be more relevant. While the original studies were carried out by means of conventional research methods, online research would make them more precise, cheaper and faster. Programme genres (Western movie, nature magazine, ballroom dancing, and others) can be illustrated by thumbnail images in a web-based questionnaire. Persons answering 'I would definitely view this type of programme' would be classified as potential viewers. Their number would describe the actual size of the respective target group and their socio-demographic structure and living habits would facilitate content planning, scheduling of transmissions and targeting TV advertising.

On the basis of scores for 'information', 'entertainment', 'art/culture' and 'practical use', a TV station could map its genres by correspondence analysis and thereby find out about strengths and weaknesses of its programme offer.

Programme Atlas

Measurement of Viewing Interest: 'Programme Atlas'

For each type of TV programme please state whether you will ...

	watch in any case	maybe	rather not	surely not
Football	○	○	○	○
Ballroom Dancing	(○)	○	○	○
Show programme	○	○	○	○
Fashion	○	○	○	○
Advanture film	○	○	○	○

One of the basic tasks of professional TV research is defining the potential audiences of important TV genres.

Solution: once a year, in an online survey, genres grouped into 'programme families' (such as entertainment, information, sport etc.) are presented to a nationwide sample.

The percentage of 'watch in any case' is called the 'programme interest' or 'potential'

'Potential' can be correlated with 'ratings' which results in the 'realization figure':

Example: if the potential of 'Ballroom Dancing' is 30% and such programme is watched by 15%, then the audience realization is 50%.

Note: only online research offers the possibility to illustrate the question with images or even videoclips!

Program Genre Mapping

For a TV station it is very important to know which programme fields it covers and which not. By scaling the 'content' of each genre, a 'genre map' can be drawn by means of a mapping programme.

Scaling is performed online similar to the programme atlas.

Please rate each programme genre by giving points between 0 and 10 for:

	Information	Entertain-ment	Art/Culture	Practical use
Football	4	6	0	2
Ballroom Dancing	2	7	5	4
Show programme	1	8	2	0
Fashion	3	6	4	6
Advanture film	1	7	1	1

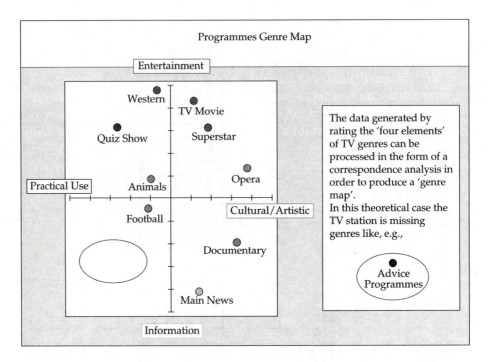

Online Appreciation Panels

In some European countries (the United Kingdom, The Netherlands, Germany, Ireland, Belgium and Catalonia in Spain) where people meters do not provide appreciation indices, online panel surveys have been used to produce appreciation scores and other qualitative data about programmes.

The first TV appreciation panel in this form was introduced in 2002 in the Netherlands after Dutch TV stations had changed their people meter contract and lost automatic appreciation measurement that had previously been done within the people meter system. The then new Dutch TV appreciation panel comprised 8,000 members.

Since 2004, the BBC has run a panel consisting of around 21,500 adults (16+) who are invited to complete a questionnaire every day to record what they thought of TV and radio offers they had been exposed to. Websites are also measured for appreciation with the help of small cross-media samples. Here is a short description of the method used.

First, using a programme chart, the respondents are asked to highlight the programmes they watched:

BBC ONE	BBC TWO	itv 1	Channel 4	CHANNEL 5	BBC THREE	BBC FOUR	sky 1	4 (E4)
18:00	18:00	18:00	18:00	18:00	18:00	18:00	18:00	18:00
18:00 BBC News at Six	18:00 Breab) 19:00 Earrannan (Gaelic)	18:00 STV News at Six	18:00 The Simpsons	18:00 Home and Away	MOTD Live: Italy v. Egypt	19:00 World News Today	18:00 Futurama	18:00 Big Brother's Little Brother
18:30 Reporting Scotland	19:30 'S Ann An Lie (Gaelic)	18:30 ITV Evening News and Weather	18:30 Hollyoaks	18:30 Zoo Days	21:30 Bizarre ER	19:30 Return to . . . Airport	19:00 The Simpsons	18:30 Friends
19:00 The One Show	20:00 Springwatch Home Movies	19:00 Emmerdale	19:00 Channel 4 News	19:00 Five News at 7	22:00 EastEnders	20:00 Hidden Histories	20:00 The Real A & E	19:00 Hollyoaks
19:30 Eastenders	21:00 Krod Mandoon and the Flaming Sword of Fire	19:30 Countrywise	19:55 Five Minute Wonder: On the Ward	19:30 Highland Emergency	22:30 The Real Hustle on Holiday	20:30 Moon Landing: Days That Shook the World	21:00 Bones	19:30 My Name is Earl
20:00 Celebrity Masterchef	21:30 That Mitchell and Webb Look	20:00 The Bill: To Die For	20:00 The Home Show	20:00 Paul Merton in India	23:05 Family Guy	21:00 Crude Britannia: The Story of North Sea Oil	22:00 Lie to Me	20:00 Friends
21:00 Occupation	22:00 Psychoville	21:00 Wild Islands	21:00 Undercover Boss	21:00 The Mentalist	23:50 Ideal	22:00 The Secret Life of the Airport	23:00 Bones	21:00 My Name is Earl
22:00 BBC News at Ten	22:30 Newsnight	22:00 News at Ten and Weather	22:00 Big Brother	22:00 Law and Order: Special Victims Unit		23:50 Crude Britannia: The Story of North Sea Oil		21:30 The Big Bang Theory
22:25 Reporting Scotland	23:00 Newsnight Scotland	22:35 Cops With Cameras	23:10 The TNT Show	23:00 Law and Order: Criminal Intent				23:30 Fonejacker
22:35 Question Time	23:30 Cricket World Twenty20	22:35 Politics Now	23:40 Derren Bown: Trick or Treat					
23:35 This Week								

This is what the programme selection screen that is sent to panel members looks like for one evening. The viewer highlights the programme he/she has watched before answering questions about their viewing experience

The respondents are then asked to answer three standard questions—to provide an overall rating 1 to 10 (1 poor, 10 excellent), then to say how much effort they made to watch (three choices—'watched because the TV was on', 'made some effort to watch' or 'made a special effort to watch', and how much attention they paid to the programme ('a lot', 'some' and 'hardly any').

They are then asked questions about a particular programme, in this case the soap East Enders. First, they are asked whether they agree or otherwise with four statements/opinions about the series, then they are asked for their opinion on the storyline and the characters and then to give any comments about what they liked or disliked.

The statements or opinions about East Enders, a popular BBC TV 'soap' were:

'It's the kind of programme I would talk to other people about.'

'The programme felt original and different from most other TV programmes I've seen.'

'This programme was inspiring.'

'This programme encouraged me to do something new.'

For each statement, the respondent panel member was asked to choose from five responses—'agree strongly', 'agree slightly', 'disagree slightly', 'disagree strongly' and 'no strong views'.

The next three questions were, in turn, about the storyline, the characters and finally an open-ended question for the respondent to write about anything else they liked or disliked. This is how the questions were put:

What was your opinion of the storyline?				
The programme had a very good storyline	The programme had a fairly good storyline	The programme had a fairly bad storyline	The programme had a very bad storyline	Does not apply/ Don't know
What was your opinion of the characters in it?				
It had very good characters	It had fairly good characters	It had fairly bad characters	It had very bad characters	Does not apply/ Don't know
What did you think about this programme? Please write in what, if anything, you liked or didn't like about it.				

The main measure, the Appreciation Index (AI) is obtained by respondents marking the programmes watched with a score between 1 and 10. The average of all these marks for a programme is then multiplied by 10 to give an appreciation index (AI). For example, when aggregating scores for all programmes together for BBC TV (as of March 2011), the average score is 8.2, which gives an AI of 82.

The answers to the final open-ended question can be presented to management and programme makers in the form of unedited comments (*verbatims*). All comments are tagged with age and gender, which enables programme makers to draw meaningful conclusions. Wordcloud can also be used to pick out frequent words and phrases that appear.

The appreciation panel enables the BBC to collect over 5,000 responses a day on TV and radio programmes. Panellists are encouraged, by means of a prize draw reward scheme, to log in at least 10 times in any one month. There are some different sets of questions within the questionnaire—some of them are constantly asked and some of them refer to the programme and may end with it. Similar methods are or have been used elsewhere in Europe, in Germany, Ireland, Spain and Belgium.

The costs of running TV and radio appreciation panels, even online, can be quite high and this stops more TV and radio stations making more use of this approach. Advertisers and agencies are the main drivers of most media research and they are not convinced of the advantages of measuring appreciation. And yet, an important and interesting feature of high appreciation scores is their value for the acceptance of TV advertising. Despite opinions to the contrary of many, if not most advertisers and agencies, a TV programme with a high appreciation score has a positive influence on ads placed immediately before or after such a programme. According to empirical studies performed in the Netherlands (Ster/Intomart/MarketResponse), adverts after well-appreciated programmes produce a higher buying intention than ads placed in other programme environments. According to these findings, even a slight increase in appreciation has a measurable effect on the propensity to buy.

One of the authors of this book, Peter Diem, has from his long personal experience with TV research, devised another model for audience appreciation research that he believes could be faster and more efficient than the ones used now.

New Way to Measure Audience Appreciation Online for TV and Radio

Like in the TV appreciation panels described above, respondents are first asked to highlight on a screen presented to them on their computer/laptop/tablet the programmes viewed or listened to on the day before. On the next screen, they are invited to rate these programmes on a scale from 0–10 by entering the points in a numeric field. Alternatively, sliders on the screen, moved by the mouse, could be used for the same purpose—they would probably be more fun, although they might require more effort and time from the respondents.

One example would be to provide questions online on a screen containing a closed question to record the most important properties or dimensions of the TV programmes viewed. This question is very simple because it requires panellists only to check those properties which they consider to fit the respective programme. The properties asked about could be, for example, 'engaging', 'entertaining', 'informative', 'well presented' and more as needed. The results of this standard question cluster would make all TV programmes comparable, and it would offer a quick explanation for good, average and bad appreciation scores. The total number of boxes checked could be also used as a measurement of attention.

As one of the parameters considers the quality of the respective programme's moderator, this measurement would also enable programme makers and management to analyse the perceived performance of moderators by simply comparing the results for the box 'well moderated'.

Music Testing

Before online research developed into what it is today, music testing was done usually through face-to-face survey methods, sometimes using handheld music players but more often at central research locations. Radio stations commissioned research whereby short extracts of music would be played to respondents who would be asked questions either through a questionnaire administered by an interviewer or else a self completion questionnaire. Sometimes called 'auditorium tests', this method usually required respondents to travel to a central location where they were asked to listen to hundreds of music samples, entering their judgement into paper-and-pencil questionnaires. The method could also be done using the telephone although because of the quality limitations of many phone lines and the recording equipment required this is not an ideal approach. These methods are relatively time consuming and expensive.

Online research has been shown to work well as a replacement method that is far superior in the time it takes, the quality of the data obtained and in the lower costs involved. Commercial popular music stations use this method to test their output, playlists and similar related programme matters. As can be seen in the graph below, in a typical music test, 10–20 second music samples (so-called 'hooks') are played online to respondents to be followed by questions about awareness, appreciation and readiness to listen to them again. Another possibility would be to provide households with music samples or upload music videos to YouTube for subsequent testing by an online survey. See sample questionnaire below. This example has three questions about awareness of a tune, liking for it and how much the respondent wants to hear it.

Do You Know This Melody? (If You Have Mediaplayer on Your PC You Can Play Samples)		How Do You Like This Melody? Rate It From 0 'Don't Like At All' To 10 'Like It Very Much'	How Often Should This Tune Be Played on The Radio?			
			As it is Now	More Often	Less Often	Not at All
Yes	No	O				
Classic Rock	O	O	O	O	O	O	O
Hip Hop	O	O	O	O	O	O	O
Reggae	O	O	O	O	O	O	O
Jazz	O	O	O	O	O	O	O
Light Classics	O	O	O	O	O	O	O

Next

Online Radio Diary

In conventional radio research, paper and pencil diaries can be used to provide qualitative feedback as well as audience measurement. As explained above, listeners can provide appreciation scores. They can also record whether they paid attention to a broadcast or had it playing in the background. Radio programmes can be rated and 'likes' and 'dislikes' can be recorded. If this is done online, the turn around and provision of data to the end user is very much faster and easier.

Using online methods for a radio diary has the big advantage that ratings can be swiftly analysed and the comments made can be instantly available. No transcription of verbal comments is required. Since the growth of the Internet into older segments of the population, online radio diaries are becoming feasible in practical radio research. See below for a simple questionnaire design.

Projective TV or Radio Programme Test

In the section on qualitative research methods elsewhere in the book, reference is made to several ways of getting respondents to use their imagination.

	What of the Following Programmes Did You Listen to at the Times Shown and How Attentive Were You?		Give Each Programme a Score 0 to 10 Where 0 is 'Very Poor' and 10 is 'Excellent'		
	Radio was on	Listened with Attention	Points 0 To 10	What was Positive?	What was Negative?
05:00-05:15 Early Morning News	O	O			
05:15-05:30 Baroque Music	O	O			
05:30-05:45 Baroque Music	O	O			
05:45-06:00 Morning News and Traffic	O	O			
06:00-06:15 Freddy's Morning Show	O	O			
06:15-06:30 Freddy's Morning Show	O	O			
06:30-06:45 Freddy's Morning Show	O	O			
06:45-07:00 Freddy's Morning Show	O	O			
07:00-07:15 Morning News and Traffic	O	O			
07:15-07:30 Favourite Classics	O	O			
07:30-07:45 Favourite Classics	O	O			
07:45-08:00 Today's Programmes in Detail	O	O			

They can be asked to imagine themselves in a defined and different situation using online questionnaire methods.

Here is an example of a 'semi-qualitative' test based on $n = 200$ online interviews in which respondents are urged to use their imagination about TV. By means of text analysis, the answers can be interpreted so as to inform programme makers of the 'real' wishes of their audience.

The respondent is presented with an online page with appropriate visual stimuli and the text reads.

Just imagine standing in front of a magic door that opens onto a land of wonder and fantasy. Close your eyes for a second. You have entered 'TV Paradise'. Without having to press any button you can order any TV programme you want. Just ask and your favourite TV programme will appear. What would they be? What shows? What stars? What is special about them for you? Tell us why you like these shows so much?

The respondent can then write answers in the space provided.

Notes and References

1. Silvey, *Who's Listening*, p. 83.
2. Here, we refer to only radio and television but the same methods can be used for all media including print and new media. The use of panels in other research areas is referred to in chapters 3, 4 and 5.
3. Peter Jenkins and Richard Windle, 'The New Listening Panel', in *Annual Review of BBC Broadcasting Research Findings* No.11 (1985): 37–44.
4. Pamela Reiss, 'Continuous Research for Television and Radio: The 1980s Approach', *Annual Review of BBC Broadcasting Research Findings*, No. 8 (1981–1982): 13–26.
5. Heloïse van den Berg and Henk van Zurksum, *Now Listen and Pay Attention* (Hilversum: NOS, .n.d.).

Chapter 9

Desk Research

What can be learned about the audience from the existing data? Do we make sufficient use of data already available, from the census, from departments of agriculture, health, housing, and so on? Sometimes new research involving fieldwork may be unnecessary because the work has already been done. It can be a very useful exercise simply to carry out an audit of what is available and what research has been done in the area you are interested in.

The Internet has made desk research a lot easier, quicker and more productive. Familiar search engines like Google, Yahoo, Lycos, Norton and others will help you find some kinds of material relevant to what you are looking for. But they will not always find everything and sometimes you will not find anything relevant. This does not mean that nothing exists and it is often worth making contact with people who are knowledgeable about the topic or area of topics you are interested in. In our experience of doing research, networking is a major part of the process of doing desk research. One asks those whom he/she knows, one contacts those whom he/she knows who may have had some experience in the topic or area concerned.

Libraries are also very important. There are standard sources of statistical and other information, not always online. Surprising as it may seem, online resources are often more difficult to use fully than a printed reference book. In the research business, one soon becomes familiar with reliable sources of information on topics from languages to ethnicity, import and export figures to data on production and consumption, data on population to data on people movement, data on holiday travel to data on leisure activities. Research may have been done into leisure, education and other aspects of daily life or any other aspect of daily routines that would be useful when planning media projects from advertising campaigns to the launch of new products and services.

Universities can be a very useful source of research and we believe it is a great weakness for both sides that there is not more cooperation between the academic communities on the one hand and media and advertising research communities on the other. Media researchers tend to look askance at the academics, accusing them of far too much theory with little empirical evidence, while academics tend to scorn media researchers' apparent lack of theoretical understanding and their apparent attachment to numbers and the single-minded pursuit of ratings or readership figures. In fact, each has a lot to offer the other. There is a wealth of important data in media organisations that is often not fully analysed because full use for media planning purposes has been made of the significant parts. For media owners, yesterday's data soon become history. At the same time, we see a lot of academic work which uses little or no empirical data in reaching conclusions about media use. The freedom academic researchers have from the day-to-day constraints and demands of a media organisation or advertising department could give them the ability to discern trends and other information from the data collected by media research departments. They could also provide the much-needed critical element into the process of media research. If there were as much cooperation in media research as there is in most other areas of scholarship—in, for example, medicine, the chemical industry or engineering—both the academic and media organisation research communities would benefit greatly.

One problem with the Internet is that all need to remember and keep in mind the difficulty of distinguishing between good quality information and the bad, inadequate or misleading. For example, put 'largest global TV audience' into any search engine and you will be given several pages of claims that are nearly all made without any evidence. At the time of writing, no globally televised TV event or programme has ever been shown to have reached more than around 900 million. And yet, claims are regularly made for audiences very much larger than this. All such claims are baseless.

The Web is free for all; anyone can post anything. How do you know that something you find through a search is reliable and the best available data? There is no simple answer. Experience is a great teacher. If you want to find out what is known about radio audiences in India, you might Google this. But you may take a long time to find something reliable. In early 2014, the first item provided by Google in response to 'radio audiences in India' was a link to the website of the national broadcaster, All India Radio, which told us nothing at all about the audiences, other than the fact that they do research into them and have done so for nearly 70 years.[1] And the suggested links that follow on Google when accessed in March 2014 provided nothing of any further enlightenment.[2]

This is not unusual. The Internet remains a very uneven source of information. There is a lot of information there, but it is very lopsided in coverage, depth or detail, and reliability.

The Internet can be quite good at providing data on media and advertising in more developed countries. But it provides very partial or actually wrong information (because data are biased by lack of detail and coverage of many areas and media) for much of the less developed world. This situation is likely to improve, however, as markets become more mature.

Global data for some things are probably quite reliable. Take, for example, global advertising spend. If you do a search for that, this is one of the results you will get from the website of the journal *Advertising Age*. This is what it says: 'The internet in 2013 passed newspapers to become the world's second-largest ad medium, behind TV, according to ZenithOptimedia. The internet now captures one in five ad dollars.'

The following table taken from Zenith data in that article and in Zenith reports shows the percentage of worldwide advertising spending that went into each medium in 2005 and 2013 (the data are for most major advertising spending and a lot of minor spending also but certainly do not cover a lot of local advertising, especially in the informal sector which is not often captured in data analyses like this). Their website predicted in 2015 that by 2017, the Internet would be taking more advertising money than any other single medium. NB. The 'Internet' here includes social media and this is where a lot of the growth is happening.[3]

Changes in Global Advertising Expenditure between 2005 and 2013[4]

	2005	2013
TV	36.8%	40.2%
Internet	5.6%	20.6%
Newspapers	29.1%	17.0%
Magazines	13.1%	7.9%
Radio	8.4%	6.9%
Outdoor	6.6%	6.9%
Cinema	0.4%	0.5%

This seems to us to be reliable. One way to test it is to see if other websites tell a similar story. But beware! It can sometimes be the case that all are getting the same (wrong) information from the same source.

But readers will look and find new sources emerging. Always take care. There are spurious data sources galore. There are two, however, which should always be looked at for some basic facts and figures on media. The first is the website of the International Telecommunications Union, the ITU. We used data from their website in the chapter on quantitative research when showing the massive global growth in the mobile phone.[5] Another useful data source is the United States Agency for International Development (USAID) website for data collected globally relating to demographic and health surveys which among many other data items collect useful data on home media access.[6]

To end this very short chapter, we append here a very good example of the data that can be culled from desk research from available sources, including the Internet. The well-known international advertising company M&C Saatchi has a division working in advocacy and communication for health, development and social progress. We were given their permission to use the following data set put together by Joe Miller about media in India. It was done in mid-2015 mainly from publicly available resources. We include it here not only as an excellent example of good desk research but also because it is about media in the most populated country on earth and one that has seen and continues to experience huge changes in media access and use.

In the previous edition of this book, we included some data on broadcast media access and use in India compiled from the available data from field research done in India on behalf of the BBC World Service. See the evidence here of what has happened in no more than 18 years. First the data from BBC surveys carried out between 1995 and 1998 in eight of the most highly populated of India's 29 states (given on Page 222).

Data were collected neither on Internet access, as it was negligible at that time, nor on mobile phones that arrived in India starting in 1995.

But now the data on media access and use in 2015 collected by M&C Saatchi:

9.1 Communication and Media Landscape in India: Joe Miller and M&C Saatchi World Services

Television

India has over 234 million television households, which account for approximately 60 per cent of the population.[7] However, this statistic varies greatly depending on which region is being analysed. New Delhi, for example, has very high television penetration, whereas in Bihar it is just 15 per cent.[8] There are over 790 satellite television channels[9] and over 65 million digital television subscribers.[10]

Doordarshan is India's biggest television broadcaster. For many years, it had a monopoly, being the state-run TV service. Today, their most popular channels are *DD1* and *DD News*. They have 11 regional satellite services, which cover the majority of widely spoken languages in India. These include *DD-Malayalam*, *DD-Bengali*, *DD-Gujarati* and *DD-Punjabi*.[11] Other popular TV stations include *CNN-IBN* (a 24-hour news channel in English), *New Delhi TV*, *Star TV* and *Zee TV*.

Media Access and Use in India—Analysis from Eight States

	All	Sex		Age			Education				Area	
		Male	Female	15–29	30–44	45+	No Formal	Primary	Secondary	Tertiary	Urban	Rural
All adults (aged 15+)	100	100	100	100	100	100	100	100	100	100	100	100
Media Equipment												
Have a Radio	35	39	31	38	34	32	20	38	58	72	49	30
Have a Television	33	34	32	34	33	31	14	36	63	79	70	19
Have Both Radio and TV	18	20	16	19	18	17	6	18	40	61	40	10
Have Neither	50	47	54	47	52	54	71	44	20	9	21	61
Weekly Audiences												
Radio	33	40	25	38	32	27	18	39	54	57	37	31
Television	48	54	41	55	47	38	24	57	80	88	78	36
Radio but not TV	12	13	10	12	11	12	12	14	10	7	5	14
TV but not Radio	27	27	26	29	27	22	17	32	36	39	46	19
Both Radio and TV	21	27	15	26	20	15	6	25	44	50	32	17
Either Radio or TV	60	67	51	67	59	50	35	71	90	95	83	51
Neither	40	33	49	33	41	50	65	29	10	5	17	49

Mobile

India has over 886 million active mobile subscriptions, which puts the penetration rate at 70 per cent.[12] It also has the third largest smartphone base in the world, with around 168 million handsets in circulation.[13] This equates to 13.4 per cent smartphone penetration for the entire population, but this is likely to increase with the development of low-price smartphones and the constantly decreasing price of mobile Internet tariffs.

While 886 million active mobile subscriptions seems to suggest that 70 per cent of India has mobile access, research has suggested that the use of multiple phones by people of higher economic status, and attractive first-time customer tariffs, means that this number is false. In fact, the mobile penetration, as defined by unique users as a percentage of the total population, is just 28 per cent.[14]

Radio

At least 90 per cent of Indians have access to radio services,[15] which is unmatched by any other medium. Crucially, radio offers a platform to disseminate information to otherwise hard to reach population in rural areas. Information from the 2011 census has shown that public and community radio stations have been able to reach almost 80 per cent of rural households through radios and mobile phones.[16] Some of the most popular radio stations include All India Radio, Radio One (6 big cities), Radio Mirchi (Mumbai, Delhi) and Radio City (Mumbai, Delhi).[17]

Online

India's 195 million Internet users account for just fewer than 16 per cent of the total population.[18] As with mobile and television penetration, this is somewhat concentrated in urban areas and bypasses more remote regions.

There are approximately 106 million social media users in India,[19] with Facebook being the most popular platform for Indians to communicate online. Pages of celebrities, such as Sachin Tendulkar (cricketer) and Narendra Modi (current prime minister) have over 20 million likes.

The BBC claims that, while there is no systematic censoring effort on the Internet, 'in late 2011, the authorities were embroiled in a dispute with leading social networks over censorship of content deemed to be offensive.'[20]

Print Media

According to the 2011 Population Census, India has a literacy rate of 74 per cent. Once again, this percentage fluctuates depending on region. Bihar has the lowest literacy rate at 63 per cent.[21]

India has thriving print media, with over 62,000 daily and periodical newspaper titles. Of these, 24,000 are in Hindi, 9,000 are in English and 28,500 are in regional languages.[22]

The most popular newspapers in widely spoken languages can be identified by their AIR. *Dainik Jagran* and *Dainik Bhaskar* are the most widely read Hindi papers, with 16 million and 13.5 million readers, respectively. *Malayala Manorama* is the most popular Malayalam paper with 9.9 million readers, and the *Daily Thanthi* and *The Times of India* are the most popular Tamil and English newspapers, with both drawing in a readership of just over 7 million people.[23]

Communication and Media Metrics for India

	India
Internet penetration	15.8% to 195,248,950[24]
Smartphone penetration	13.4% to 167,900,000[25]
Active social media users	8% to 106,000,000[26]
Active mobile subscriptions	70% to 886,300,000[27]
Active mobile social users	7% to 92,000,000[28]
Literacy rate	74%[29]
Television penetration	60%[30,31]
Number of television households	234,000,000[32]
Digital television subscribers	65,000,000[33]

Following table shows the top seven newspapers by AIR in India.

Newspapers with Highest Average Issue Readership in India[34]

Newspaper	*Language*	*Reach (average issue readership)*
Dainik Jagran	Hindi	16,000,000
Dainik Bhaskar	Hindi	13,500,000
Hindustan	Hindi	10,800,000
Malayala Manorama	Malayalam	9,900,000
Amar Ujala	Hindi	8,600,000
Daily Thanthi	Tamil	7,200,000
The Times of India	English	7,300,000

Newspapers with Highest Average Issue Readership in Bihar[35]

Newspaper	Language	Reach (average issue readership)
Hindustan	Hindi	4,842,000
Dainik Jagran	Hindi	2,727,000
Prabhat Khabar	Hindi	426,000
AJ	Hindi	286,000
The Times of India	English	162,000
Rashtriya Sahar	Hindi	119,000
I Next	Hindi	92,000

Notes and References

1. http://allindiaradio.gov.in/Information/Pages/Audience%20Research%20Survey.aspx (accessed 16 September 2015).
2. In fact, the only url provided that led to anything at all about radio audiences in India was Google suggestion #5, which took you to the online version of the second edition of this book, the last chapter of which provided some detailed demographic analysis of radio and television audiences in a large number of the more populated states.
3. Zenithoptimedia (advertising expenditure forecasts, December 2013). Also see similar sets of data at www.mckinsey.com and Advertising Age, http://adage.com/ (accessed 16 September 2015).
4. http://adage.com/article/global-news/10-things-global-ad-market/245572/ (accessed 16 September 2015).
5. http://www.itu.int/en/ITU-D/Statistics (accessed 16 September 2015).
6. http://www.dhsprogram.com/Data/ (accessed 16 September 2015).
7. KPMG, *The* Industry *Stage is Set*, FICCI-KPMG Indian Media and Entertainment Report (New Delhi: FICCI-KPMG, 2014). Available online at https://www.kpmg.com/IN/en/Topics/FICCI-Frames/Documents/FICCI-Frames-2014-The-stage-is-set-Report-2014.pdf (accessed 20 April 2015).
8. Shrinivasan, R., '200 million Indians have no TV, Phone or Radio', *The Times of India,* 14 March 2012. Available online at http://timesofindia.indiatimes.com/india/200-million-Indians-have-no-TV-phone-or-radio/articleshow/12253614.cms (accessed 20 April 2015).
9. Mahajan, A.C. 'The Growth in Internet and Telecom Users in India during Q2 2014 Disappoints', 2014. Available online at http://dazeinfo.com/2014/11/19/growth-internet-telecom-users-india-q2-2014-disappoints/ (accessed 20 April 2015).
10. IndianTelevision.com. 'Only 70 per cent of the Indian pay-TV market will be digitised by 2023: MPA report', 2014. Available online at http://www.indiantelevision.com/cable-tv/msos/only-70-per-cent-of-the-indian-pay-tv-market-will-be-digitised-by-2023-mpa-report-140728 (accessed 20 April 2015).
11. India.gov.in. 'Television—Doordarshan', 2010. Available online at http://www.archive.india.gov.in/knowindia/television.php (accessed 20 April 2015).
12. Srivastava, B. 'Mobile and Internet in India 2014: 349 Unique Mobile Phone Users, 70% Traffic From Mobile', 2014. Available online at http://dazeinfo.com/2014/07/11/mobile-internet-india-2014-349-million-unique-mobile-phone-users-70-traffic-mobile-india-shining-infographic/ (accessed 20 April 2015).
13. Ghosh, M. '204m Smartphone Users in India by 2016', 2014. Available online at http://trak.in/tags/business/2014/12/23/smartphone-users-india-global-growth-chart/ (accessed 20 April 2015).

14. Srivastava, 'Mobile and Internet in India 2014'.
15. Gaurav1019. *Indian Radio Industry.* 2010. Available online at http://www.slideshare.net/Gaurav1019/indian-radio-industry (accessed 20 April 2015).
16. Sesame Workshop India. 'Talking to the FM airwaves with songs, smiles, and health awareness', 2014. Available online at http://www.sesameworkshopindia.org/what-we-do/radio/ (accessed 20 April 2015).
17. BBC. 'India profile—Media', 2015. Available online at http://www.bbc.co.uk/news/world-south-asia-12557390 (accessed 20 April 2015).
18. Internet World Stats, 'ASIA', 2015. Available online at http://www.internetworldstats.com/asia.htm#in (accessed 20 April 2015).
19. Srivastava, 'Mobile and Internet in India 2014'.
20. BBC, 'India profile'.
21. India Online Pages, 'Literacy Rate in India', 2015. Available online at http://www.indiaonlinepages.com/population/literacy-rate-in-india.html (accessed 20 April 2015).
22. Aidem, 'India Media Scenario', 2011. Available online at http://www.aidem.in/downloads/Indian%20Media%20Scenario.pdf (accessed 20 April 2015).
23. ———., 'India Media Scenario'.
24. Internet World Stats, 'ASIA'.
25. Ghosh, '204m Smartphone Users in India by 2016'.
26. Srivastava, 'Mobile and Internet in India 2014'.
27. Ibid.
28. Ibid.
29. India Online Pages, 'Literacy Rate in India'.
30. KPMG, *The Stage is Set.*
31. Shrinivasan, '200 million Indians have no TV, phone or radio'.
32. TAM Media Research, 'TAM Annual Universe Update—2014', 2015. Available online at http://www.tamindia.com/webview.php?web=ref_pdf/Overview_Universe_Update-2014.pdf (accessed 20 April 2015).
33. IndianTelevision.com, 'Only 70 per cent of the Indian pay-TV market will be digitised by 2023'.
34. All information in this table comes from Aidem, 'India Media Scenario'.
35. All information in this table is taken from the following website—Best Media Info. *IRS Q2 2011: Top 10 dailies in Bihar*, 2011. Available online at http://www.bestmediainfo.com/2011/10/irs-q2-2011-top-10-dailies-in-bihar/ (accessed 20 April 2015).

Chapter 10

Data Analysis

10.1 Some History

The rapid advances of computer technology have opened up enormous opportunities for all kinds of research. Data analysis was previously a very complex and time-consuming activity. Completed questionnaires had to be hand counted and checked. The answers had to be coded and data written onto large sheets of paper, not unlike doing accounts by hand, or punched on cards or paper tape. Early computers, from some 60 years ago, made a lot of this work easier. But the whole process of data analysis was still quite time consuming. And there were limits on the analysis one could do. This was because researchers did not usually have direct access to computers themselves. The results from the questionnaires had to be coded onto punched tape or cards, but at that point, computer specialists took over. We can illustrate this by giving the example of how Graham Mytton, one of the co-authors of this book, analysed the results of his first survey. This was of media access and use in Tanzania in 1967–68. He returned to Manchester University from Dar es Salaam University in July 1968. The nearly 1,000 questionnaires were all coded and the data punched onto nearly 2,000 cards, two for each respondent. He then went to the Manchester University Computer Centre to arrange for the cards to be read and analysed. This part he could not do himself. Instead he had to explain carefully and precisely what analyses he wanted—how he wanted the results to be tabulated, what demographic breaks he required, whether any weighting was to be applied and more. The computer staff, then, wrote computer instructions and the data set was run on the famous Atlas computer at some date booked several weeks in advance.[1]

Everyone who used that computer spoke in almost hushed and awe-struck tones about what was then one of the most powerful machines of its kind in the world. Now, 50 years later, computers of a far greater capacity and speed than Manchester University's Atlas which, incidentally occupied quite a large building, can be bought for a few hundred dollars and taken around in a small bag, or even in your pocket.

The personal computer has meant a revolution in market research. All researchers can now do their own analyses. What is more, they can do several repeat analyses of the same data without difficulty. When Mytton took those Tanzanian questionnaires and the accompanying coded cards to the Manchester computer in 1968, he had to know exactly what he wanted. He could have gone back later and run the data again to look at things in a different way. But this was not something that could be done very often. Computer time was expensive and limited. Sometimes one could wait for several weeks until time was again available. Manchester's Atlas computer, now a museum piece, was like the few other large computers in use at that time, in constant demand running for 24 hours every day of every week.[2]

Personal computers speed up and simplify research analysis and report writing. They have also made possible the development of databases for the continuous analysis of market trends as well as many more powerful facilities relevant to all aspects of media research. Formerly, research was reported in long and comprehensive papers and documents. This is still done, but it is not always necessary or desirable. Data can be stored and information provided on request when it is needed. Surveys almost always provide far more information than can be digested in a single report. A comprehensive database can be maintained and kept up to date, end be used to answer questions as they occur.

10.2 Interpretation and Terminology

Most audience research activity is quantitative. Many figures are produced. What do they mean and what do we do with them? If we say that the evening news on television's main national channel had a 20 per cent audience, what does this mean?

The first point to make sure we are quite clear about the coverage of any piece of data. What is the universe? Twenty per cent of what? It could be the population aged 4 and over, 12 and over, 15 and over, depending on the age covered by the research method. Is it 20 per cent of everyone over that age, or 20 per cent of people in TV households? Figures are usually given for whole populations, but one must make this clear. The figure could mean 20 per cent of those watching any TV at that time. Twenty per cent of those watching TV can be a 'very' different thing from 20 per cent of the population over the age of 15.

There are other things we need to know about the meaning of this 20 per cent. Does it mean that 20 per cent watched the entire news programme? Or does it mean that 20 per cent watched any part of the programme? Or is it the average audience for the programme?

As you can see, there are rather a lot of things we need to know about the meaning of any data. It is a good discipline whenever dealing with any market research data to make sure that nothing is taken for granted. Make sure always that the bases to which the data relate are clearly stated. If you are given data by others that do not provide this information, make sure you demand it. Quantitative research data are not really useable unless you know precisely what they mean and on what they are based.

Let us suppose that in the above hypothetical case, the data mean that 20 per cent of the population aged 15 and over watched at least some of the particular news bulletin. Is this information enough? Are there any further things we need to ask? What do we mean by 'watch'? What do we mean by 'at least some'?

If the data have come from a people meter system, 'watch' probably means presence in the room where the television was switched to this particular channel at this time. If the data have come from a self-completion diary, it means that this percentage reported watching this channel at this time. But if someone watched for only one minute a news programme lasting half an hour, did he or she 'watch' the programme? What if he or she watched for 10 minutes? What about 15 minutes? At what stage do we admit the person to membership of the audience to the programme? These are important questions for which answers must be given. Once again, there is no correct answer; the users of research need to say what they want to measure and report.

Try this. One might ask the question 'How many people in Zambia listen to the national broadcaster's main radio service, *Radio Four*?' What is meant by this question? What would it mean if we said that half the adult population listens to *Radio Four*? We might mean that on an average day, half the population listens to at least one programme on *Radio Four*. Or we might mean that on average, each week half the population listens. Or we could mean that of all the radio listening that occurs, half of it is to *Radio Four*. Or we could mean that on average, at any time, about half the radio listening is to *Radio Four*.

All these measures, and there are more, are used and you will come across all of them. But they mean different things. They have different uses. A TV station may reach at least half the population in a week, but only 20 per cent of them on an average day. It may reach less than 5 per cent of the TV audience watching at any time and have an even smaller overall share of all TV viewing. Note the uses of these words 'reach' and 'share'. They are used a lot in audience research, and we will see how they are calculated shortly. Other measures exist and new measures could still be devised for new requirements, especially in underdeveloped regions where special audience research needs may emerge.

Different kinds of people in broadcasting organisations and different kinds of broadcasting organisations require different kinds of information for different purposes. Producers of programmes require different information from those who plan the schedules. Those responsible for raising advertising revenue will have special data requirements. Services funded by advertising or sponsorship need audience measurement data for their advertising sales teams to show potential customers what audiences are reached at different times of the day by different networks. Those who buy and sell advertising time on radio and television are especially interested in Share, Ratings (and Gross Rating Points [GRPs]) and Demographics. Publicly funded public service broadcasting organisations like the BBC are more interested in Reach, Demographics and, to a lesser extent, Share. Programme makers and schedulers are also interested in assessing or measuring appreciation.

10.3 Ratings and Gross Rating Points

Ratings and GRPs are widely used by those who buy and sell TV and radio time for advertising. Most American literature on audience research tends to concentrate on ratings when covering the quantitative aspects of the subject.[3] 'Ratings' are obtained in the same way as 'Reach' (see later), but the word is usually used to describe what happens at a particular time of day, or in the word often used in advertising, 'daypart'. An audience rating is usually given as an average percentage of people in a given population listening or watching a TV or radio station within a given time period. The rating is calculated by dividing the estimated number of people in the audience by the number of people in the population and multiplying the result by one hundred. The process depends, of course, on the assumption that in quantitative research, our sample represents the population as a whole and the sub-samples who listen or watch represent the respective audiences. Let us take the following hypothetical example to illustrate.

We have data for a country that has six main television channels. The audience measurement system uses a representative sample of households and covers individuals in those households aged four and over. The population thus covered is 12 million. The sample used for the research is 2,000 individuals. (The measurement methods used, while very important, do not substantially affect the point we are demonstrating here. These data could come from diary, face-to-face interview or meter methods.)

Let us suppose that we want to provide ratings for a Monday evening at 2100. Looking through the analysed data, we find that out of the 2,000 interviewed, the following numbers were viewing TV at that time, broken down by the different available channels:

Channel 1	305
Channel 2	298
Channel 3	236
Channel 4	132
Channel 5	15
Channel 6	34
Other Channels	20
Total Viewing any TV	1,040
Not Viewing any TV	960
Total	2,000

The sample represents the population. Therefore, each sub-sample of the viewers of each channel represents all those viewing each channel in the population. We calculate the rating by the following formula:

$$\text{Rating} = \frac{\text{People}}{\text{Population}} \times 100$$

So the rating for Channel 1 is calculated as follows:

$$\frac{305}{2,000} \times 100 = 0.1525 \times 100 = 15.25$$

And for Channel 2:

$$\frac{298}{2,000} \times 100 = 0.149 \times 100 = 14.9$$

Continuing with the same formula, we obtain the following ratings for each channel.

	%
Channel 1	15.25
Channel 2	14.9
Channel 3	11.8

(Continued)

(Continued)

	%
Channel 4	6.6
Channel 5	0.75
Channel 6	1.7
Other Channels	1.0
Total Viewing any TV	52.0
Total Not Viewing any TV	48.0
Total	100.0

Note that the total rating—all those viewing any television—is 52. This means that just over half the population in the area of our survey was watching television at 21:00 on the Monday in question.

As we should expect (and it is always wise to check to confirm the accuracy of ones calculations!), the ratings together with the figure for non-viewers add up to 100. A rating is actually a percentage figure and each rating represents the percentage of the population (in this case, everyone aged four and over in the coverage area). Therefore, these rating percentages can be used to calculate estimates of the numbers of people who were watching each channel at the time in question. This is done by the following formula:

Numbers of People = Network Rating × Population ÷ 100

Channels 1, 2 and 3 are in fairly close contention for being the leading channels at 2100 on Monday evenings. Using this formula, we can estimate their audiences.

Channel 1: 15.25 × 12,000,000 ÷ 100 = 1,830,000
Channel 2: 14.9 × 12,000,000 ÷ 100 = 1,788,000
Channel 3: 11.8 × 12,000,000 ÷ 100 = 1,416,000

Advertisers use ratings to work out how much it costs to reach their target audience. They need to be able to work out the 'efficiency' of an advertising placement on radio or TV to determine which selected spot is the most cost-effective. One way to do this is to compute the *Cost per Thousand*—that is, what it costs the advertiser to reach one thousand people. It is calculated as follows:

$$\text{Cost per thousand} = \frac{\text{Cost of advertisement}}{\text{Audience size (in thousands)}}$$

A term often used in the buying and selling of advertising spots is 'GRP'. An advertiser or an advertising agency or 'media buyer' typically does not buy single advertising spots, but many at a time for a product campaign. An advertiser may want, for example, to buy 15 placements for an advertisement on a radio channel. He/she will want to know the gross audience they are likely to reach. Ratings data for past weeks will be used to calculate what can be expected.[4]

Daypart	Number of Advertisements	Rating %	GRP %
Weekday 0700–0800	5	8.6	43
Weekday 0800–0900	5	6.7	33.5
Weekday 0900–1000	2	4.1	8.2
Saturday 1200–1300	1	2.1	2.1
Sunday 1200–1300	2	3	6
Totals	15	(Average) 6.19	92.8

These give a total GRP for the 15 advertisement campaigns of 92.8 (the total in the right-hand column). This does not mean, of course, that nearly 93 per cent of the population will hear at least one commercial. Many will hear the advertisements more than once and many others not at all. But it is a measure by which advertisers can get some idea of the overall exposure achieved by a campaign. There are other ways of making estimates of how many people are likely to actually hear at least one advertising spot, but those are beyond the scope of this manual.

10.4 Amount of Listening or Viewing, and Share

We can also use the figures from the imaginary TV market shown previously to compute the 'share' of viewing at this particular time. For convenience, I repeat the ratings chart here.

	%
Channel 1	15.25
Channel 2	14.9
Channel 3	11.8

(Continued)

(Continued)

	%
Channel 4	6.6
Channel 5	0.75
Channel 6	1.7
Other Channels	1.0
Total viewing any TV	52.0
Total not viewing any TV	48.0
Total	100.0

First, we have to exclude the non-viewers and recalculate the percentages. Note that share is defined as a measure of viewing or listening. The measure is derived from the commercial world where, for example, we might speak of the market share of soft drinks and mean by this the proportions of sales of soft drinks by each brand name or manufacturer. What we attempt to do here is to compute what share of all viewing is accounted for by each channel, just as we might use sales figures to work out what share of the soft drinks market was accounted for by Fanta, Pepsi Cola and so on.

With television and radio, this is how we calculate share for viewing at a particular time:

$$Share = \frac{Channel\,Rating}{Total\,Rating} \times 100$$

So Channel 1's share would be:

$$\frac{15.25}{52} \times 100 = 29.3$$

You can work this out in another way and get the same result.

$$Share = \frac{Number\,Viewing\,Channel}{Number\,Viewing\,Any\,TV} \times 100$$

In our sample representing the entire population, 305 people were watching Channel 1 and 1,040 people (2,000 less 960) were watching TV.

$$\frac{305}{1,040} \times 100 = 29.3$$

Doing the same calculation for all the channels, we get the following results[5]

	%
Channel 1	29.3
Channel 2	28.7
Channel 3	22.7
Channel 4	12.7
Channel 5	1.4
Channel 6	3.3
Other Channels	1.9
Total	100.0

In the example I have used here, share has been worked out by using data from a particular time of day or 'daypart' (a word often used in the advertising industry when talking about radio or television use). In this hypothetical case, the time used was 2100 or 9.00 PM. But share is more often used as a measure of channel use over a longer period of time, usually a day or a week.

To illustrate this and to show how share can be calculated, I will take the figures produced for television in the United Kingdom for the week ending 9 March 2014. BARB, the Broadcasters' Audience Research Board, produces these figures every week. BARB is a joint company owned by the main TV channels and advertisers. The data are supplied by two research companies, RSMB, Ipsos MORI, and Kantar Media, and are obtained from a representative sample of households where all the televisions are fitted with the TV meters described earlier.

UK Weekly Viewing Hours (including time shift[6]) in March 2014[7,8]

	Weekly Viewing (Hours: minutes per person)
BBC1	06:01
BBC2	01:25
Other BBC	00:51
Total BBC	08:17
ITV1	03:38
Other ITV	02:12
Total ITV	05:50
Channel 4	01:13
Other Channel 4	01:32
Total Channel 4	02:45
Channel 5	00:59
Other Channel 5	00:13
Total Channel 5	01:12

(Continued)

(Continued)

	Weekly Viewing (Hours: minutes per person)
All Sky	01:55
All Other TV	05:54
Total TV Hours/minutes	25:55

It is important to note what these figures mean. The data are obtained from the BARB people meter panel of 5,100 homes. The figures are obtained by adding up all the viewing by individuals in these homes to each channel and dividing the total by the number of individuals involved. They tell us that the average person in the UK living in a home with TV watched for 25 hours and 55 minutes in March 2014.[9] Some watch a lot less and, by the same token, some a lot more. Some people devote most of their viewing to one or two channels. Others watch several. This table tells us, and it is quite a lot, that this is what British TV viewers as a whole do.

We can use these average weekly viewing times to work out share. This is done by calculating each channel's viewing hours and minutes as percentages of all viewing. One way of doing this on your computer is to convert each figure into minutes—remember that time is not decimalised.[10]

The total amount of viewing, 25 hours and 55 minutes becomes for our calculations 1,555 minutes. Let us take BBC1 and calculate its share. Six hours and 1 minute is 361 minutes.

$$\frac{361}{1,555} \times 100 = 23.2$$

BBC1' share of viewing is 23.2. This means that of all viewing in that week, BBC1 accounted for 23.2 per cent. The following table gives the results for all the channels or groups of them.

UK Share of TV Viewing by Channel (including time shift) in March 2014

	Share of Total Viewing %
BBC1	23.2
BBC2	5.5
Other BBC	3.3
Total BBC	32.0
ITV1	14.1
Other ITV	8.5
Total ITV	22.6

(Continued)

(Continued)

	Share of Total Viewing %
Channel 4	4.7
Other Channel 4	5.9
Total Channel 4	10.6
Channel 5	3.8
Other Channel 5	0.8
Total Channel 5	4.6
All Sky	7.4
All Other TV	22.8
Total TV	100

Reach

This measure is used to refer to the percentage of the population (aged over 4 or 12 or 15 or whatever lower age the measurement system uses) who listened to or watched at least some of a programme, or a network, or service or group of services during a day or week. Thus, we have four common uses:

1. Programme Reach: The percentage for those who watched or listened to at least some of the programme. (A minimum period needs to be defined. It could be a minute, or it could be at least five minutes. Practice varies.)
2. Network/Station Reach: The percentage of the population who watched or listened to at least some of a station or network's output over a given period.
3. Daily Reach: The percentage of the population who watches or listens at least once to the network in question in a day. Sometimes a group of services or networks may be taken together. We might produce a figure giving reach for all or any BBC radio or TV service.
   Note: With meter-measured TV data, 'reach' is commonly defined as viewing for at least one consecutive minute.
4. Weekly Reach: The percentage who watches or listens at least once in a week.

Note that we can use reach to also refer to any use of TV or radio. We might want to know what the weekly reach of any radio is in any selected country—that is what percentage of the adult population listens to at least some radio, no matter what network or station, within an average week.

Reach is a measure used in a variety of ways. Some public service broadcasters view it as particularly valuable and important. They need to know if their services are reaching the majority of the population who pay for them. They will usually also want to see if their reach is satisfactory among all segments of the population. Publicly funded broadcasters need to be able to show that they are serving all sections of the society. It may be that no single programme on a public service network enjoys the largest audience figures. But if a network or perhaps a group of networks run by the same company are appealing to many different tastes and interests, they can, across a day or, even more so, a week, have an impressive reach. Thus, if we take BBC *Radio Four* in the United Kingdom, we find that at no time does its audience rating exceed 5 per cent. That is to say that at no time is more than 5 per cent of the population listening. However, it has a weekly reach of 17 per cent of the population. In fact no BBC Radio network normally reaches an audience higher than about 5 per cent at any time, but the weekly reach of each network as well as the commercial competition is shown in the following table.

Weekly Reach of Radio in the UK in Millions and Percentage of Population Aged 15+ in the 4th Quarter of 2013.[11]

15+ Population (000s)	53,205
Reach 000s	
All Radio	48,375
All BBC	36,219
All Commercial	34,914
Other Listening	3,472
Hours 000s	
All Radio	1,029,690
All BBC	568,433
All Commercial	433,520
Other Listening	27,737
Reach%	
All Radio	90.9%
All BBC	68.1%
All Commercial	65.6%
Other	6.5%
Share of Listening	
BBC	55.2%
Commercial Radio	42.1%
Other	2.7%
Hours per Head	19h 16m
Hours per Listener	21h 18m

We can look at the same data set and see the results for some of the BBC stations. We could do the same for the commercial and other stations, but there is not enough room here. But readers can do these themselves on the RAJAR website where a lot of data, both current and historic are provided to anyone visiting the website.

It is important for a broadcasting institution, funded by the public, to show that it serves all sections of the public. The following table shows the demographic profile of BBC TV channels and radio networks in 2014.

	Reach ('000s)	Reach %	Average Hours per Head	Average Hours per Listener	Total Hours ('000s)	Listening Share in TSA
All Radio	48,375	91	19.4	21.3	1,029,690	100
All BBC Radio	36,219	68	10.7	15.7	568,433	55.2
All BBC Network Radio	33,126	62	9.1	14.5	481,969	46.8
BBC Local Radio	9,321	18	1.6	9.3	86,464	8.4
All Commercial Radio	34,914	66	8.1	12.4	433,520	42.1
All National Commercial	17,635	33	2.6	7.8	136,744	13.3
All Local Commercial (National TSA)	27,594	52	5.6	10.8	296,776	28.8
Other Radio	3,472	7	0.5	8	27,737	2.7
BBC Radio 1	10,969	21	1.3	6.4	70,628	6.9
BBC Radio 2	15,513	29	3.4	11.7	181,022	17.6
BBC Radio 3	1,992	4	0.2	5.6	11,127	1.1
BBC Radio 4	11,205	21	2.4	11.5	128,922	12.5
BBC Radio 4 (including 4 Extra)	11,494	22	2.6	12.1	138,704	13.5
BBC Radio 4 Extra	1,646	3	0.2	5.9	9,782	1
BBC Radio Five Live	6,285	12	0.8	6.9	43,388	4.2
BBC Radio Five Live (including Sports Extra)	6,529	12	0.9	7	46,002	4.5
Five Live Sports Extra	889	2	*	2.9	2,614	0.3
BBC 6 Music	1,962	4	0.3	9	17,688	1.7
1Xtra from the BBC	1,094	2	0.1	4.6	5,069	0.5
BBC Asian Network UK	668	1	0.1	6.8	4,515	0.4
BBC World Service	1,413	3	0.1	5.1	7,215	0.7

Note: * less than 0.5%.

There are now several Web-based services that will help you do your analysis. There are several of these, but one that we think is attractive, easy to use and inexpensive is Statwing. www.statwing.com—at the simplest level is free. There are two higher levels for which you pay a monthly fee according to the level of analysis required.

There are also many open source statistical packages available on the Web. For more about these, look at Wikipedia's list en.wikipedia.org/wiki/List_of_statistical_packages

Notes and References

1. Readers can see more about this historic computer by searching online with the phrase 'Manchester's Atlas Computer', which is now in a museum.
2. For more on this topic, see many references on the Web. For example, http://www.bbc.com/news/technology-20585395 and http://www.manchester.ac.uk/aboutus/news/archive/list/item/?id=9165&year=2012&month=12. It was installed in 1962 and said to be both the fastest and largest computer in the world at that time. It was decommissioned in 1972.
3. Two books are recommended for students wishing to understand media research from a wholly commercial and US perspective. Both have been produced for students of the subject. They are Hugh Malcolm Beville Jr., *Audience Ratings: Radio, Television, Cable*, Revised Student Edition (Hillsdale, New Jersey, 1988); and Roger D. Wimmer and Joseph R. Dominick, *Mass Media Research: An Introduction*, Third Edition (Belmont, California: Wadsworth, 1991).
4. N.B. Radio audience data are often provided in three-day-type categories—weekdays and Saturdays and Sundays. In this hypothetical example, we have ratings for different hour periods or dayparts.
5. Note that here and elsewhere I have used only one decimal point. In my view to use more implies a level of accuracy, which is rarely, if ever, justified.
6. Timeshift refers to programmes that are video-recorded at the time of transmission and viewed later. People meters are able to measure this and will report if the programme(s) recorded are actually viewed.
7. BARB, *This Week's Viewing Summary*, Week Ending 26th April 1998. This chart and the following one include what is referred to as 'timeshift' viewing. People who use their video-recorder to record a programme in order to watch later are included in the audience figures for that programme, provided that the programme is actually viewed within a certain period of time. The TV meters are designed to measure and record this behaviour.
8. http://www.barb.co.uk/viewing/weekly-total-viewing-summary, March 3rd to 9th inclusive. The BARB panel consists of 5,100 homes in which all viewing devices are metered. More than 30,000 devices are involved. The resulting data can be reliably projected to the estimated 26 million households in the UK which have at least one TV receiving piece of equipment
9. Total TV viewing hours, despite the huge changes in the number of channels and the means whereby one can watch over the last 16 years, have changed very little. In the previous version of this book, the average viewing time per week was 25 hours and 11 minutes in April 1998, which means an increase of less than 3 per cent over this period.
10. If you are using Excel, you can avoid converting and reconverting hours and minutes by changing the format from decimal numbers to time. Go to Format/Cells/Custom and select hh:mm.
11. RAJAR dataset accessed March 2014. Much data are also available to anyone at www.rajar.co.uk

Chapter 11

Adapting Media Research to Different Cultures

This final chapter is about how there can be difficulties and mismatches between the research we do and the complex realities of human societies and the steps we can take to stand back from what we are doing to examine critically how we need to amend our work to take account of human differences. In an increasingly globalised world, we have to remember that differences remain; human life is wonderfully diverse and multifaceted. This is not a negative thing. It is something to treasure and enjoy.

Media and market research have developed in industrialised countries and many of the disciplines and procedures, as well as many of the assumptions on which it is based are derived from these countries. You may have noticed that there is a strong emphasis on the 'individual' in a lot of the research methods and processes we have described. This derives from the importance industrialised, liberal democratic systems place on individual choice and decisions. Some cultures, especially in Africa and Asia, place significantly more emphasis on group responsibilities and decisions. It is, therefore, important to be ready to adapt research methods accordingly. But how can this be done? To adapt appropriately requires a thorough understanding of how different societies operate. But thorough studies by anthropologists may not exist already and can take a long time to complete.

A leading advocate of the cultural adaptation of market research methodology in less developed, non-industrial societies is the late Scarlett Epstein, who has offered a very useful, practical and relatively simple approach. She provides a valuable checklist of what she calls 'Key Cultural Variables'. We reproduce this in the following chart together with, first, her explanation of it.

[The Chart] sets out some of the most important cultural variables together with the extremes of possible options. It must be stressed here that this is not meant to represent an exhaustive list nor is it an attempt to predetermine cultural responses. All the list tries to do is to provide a set of key cultural variables that need to be considered when tackling the cultural adaptation in the limited time allocated to [market research]. With experience this list will of course be refined.[1]

Cultural Variable	Extremes of Possible Options	
Unit of decision-making	individual	group
Ethos of social organisation	egalitarian	hierarchical
Patron-client relationships	situational	continuous
Allocation of status	achieved	ascribed
Prestige criteria	behaviour	expenditure
Kinship structure	patrilineal	matrilineal
Family organisation	nuclear	extended
Marriage arrangements	monogamy	polygamy
Residence pattern	patrilocal	uxorilocal
Gender relationship	equality	subordination
Land tenure	individual	group
Factionalism	interest-based	kin-based
Colonial experience	enlightened administration	exploitative administration

Not all of these are of major importance in relation to the way media are used. However, you cannot make any assumption about this matter (the importance or relevance of such variables for the way that people use media) without doing some investigation and enquiry. The checklist above is not comprehensive; there may be other aspects of culture that have some impact and importance. We reproduce the list in order to remind us that societies can vary greatly. New media have gone global, just as radio and television did earlier during the 20th century. The difference with new media is that they are more interactive. Social media, by their very designation and mode of operation, remind us that they reproduce to some degree, or perhaps more accurately pretend to do so, social relationships of the face-to-face and traditional variety. But they are not the same. New kinds of relationships are created that are different. These are early days in the history of these new media. Readers of this book will be among those who will be researching and seeking to understand these new relationships. It is an important part of what you will be doing to seek to relate new communications activities to the existing social relationships and practices and see how the old and the new inter-relate.

There is a more general point to be made about the way that media and market research is done, and this is especially true for quantitative research. The way that research is done is itself a cultural indicator and artefact. Some scholars have made an interesting study of what they call the social history of research and have especially focussed on the way that it has developed in the Western liberal democracies. The format and approach of this research, especially in its commercial applications, and also beyond that, tends to consider the individual consumer as a separate decision-making unit. Equal weighting is given to each individual response. But we know that even in the most egalitarian, democratic societies, things are not in reality entirely like this. People often defer to others, within families as well as other social groups. In some societies, decisions are made jointly after discussion.

This is also true in the way media are used. Some media are more personal than others. Radio or television sets can be used at the same time by many people. A mobile phone or a personal computer are more obviously personal media to be used by one person at a time. Even so, for all media, the way they are used can be profoundly influenced, if not actually controlled, by relationships between members of a household. The story was told elsewhere in this book about the radio set in a Moroccan home that was locked away and, therefore, accessible only to its owner. BBC research among Afghan refugees in 1986 found that some husbands prevented their wives from listening independently to the radio because, as one man put it, 'I do not wish my wife to listen to a strange man without me being present'.

Traditional patron–client relationships, criteria for status and prestige, and kinship structures can also have a considerable influence on the ways in which media are used within a household and within a social situation. For example, patron–client relationships and ascribed social status in some societies cut across linguistic and ethnic divides. You may also find that the connected power relationships in that society are reflected in what is and is not available through the media. The subordinate group may be left out of the media or served only inadequately.

Family organisation can be another important variable in understanding the way the media are used. In many societies, the care of the aged is a family responsibility. The elderly do not, as a consequence, live alone. In other societies, older people tend to be independent and live alone. Media and access and use will be much affected by these differences. Extended families have an even greater impact. When in 1970 Mytton was carrying out a survey of Lusaka, Zambia, the number of poor and ill-educated people who were claiming to watch television at least once per week surprised him. On further examination—follow-up interviews with some of the people concerned—he discovered how some of this was happening. Television sets in those days were almost entirely confined to the homes of expatriates and wealthy Zambians. Wealth in Zambia was and is strongly correlated with education. But educational achievement was not closely related to caste, family or ethnicity. People with a university degree or other higher education with well-paid jobs always had relatives, sometimes quite close ones, with no education. The extended family would almost always include some who were very poor. Under the traditions of most Zambian ethnic groups, members of an extended family felt entitled to visit and watch television at the home of a better-off relative, and many did so.

The colonial experience of different countries had great influence on the development of modern media, an influence that continues today. Countries with French and Portuguese connections tended to give less importance to indigenous languages in their media. This is because under the French and Portuguese, indigenous languages tended to be neglected on the media in favour of French or Portuguese. The British system of indirect rule tended (not in all cases) to give greater emphasis to indigenous languages.

Research should always have the purpose of enlightenment—to throw light on a subject—not to obscure things. And yet, if we use research tools in a mechanistic way and do not make the necessary adaptations that are called for in different circumstances, we will not be doing our work professionally. The good audience researcher is always alert to the cultural and social realities in the societies he studies and is always ready to adapt his research methods and approaches accordingly. The exciting thing about audience research is that you are always breaking new ground. Nothing is the same everywhere. All social situations are different. People are wonderfully different and never stop being so. Your task is to use your skills to understand and, through research, help others also to do so.

Reference

1. T. Scarlett Epstein, *A Manual for Culturally Adapted Research (CMR) in the Development Process* (Bexhill-on-Sea: RWAL Publications, 1988), p. 27. Also see T. Scarlett Epstein, Janet Gruber and Graham Mytton, *A Training Manual for Development Market Research (DMR) Investigators* (London: BBC World Service, 1991).

APPENDIX

Random Numbers

You often need random numbers in quantitative research to make selections free from bias. It may be to make a sample, or choose a place to start a sample or make a choice of clusters for sampling when you have stratified the sample for a large country and need to select areas for research. Many computer programmes can generate random numbers. They are also printed in some books on statistics. And you can easily obtain them online.[1] But here we provide a handy loss of random numbers generated by one of these programmes. You can use them for any project where you need to choose something randomly. You can start at any number of course.

List of 400 Random Numbers between 1 and 1,000							
885	277	506	74	975	411	335	358
157	615	524	699	464	577	597	59
453	88	272	396	902	895	696	180
613	813	721	576	824	16	66	610
15	403	148	950	470	224	187	718
353	159	384	371	411	786	622	104
675	196	818	554	885	525	851	613
158	942	464	233	589	6	52	724
951	314	338	784	333	878	496	477
583	236	627	341	528	992	91	305
369	817	8	803	230	859	618	415
745	309	710	37	679	828	684	341
555	128	903	909	126	311	686	458
193	676	741	332	566	437	415	169
775	345	164	304	900	347	936	426
32	280	355	524	136	309	933	367
368	786	783	392	681	538	883	896
375	781	696	998	967	420	215	195
68	348	515	709	557	569	461	639
781	898	415	464	995	326	992	499

(Continued)

(Continued)

List of 400 Random Numbers between 1 and 1,000							
168	264	199	852	959	966	338	248
734	106	472	879	385	671	759	374
89	869	422	43	242	193	166	589
919	283	377	911	827	17	320	612
189	978	765	862	834	910	803	351
83	608	939	858	700	977	30	932
496	737	283	241	448	72	205	839
220	586	635	190	646	556	131	796
118	877	151	961	528	52	687	466
135	24	106	817	915	86	299	956
24	258	652	662	679	401	522	308
11	307	134	473	717	61	731	86
195	807	521	232	964	387	25	780
244	929	403	357	832	126	486	893
862	136	525	683	196	540	321	644
773	710	863	410	509	681	155	907
559	851	359	320	117	124	173	451
334	515	822	510	711	92	250	320
669	272	964	750	793	814	37	465
426	56	482	605	684	320	35	997
850	414	444	661	66	131	645	247
919	375	884	634	833	72	896	929
745	1	979	858	351	191	338	228
950	643	214	416	541	879	452	44
548	783	937	435	534	992	115	44
894	422	171	71	330	737	238	533
604	993	388	785	93	478	141	388
408	134	704	927	570	646	571	601
934	124	219	550	937	526	311	314
300	846	300	842	529	668	998	256

Reliability of Estimates

The following two tables derived from well-established statistical formulae should be used to help you and those who use your quantitative results to determine the strength and reliability of the data. The first table helps you to estimate the 'sampling error' for any single result—that is the likely true figure within a probable range of numbers.

Confidence Levels for a Single Percentage Result for Different Sample Sizes at the 95% Level.[2]

%	50	100	150	200	250	300	400	500	700	1,000	1,500	2,000	3,000	5,000	%	
50	14.1	10.0	8.2	7.1	6.3	5.8	5.0	4.5	3.8	3.2	2.6	2.2	1.8	1.4	50	
60	13.9	9.8	8.0	7.0	6.2	5.7	4.9	4.4	3.7	3.1	2.5	2.2	1.8	1.4	40	
70	13.0	9.2	7.5	6.5	5.8	5.3	4.6	4.1	3.5	2.9	2.4	2.0	1.7	1.3	30	R
80	11.3	8.0	6.5	5.7	5.1	4.6	4.0	3.6	3.0	2.5	2.1	1.8	1.5	1.1	20	E
85	10.1	7.1	5.8	5.0	4.5	4.1	3.6	3.2	2.7	2.3	1.8	1.6	1.3	1.0	15	S
90	8.5	6.0	4.9	4.2	3.8	3.5	3.0	2.7	2.3	1.9	1.5	1.3	1.1	0.9	10	U
92	7.7	5.4	4.4	3.8	3.4	3.1	2.7	2.4	2.0	1.7	1.4	1.2	1.0	0.8	8	L
94	6.7	4.7	3.9	3.4	3.0	2.7	2.4	2.1	1.8	1.5	1.2	1.1	1.0	0.7	6	T
95	6.2	4.4	3.6	3.1	2.8	2.5	2.2	1.9	1.6	1.4	1.1	1.0	0.9	0.6	5	
96	5.6	3.9	3.2	2.8	2.5	2.3	2.0	1.8	1.5	1.2	1.0	0.9	0.7	0.6	4	
97	4.8	3.4	2.8	2.4	2.2	2.0	1.7	1.5	1.3	1.1	0.9	0.8	0.6	0.5	3	
98	4.0	2.8	2.3	2.0	1.8	1.6	1.4	1.3	1.1	0.9	0.7	0.6	0.5	0.4	2	

The R E S U L T labels appear down the left margin, and R E S U L T down the right margin.

For any percentage result you wish to check, you obtain the confidence interval or margin of likely error with a 95 per cent degree of confidence by reading off the figure against the column with the appropriate sample size.

Exercise

Your survey of 1,000 randomly selected adults produces a figure of 10 per cent for household ownership of at least one colour television set. What is the confidence interval and what does this mean?

Comment

We can be 95 per cent confident that the true picture lies somewhere between 8.1 per cent and 11.9 per cent because the confidence level for 10 per cent (or 90 per cent) with a sample of 1,000 is 1.9.

But remember that in all cases, the sample size you should use when employing this table will not be the entire sample. Let us suppose that you are dealing with a sub-sample. Of those with a colour television, 40 per cent have the capacity to receive the new digital transmissions. What is the probable range of the true figure now? The sub-sample size is 100—those with at least one colour TV—10 per cent of 1,000. The chart shows you that the probable margin of error is much larger, at 9.8 per cent so that we can say that the 'true' figure for colour set owners with digital capability lies somewhere between 30.2 (40–9.8) and 49.8 (40+9.8).

When we want to compare two results taken from different samples of the same or different sizes, we can do two things. You could use the above table and use it for each result. The test is simple. Is the margin of error you obtain with each greater or less than half the difference between the two results? If it is greater, then we have to say that the difference between the two results may not represent any real change. If, however, the two figures we get from the table are less than half the difference between the results, then we can be 95 per cent sure that the difference represents a real one.

Let us try this out with the real example used in the text. The radio station's weekly reach had fallen from 43 per cent to 37 per cent. Both samples were 2,000. We have not produced a full set of possible percentage results on this table, not even of whole numbers because there is no space for this kind of detail. However, this does not matter very much. We choose the nearest percentage—40 per cent. The plus or minus margin of error for this result with this sample size is 2.2. This is less than half the difference between the two results (half of 6 is 3), so we can be 95 per cent confident that this radio station's weekly reach really has fallen. If the sample size were only 1,000, the margin would be 3.1 per cent—greater than half the difference, although only just!

If the sample sizes are different, proceed in the same way, but remember to use the different columns for the different sample sizes. If with our radio station example, the first sample had been 1,000 and the second 2,000, we would obtain two margins of error—3.1 and 2.2, respectively. The average of these two is 2.65 less than half the difference between the results, so we would be able to say that the change in audience figure is significant.

Another way to discover whether any difference between two results is significant is to use the χ^2 or chi squared test. There are several uses of this formula, but one of the most common is in the analysis of survey data. The chi-squared test is used to determine whether one result differs from another more than is likely to be the result of chance.

There is not the space here to explain the chWe squared formula, but below is a much-simplified table derived from it. It is not possible in limited space to give more than a few sample combinations. Choose the ones nearest that apply.[3]

Results:	10 or 90	20 or 80	30 or 70	40 or 60	50
Sample Sizes:					
4,000 and 4,000	1.3	1.8	2.0	2.1	2.2
2,000 and 2,000	1.9	2.5	2.8	3.0	3.1
2,000 and 1,000	2	3	3	4	4
2,000 and 500	3	4	4	5	5
1,500 and 500	3	4	5	5	5
1,000 and 1,000	3	4	4	4	4
1,000 and 500	3	4	5	5	5
1,000 and 100	6	8	9	10	10
750 and 750	3	4	5	5	5
750 and 250	4	6	7	7	7
500 and 500	4	5	6	6	6
500 and 250	5	6	7	7	8
500 and 100	6	9	10	11	11
250 and 250	5	7	8	9	9
250 and 100	7	9	11	11	12
100 and 100	8	11	13	14	14

The formulae used to create these tables and other formulae like them for calculating confidence levels, margins of error and significance are to be found in any good book on statistics. There are some suggested titles in the bibliography.

Examples of Audience Research in Action

In this section, we have used examples from audience research practice around the world, first to give some examples of questionnaires that have been used and then to give some examples of the presentation of results. The section focuses on quantitative research.

Examples of a Face to Face Questionnaire and a Radio Diary

On the following pages are two examples from questionnaires used in audience measurement. Some notes about them will help.

Media Survey Questionnaire in Zambia

This was used in an 'ad hoc' survey conducted face to face with a sample of adults throughout Zambia in 1995. This was produced a long time ago, but it was well designed and is still a good example. It was in the previous editions and is reproduced again here. We have reproduced the first five pages. Note the Kish Grid method of choosing the respondent at each household (S4). Also note the clear interviewer instructions which say where to go next when there is a Yes/No question or one with alternatives which require different questions to follow (Qs. 5, 8, 11 and 14). Note that with Q. 15, three questions are asked about yesterday radio listening—two linked questions about times of listening, and the station(s) listened to. Note also that in this survey, the intervals are of 30 minutes.

Radio Listening Diary from the United Kingdom

This double page from the self-completion diary is the example instruction page in the front of every diary used by the RAJAR panel members. The example is for Monday. Instructions are given in the panels printed over the diary grid. Note, especially, how the diarist is asked to record all listening with an X at the start of each period and an X at the end, with a line between the two. The 15-minute intervals are printed down the left-hand column starting at 0400. (The convention is to 'begin' the day at 0400 rather than at midnight in most but not all daces. Note that in the Zambia questionnaire the day 'begins' at 0500.)

In the days when they could be fitted in, all radio stations available in the locality of each diary would be listed across the top of the page. Now that there may be as many as 50 or more locally transmitted and of course very many more online, the practice is now to provide the panellists with a set of radio station stickers to choose and stick in the boxes across the flap at the top. These would be the result of the respondent, saying which radio stations he/she ever normally listened to. The flap is at the front of the diary booklet and the panellist chooses his/her own repertoire of listened-to stations and records each episode across the entire 24-hour period. The flap is used each day at the top of the relevant double page. Note that the diary keeper is also asked (at the right of the flap) to say where he/she listened and the 'platform' used. Note that there is not enough room for the entire 24 hours on this diary page. Each day requires two double pages like this. Look at the time periods of 15 minutes each down the left-hand side of the double page.[4]

Media Questionnaire in Zambia

Selection Procedure

Speak to any Responsible Member of the Household.

I am working for a group of radio and television companies. We are conducting a survey of radio, TV, etc. and would like to ask you a few questions (or an alternative, introduction).

S1   May I know the name of the head of this household? Please tell me the full address of this house.

Name ....

Address ....

Telephone Number...

S2   How many are there in your household? Please include children and lodgers and anyone who shares your kitchen, but exclude guests and servants who have their own homes.

S3   Among these, how many children are there below 15 years of age?

.... /........................ /.

S4   Please tell me the names and ages of all males/females who are 15 years and over.

Enter the names and ages of people in the household aged 15 years and over, starting with the oldest and working down to the youngest.

Name	Age	1	2	3	4	5	6	7	8	9	0
1		1	1	1	1	1	1	1	1	1	1
2		2	1	2	1	2	1	2	1	2	1
3		3	1	2	3	1	2	3	1	2	3
4		2	3	4	1	2	3	4	1	2	3
5		1	2	3	4	5	1	2	3	4	5
6		4	5	6	1	2	3	4	5	6	1
7		7	1	2	3	4	5	6	7	1	2
8		5	6	7	8	1	2	3	4	5	6
9		4	1	2	3	4	5	6	7	8	9
10		1	2	3	4	5	6	7	8	9	10

Look along the row of the last person in the list. Where this meets the column of the last digit of the questionnaire number is the number of the person in the list to be interviewed.

The rest of the questionnaire is to be administered to the selected member.

If selected member is not available, two more attempts are to be made at times when he/she is likely to be at home.

If you are not able to interview the selected member, note the reason below and substitute with a new household.

Respondent's name (Original/substitute)...............................
Address of substitute..
....

Reason for substitution:
Could not contact ....
Away from home ....
Refused ....
Other ....

ASK ALL RESPONDENTS

Q1   What is your main source of entertainment?

Do not read out list- multiple answers possible—Circle all codes which apply if respondent says he/she enjoys listening to radio, ask if that is Zambian or Foreign Radio and code accordingly.

Visit friends/relatives' houses	1
Go to the local pub/bottle store	2
Watch television	3
Watch video	4
Listen to ZNBC radio	5
Listen to foreign radio stations	6
Go to the cinema	7
Visit night clubs/discos	8
Read books/newspapers	9
Play sports	A
Listen to records or cassettes	B
Other (Write In)	C

Q2   I am going to read to you a list of topics. For each one, please tell me if you are interested in it or not.

Circle code for each one interested in, read out list. Rotate start of list for each interview and mark where you begin. Multiple Answers possible.

Football commentaries	1
Other sports	2

Medicine/Health	3
Political events in Africa	4
Political events in Zambia	5
Economic issues in Zambia	6
Relationships between men and women (e.g., problems in marriage, at work, etc.)	7
Relationships between generations (e.g., problems between youth and elders)	8
Scientific/technological advancement	9
Agriculture	A
AIDS	B

Q3   I am now going to read to you a list of different types of music. For each one, please tell me if you enjoy listening to it or not.
Circle code for each one enjoyed. Read out list rotate start of list for each interview and mark where you begin. Multiple answers possible.

Zambian music	1
Reggae	2
Calypso	3
Disco	4
Pop	5
Rhumba	6
Rock	7
Classical	8
Soul	9
Country	A
Gospel	B
Jazz	C
Traditional music	D
Other music (specify)	E

Q4   Have you ever heard of any of the following magazines (It does not matter whether you have read them or not)?
Circle appropriate code. Read out list.

Magazine	Aware of Magazine?	
	Yes	No
Newsweek	1	2
Jeune Afrique	1	2
Time	1	2
Focus on Africa	1	2
Economist	1	2

Q5   Have **you read** any newspapers or magazines in the last 12 months?

Yes	1	*Continue to Q6*
No	2	*Go to Q11*

Q6   Which, if any, of the following newspapers or magazines have you read in the last 12 months *READ LIST*

Q7   When did you last read .... (Mention each newspaper or magazine read in the last 12 months) fit answer to codes in grid below

Names of Newspapers/magazines	Q6 Read in Last 12 Months		Q7 Last Read			
	Yes	No	Yesterday	Past Week	Past Four Weeks	Past Year
Times of Zambia	1	2	1	2	3	4
Zambia Daily Mail	1	2	1	2	3	4
Financial Mail	1	2	1	2	3	4
The Post	1	2	1	2	3	4
The Chronicle	1	2	1	2	3	4
The Sun	1	2	1	2	3	4
Focus on Africa	1	2	1	2	3	4
The National Mirror	1	2	1	2	3	4
Beauty/Fashion magazines	1	2	1	2	3	4
Other (please specify)	1	2	1	2	3	4
Other (please specify)	1	2	1	2	3	4
Other (please specify)	1	2	1	2	3	4
Other (please specify)	1	2	1	2	3	4

Q8   How do you get to read newspapers? Do you buy your own, borrow from friends or available at work?
Multiple Answers Possible Circle all Codes which Apply

I buy my own	-~	1 *Ask Q9*
I borrow from friends		2 *Go to Q10 if code '1' not circled as well*
I read newspapers available at work		3 *Go to Q10 if code '1' not circled as well*

Q9   How many other people read your newspapers after you have finished?

No-one else	1
One or two others	2

Three or four others	3
Five or more others	4

Q10   Which sections of the newspaper do you pay particular attention to?
Multiple Answers Possible, Circle all Codes which Apply

Front page	1
Sports	2
Business section	3
Features	4
Classifieds	5

Q11   Now I will ask you some questions about radio listening. Have
you listened to the radio in the last 12 months? It does not matter
whether you listened to it at home or somewhere else.

Yes	1	*Continue with Q12*
No	2	*~Go to Q20[5]*

Q12   Where do you usually listen to the radio?
Multiple answers possible. Circle all codes which apply.

At home	1
At friends, relative's house	2
At work (office, field etc.)	3
At school/college	4
In a bar/restaurant	5
In a car	6
On a bus	7
Other (write in)	8

Q13   How often do you listen to the radio? Would you say...........? *Read
list and fit answer to codes below*

Almost everyday (6 or 7 days a week	1
Most days	2
At least once a week	3
At least once every 4 weeks	4
Less often than that	5

Q14   Apart from today, when did you last listen to the radio?
Fit Answer to Codes Below

Yesterday	1	Ask Q15
Within the last 7 day	2	Go to Q16
Within the last 4 weeks	3	Go to Q16
Within the last 12 months	4	Go to Q16[6]

Q15 Please think about the times that you listened to radio yesterday. At what time did you first begin listening to the radio yesterday and at what time did you stop listening?

Once the respondent has given the first time of listening, ask:

When did you next listen to the radio yesterday? And when did you stop listening?

Repeat until the respondent has given all the times of listening to the radio yesterday and write '1' next to all times given by respondent under the first column ('all listening')

You said that you listened to the radio at .... (Give first time listened to) yesterday. Can you remember which station or stations you were tuned into at that time?

Mark the column of the station or stations named. Repeat for each time that the respondent listened to the radio yesterday.

All Listening	ZNBC 1	ZNBC 2	ZNBC 4	BBC	Phoenix	Icengelo	Christian Voice	Channel Africa	Other	Don't Know
0500–0530										
0530–0600										
0600–0630										
0630–0700										
0700–0730										
0730–0800										
0800–0830										
0830–0900										
0900–0930										
0930–1000										
1000–1030										
1030–1100										
1100–1130										
1130–1200										
1200–1230										
1230–1300										
1300–1330										
1330–1400										
1400–1430										
1430–1500										

(Continued)

(Continued)

All Listening	ZNBC 1	ZNBC 2	ZNBC 4	BBC	Phoenix	Icengelo	Christian Voice	Channel Africa	Other	Don't Know
1500–1530										
1530–1600										
1600–1630										
1630–1700										
1700–1730										
1730–1800										
1800–1830										
1830–1900										
1900–1930										
1930–2000										
2000–2030										
2030–2100										
2100–2130										
2130–2200										
2200–2230										
2230–2300										
2300–2330										
2330–2400										
2400–0030										
0030–0500										

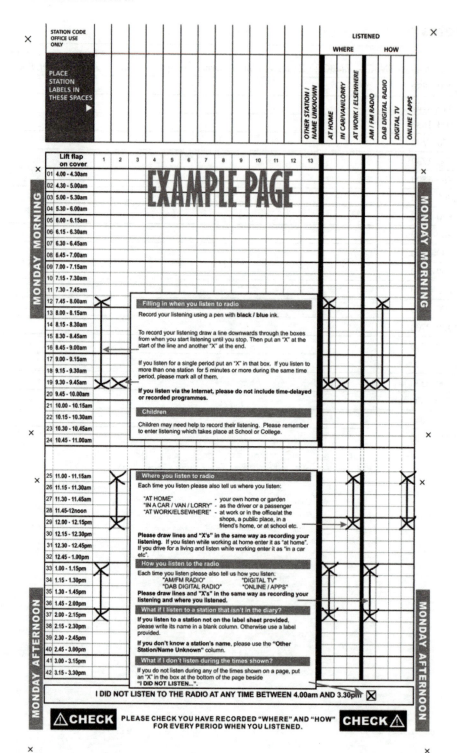

Notes and References

1. For example, www.random.org where the service is free of charge.
2. This table was provided by Continental Research, a major media and market research agency in the UK, now BRDC Continental.
3. This table was provided by MORI, another major media and market research agency, now part of Ipsos MORI.
4. RAJAR, the JIC for radio audience measurement in the UK, gave permission to use this sample page here. Readers can learn more about RAJAR and radio audience research in the UK at www.rajar.co.uk.
5. Question 20 comes after the section of this questionnaire reproduced here.
6. Question 16 also comes after the section reproduced here.

GLOSSARY

Access Panels. Typically, these are the panels created for online research. Access is for people with certain qualities, in this case Internet users.

Ad Hoc. Latin phrase meaning 'for this'. The term is used to refer to a single project, usually a quantitative survey, designed for a specific purpose and not a continuous, repeated or similar project. A 'one-off'.

Algorithm. The word is used very widely in electronics and computer science. It refers to the step-by-step procedures required in a programme or process expressed usually in the series of binary choices. 'A set of rules that precisely defines a sequence of operations'.[1]

Application Programming Interface (API). This allows different software programmes to interact with each other and exchange data automatically, without the need for manual exports and imports.

Audience Share. The share of the total viewing or listening audience at a certain time or over a certain time period, viewing a particular TV channel or listening to a particular radio station.

Average Hours per Head. The average length of time a person spends listening to a station. This is calculated by dividing the weekly hours by the population.

Average Hours per Listener. The average length of time that listeners spend on a station. This is calculated by dividing the **weekly hours by the weekly reach.**

Average Issue Readership or AIR. The calculated average number of people who see an issue of a particularly published periodical—used for daily newspapers as well as weekly and monthly magazines.

Back Check. A check by a fieldwork supervisor or someone else appointed for the purpose to confirm that an interview, usually part of a quantitative survey, has been properly carried out. It can be done by telephone or in writing but is often done face to face.

Base. This term usually refers to the base number of respondents in a quantitative survey who have been contacted and interviewed successfully and whose responses are included in the analysis. Sometimes you will see references to an unweighted base and a weighted base. The former is the real number of respondents who were contacted, interviewed and whose responses have been recorded and included. The weighted base, if used (it is not always necessary), is the number as used after weighting in the data analysis.

Before and After Test or Before/After Test. A study carried out before and after some initiative. It could be before and after an advertising campaign for a new product or service, before and after a health campaign or similar. The purpose is to detect changes in knowledge, attitudes and behaviour. It is a popular approach in advertising studies, but it is now increasingly being used with, for example, health campaigns and similar non-profit activities in areas of need, poverty and deprivation.

Bivariate Analysis. Bivariate data consist of observed or measured pairs of values for two variables or attributes from which it might well be possible to work out a relationship between them.

Bounce. This is a term used in Internet or Web traffic analysis. It represents the percentage of visitors who enter a site and 'bounce' (leave the site) rather than continue viewing other pages within the same site.

Buzz. The word seems to be used in many different ways in media research. However, this definition provided by Wikipedia seems to express best the way we are using the term. It is the interaction of consumers and users of a product or service, which amplifies or alters the original marketing message. This emotion, energy, excitement or anticipation about a product or service can be positive or negative. Buzz can be generated by intentional marketing activities by the brand owner or it can be the result of an independent event that enters public awareness through social or traditional media.

Call Back. This is when after an attempt to make contact with a selected respondent has failed either because the respondent is not at home or because for some reason the interview could not take place. It can also refer to a second interview later than the first one and done to continue the same enquiry at a different stage.

CAPI. Computer-assisted personal interview. The interviewer uses a laptop or similar device where the questionnaire is displayed and answers can be entered. See also mCAPI below.

CASI. Computer-assisted self interview. The respondent answers a computer-delivered questionnaire that has come by email or is accessed through the Internet. The questions are answered by the respondent without any interviewer being present. It could be called a Computer-assisted Self-completion Questionnaire, but this is longer and clumsy.

CATI. Computer-assisted telephone interview. The questionnaire is on a computer at the interviewer end, while the respondent answers verbally and the responses are recorded on the computer by the interviewer.

Census. Any enumeration of all individuals in a population is a census, although the term is usually used to refer to a national census. An accurate census is a major and vital tool for all quantitative research.

Chat Rooms. See also Message Boards. The chat room is an online facility for the exchange of ideas, comments and other information. They can involve games and other kinds of entertaining exchange. The terms Chat Room and Message Board seem to be used interchangeably, although some sources say that the latter should refer to exchanges that happen over periods of time and allow more content, whereas chat rooms are usually in real time and are more ephemeral. One analogy that makes some sense is that chat rooms are more like phone calls, while message boards are like letters.

Churn. This means turnover of audiences, often used to refer to the reality that any medium gains as well as loses audience. The churn rate may be steady so that the audience size does not change, although its composition will do so. Certain kinds of audience measurement can show the rate of loss or gain. Churn can also be used to refer to the turnover within a panel being used for research.

Clickstream. This is the recording of the parts of the screen a computer user clicks on while Web browsing or using another software application. As the user clicks anywhere in the webpage or application, the action is logged on to the web server, as well as possibly the web browser, router, proxy server or ad server. Clickstream analysis is useful for web-activity analysis, software testing, market research and for analyzing employee productivity.

Click through Rate (CTR). This is an often used way of measuring the success of an online advertising campaign for a particular website, as well as the effectiveness of an email campaign, by measuring the proportion or number of users who clicked on (i.e., 'went through') a specific link.

Codes and Coding. A code is a symbol used to classify data so that it can be analysed. Coding is the process of assigning codes to a set of responses. Very often, responses have to be grouped into coding categories to make the analysis possible, even though in this process, we do often lose a lot of subtlety and difference between people. Subtleties and differences are not always best understood through quantitative means; qualitative research provides better insights and understanding of the variety in human experiences.

Contact Sheet. A record needs to be kept of all contacts and attempted contacts by the interviewer during the course of any survey.

Continuous Research. Research that is done on a continuing basis either happening all the time or repeated frequently. Examples are the RAJAR radio diary used in the UK and the people meter systems used in some countries to measure TV viewing.

Crawler. A crawler is a robotic software device (or 'bot') that automatically surveys the World Wide Web looking for items to index.

CAWI. Computer-assisted Web interview. The same as CASI above.

Data Fusion. The bringing together of data from different sources into a single database.

Dayparts. A term used in broadcasting advertisement sales and placements. Rather than referring to precise times, time slots are often sold in dayparts, time categories or slots typically as follows: Of course, any such scheme can be varied to suit requirements and circumstances:[2]

Day	Description	Times
Weekday	Breakfast Peak	0600–1000
	Mid Morning	1000–1300
	Afternoon	1300–1600
	PM Drive	1600–1900
	Evening	1900–2400
	Overnight	0000–0600
Saturday	Breakfast Peak	0600–1000
	Mid Morning	1000–1300
	Afternoon	1300–1900
	Evening	1900–2400
	Overnight	0000–0600
Sunday	Breakfast Peak	0600–1000
	Mid Morning	1000–1300
	Afternoon	1300–1900
	Evening	1900–2400
	Overnight	0000–0600

Delphi Studies. This refers to a structured communication technique, originally developed as a systematic, interactive forecasting method, which relies on a panel of experts.

DPI. Deep Packet Inspection. Also called complete packet inspection and Information extraction or IX) is a form of computer network packet filtering that examines the data part (and possibly also the header) of a packet as it passes an inspection point, searching for protocol non-compliance, viruses, spam, intrusions or defined criteria to decide whether the packet may pass or if it needs to be routed to a different destination, or, for the purpose of collecting statistical information.

Earned Media. A term used in advertising and public relations to refer to publicity gained through promotional efforts other than advertising. It is a significant factor when looking at social media, and companies make considerable efforts to 'earn' their place on these platforms.

Efficiency Factor. The Efficiency Factor indicates the all-time efficiency of a broadcasting station at delivering a given Target Market. This is calculated by dividing the All Adult Weekly Hours by the Target Market Weekly Hours.

Establishment Survey. An essential element of much panel-based research. For example, before creating a panel of TV homes for a people meter system, an establishment survey is needed to establish a reliable and accurate estimate of the number of homes with TV sets, the proportion of multiset homes, the proportions with cable or satellite access, the proportions with smart TVs and so on. This is so that the panel chosen to have people meters attached to all receivers is representative of the TV set owning public in households.

Face-to-face Interview (F2F). This better describes the activity than 'personal interview' since the latter can include telephone interviews. The phrase explains itself. The interviewer and interviewee are literally face to face.

Focus Groups or Group Discussion. The term 'Focus Group' is more often used nowadays. A basic method in qualitative research whereby small groups of people, usually with something in common, are brought together to discuss topics relevant to the research project's theme or purpose.

Hall Test. This is a term used throughout the market research industry to refer to the tests using selected and invited respondents, who come to a central location or 'hall' to test or evaluate a product or service.

Household. We use the term a lot in all kinds of market research. How does one define a home, given the fact that practices are sometimes quite different between different cultures? The widely accepted practice is to define a household as one or more people living together who share the same arrangements for the preparation of food and other household expenses and activities.

Hours Index. The average hours for a station against a Target Market indexed against the All Adult Average Hours for that station. This indicates whether a target market is likely to listen to a given station for more or less time, with 100 being the norm.

Incentives. This term is almost always used in research to refer to inducements or compensations to respondents to take part in research.

Joint Industry Committee or JIC. A JIC (Joint Industry Committee) is a non-profit, neutral organisation formed to be responsible for shared quantitative research for relevant media in which all key players in a market or country—normally media owners, advertisers and advertising agencies are represented. For more, go to the international association for JICs at www.i-jic.org. However, this organisation has only a limited membership. There are many more. The best known are perhaps BARB and RAJAR in the UK, responsible for TV and radio audience measurement, respectively, SAARF in South Africa responsible for all media measurement, Auditel for TV audience measurement in Italy and BBM for all broadcast audience measurement in Canada. You can find more by putting these names into any search engine.

Kish Grid. A method for randomising the choice of respondent within a contacted household.

Main Shopper/Housewife. Nowadays the term 'housewife' has largely fallen out of favour. Many research agencies now use the term 'main shopper' in a survey questionnaire, and it can be either male or female. The term 'housewife' is sometimes replaced by 'home keeper' or similar.

mCAPI. mobile Computer-assisted Personal Interviewing is a form of computer-assisted interviewing though a mobile phone—smartphone or, more rarely, an ordinary mobile or cell phone.

Message Boards. Otherwise known as Online Forums or Internet Forums are online facilities or sites where Internet users can have online conversations. They are similar to the Chat Rooms, but allow longer sentences. Message boards may be monitored so that abusive or inappropriate comment can be blocked or removed.

Mystery Shopping. Mystery or secret shopping is a research tool used in market research to find out about how goods and services appear to consumers. The mystery shopper doing the work operates anonymously and is generally not known by the establishment or service being evaluated. Quality of service, or compliance with regulation, or to gather specific information about products and services are typical examples of the use of mystery shopping. Its use in media research is limited but not absent. Mystery shoppers perform specific tasks such as purchasing a product or service, asking questions, registering complaints or behaving in a certain way, and then providing detailed reports or feedback about their experiences.[3]

National Readership Survey or NRS. This often refers to the British NRS which is a continuous nationwide readership measurement survey carried out for the JIC (qv) for press readership research in the UK. As this book was going to press, it was announced that the UK NRS would become PAMCO, the Publishers' Audience Measurement Company in 2016. Evidently, it will remain a JIC as before. There are similar systems of press readership measurement, often called NRS in several other countries, including India, several Middle East countries and others. For more information on the India Readership Survey, by far the largest media survey done in the traditional (face to face interviewing) way, go to http://www.mruc.net/

Non-response. The part or section of any sample from which no response has been obtained, or it can refer to questions on a questionnaire to which no response has been obtained or given.

Normal Distribution. In probability theory, the normal (sometimes called Gaussian) distribution is an expression describing what probably happens. It is used to help us to work out the probability or likelihood that any real observation will fall between any two real limits or real numbers, as the curve approaches zero on either side. Normal distributions are very important in statistics and are used in quantitative research to estimate random variables whose distributions are not known.

Online Address Pool. A list of potential respondents whose demographic characteristics are known and who have been recruited and have agreed to being contacted for research purposes.

Opportunity to Hear (OTH). Opportunity to hear. Whether or not someone hears a broadcast, does he/she have the opportunity to do so?

Opt-out Service. Some radio or TV stations at certain times of the day switch their broadcast to a different station, or they may opt out and transmit locally relevant programming. In the UK, the radio measurement JIC called RAJAR is often unable to measure these opt-outs when the market concerned is too small to report separately.

Other Listening/Other Viewing. Any station that is not surveyed by a research agency but which is nonetheless measured as 'Other' is reported as such. Very often, these are foreign stations, radio or TV stations from neighbouring areas, distant stations heard through the Internet or via satellite, short-term licences, etc. 'When "Other" becomes large enough to be significant in local market terms it may become necessary to measure the services with the larger audience separately and specifically rather than recording them as "other".'

Panels. A recruited group of people who have been selected (using purposive criteria) to represent a defined universe who are then regularly called on for research purposes.

Pilot. A pilot is a small-scale preliminary activity before a main survey, whereby the questionnaire is tested to see if it works as intended. Piloting can also test sampling frames and methods before going into full fieldwork.

Placement Test—Sometime Product Placement. This is a research method whereby a product or service is offered to respondents for them to test and provide opinions, experiences and responses. It is a method sometimes used in media research to test new programmes, music or other content.

Preroll. An online commercial that is displayed before viewing, for example, a YouTube video. Typically, they are of 10 to 15 seconds in duration.

Probe and Prompt. To 'probe' means during an interview to use stimuli, usually by word of mouth, to obtain further detail or elucidation from a respondent about the topic, subject or theme being asked about. It is non-directive. Whereas a 'prompt' is when a method is used to suggest or lost possible answers to a question. Prompts are often read out or shown on a prompt card to a respondent, or might, for example, be on a self-completion questionnaire.

Population. This term is used in research often to define the measured universe. The number of people of the ages included who live within the TSA (total survey area) of what is being measured.

Probability. We use this term a lot when analysing quantitative data. It is a basic concept expressing the likelihood that something will happen. It is often used to express the likelihood that a result from quantitative research represents the reality. See the section on Data Analysis.

Product Test. See Placement Test.

RAJAR IR Regions. The 11 RAJAR IR regions (independent radio regions) are created from the existing commercial stations' TSA. As such, they overlap and their geography varies along with TSA changes. The other regions available on RAJAR are the BBC Editorial Areas and the new non-overlapping ITV regions that were introduced by BARB with their new 2010 contract.

Random Digit Dialling. A computer-driven method of randomising and selecting landline phone numbers to call for interviews.

Random Walk. Sometimes it is referred to as 'random route'. This is a method of selection of dwellings in a survey using face-to-face questionnaire, whereby the interviewer is required to follow procedures that prevent him/her in choosing where to go. The term has come from the writings of Karl Pearson, a statistician of the late 19th and early 20th centuries. The idea has been widely adopted in molecular physics among many other fields. In the social sciences and market research, it is generally used to denote the method or methods whereby an interviewer selects households where an interview takes place. This is how a major market research reference book describes the choice of a starting point and what follows. 'The interviewer is given a random address at which to conduct the first interview and thereafter a set of rules to follow to obtain the other addresses. Basically the interviewer continues to interview at every nth address in the street, alternatively turning left and right into other streets when he meets them.'[4]

Ratings. An audience rating is usually given as an average percentage of people in a given population listening or watching a TV or radio station within a given time period. The rating is calculated by dividing the estimated number of people in the audience by the number of people in the population and multiplying the result by one hundred.

Reach. This is usually expressed within a time frame—typical, daily, weekly or monthly. Weekly reach means the number of people within the measured age range and area, usually expressed as a percentage, who are reached by the measured medium within a period of seven days. In the case of RAJAR in the UK, it means those who have tuned to the particular radio station for at least 1 quarter-hour period over the course of a week. Weekly Reach is typically expressed as a percentage of the population within the relevant service area. The same definition works for daily reach, monthly reach, and so on.

Reach Index. The weekly reach per cent of a station against a Target Market indexed against the All Adult Weekly Reach per cent for that station. This indicates whether a Target Market is more or less likely to listen to a given station, with 100 being the norm.

Refusal Rate. The number of people who refuse to be interviewed is usually expressed as a percentage of the total number of respondents selected for interview or of the number actually participating. Refusal rates for face-to-face and telephone interviewing are now rather high in most developed countries, largely because of the negative effect of visits and calls that are not market research related but which pretend to be. Refusal rates are generally very low in less developed countries as the experience of being interviewed is still novel and also because there is very little misuse of interviewing for non-research purposes when calls and contacts are made with the purpose of selling goods or services.

Response Rate. The number of adequately completed interviews expressed as a percentage of all contacts made in the sampling process.

Sample. Instead of asking everyone in a population, we take a sample of it. A sample aims to be a subset of a population and to be representative of it. There are many different types of sampling—cluster, multistage, stratified, quota and more.

Sampling Error. A measurement from any sample is likely to be different in some degree from the true value for the universe being studied. This margin of error can be calculated. See the section on data analysis and the quick calculation tables provided in the appendix.

Sampling Frame. The device used to create a sample. It can be a population list, a census report with enumeration areas defined with their populations, a directory, a voters' list, a phone directory, and so on. Google Maps now provide a ready sampling frame for sampling dwellings.

Self-completion. Any questionnaire or diary or similar survey instrument, which is completed by the respondent with no interviewer being present. All online questionnaires are by their very nature, self-completion.

Segmentation. The division of any 'market' or geographic location or group or category of people being studied, into parts or segments for analysis. Segmentation can be by standard demographics of age, gender, education, socio-economic status, ethnicity, religion, and so on. But one can often segment by levels of usage of the product or service being studied. For example, when studying online activity, we may usefully segment by levels of online activity—heavy, medium and low.

Semi-structured Interview. Semi-structured interviews will often be used with many of the questions structured—that is with coded answers and with everything preformed and specified. But there will be questions that allow for open-ended answers and also allow probing by the interviewer to find out more detail on points of interest or importance. There is usually extensive use of probing techniques.

Share. The share of a particular market taken by each competing product or brand. In broadcasting, it is the percentage of all radio or television listening or viewing hours that a station accounts for within its transmission area. This can be calculated for any target market across any area.

Share Index. The Market Share per cent of a station against a Target Market indexed against the All Adult Weekly Reach per cent for that station. This indicates whether a Target Market is more or less likely to listen to a given station for more or less time, with 100 being the norm.

Share in TSA. This is a term used by RAJAR in the UK. It refers to the percentage of total radio listening time accounted for by a station in its Total Survey Area in an average week. This is obtained by dividing the station's total hours by the All Radio total hours in the station's TSA.

Standard Deviation or Standard Error. The two terms are often referred to as if they were the same. Actually, they are not. The Standard Deviation (SD) is the measure of the variability of data collected, otherwise known as the scatter of data. The Standard Error (SEM) quantifies the precision of your data. It is a measure of how far your data are likely to be from the reality. SEM will always be smaller than SD.

Storyboard. In film and video making, storyboards are used to outline a proposed production sequence. Storyboards can and often are used to test with potential target audience members.

Stratification. This technique is sometimes used in sampling (qv) to ensure that the sample is representative in terms of the categories chosen to stratify by. For example, a purely random sample may exclude people of a certain ethnicity or it may insufficiently represent hard-to-reach categories. It can under-represent certain geographic subsamples. To avoid this, one can ensure the inclusion of all such categories by stratifying the sample; this means that the sample is specially designed to include all strata required in proportion to their numbers in the overall population. Sometimes it may be necessary to include some strata in numbers greater than their proportion in the total population. This is done when detailed analysis of such strata is deemed necessary. In these cases, when analysing and producing results for the whole sample, weighting is used to redress and correct any imbalances.

Street Interview. A short interview conducted in a street or shopping mall or similar away-from-home location. Usually quota samples are used.

Survey Period. Again using RAJAR as our example, depending on the size of their Total Survey Area, stations are reported on a sample based on 3,

6 or 12 months. This is the survey period and is denoted by the letters Q (Quarter), H (half yearly) and Y (yearly).

Total Survey Area (TSA). The area within which a station's audience is measured. As an example, in the UK, this is defined by RAJAR (responsible for radio audience measurement) as being something that the station itself describes or delineates using postcode districts as building blocks.

Total Weekly Hours. The total number of hours that a station is listened to over the course of a week. This is the sum of all times for all listeners or viewers.

Unique Visitor (UV). An Internet term referring to one user visiting a site or page and who is counted once no matter how often the same page or site is visited. UVs are typically measured on a daily, weekly or monthly basis. Derived from this are two other terms—MAU (Monthly Active Users) and DAU (Daily Active Users). Unique Visitors are sometimes referred to simply as 'uniques'.

Universe. The universe consists of all survey elements that qualify for inclusion in the research study. The precise definition of the universe for a particular study is set by the research question, which specifies who or what is of interest.[5]

Variance. This is a statistical concept and is a measure of the variability or dispersion of a set of numbers in the data. It is the arithmetical mean of the squared differences between each number and the mean of all the numbers.[6]

Weighting. The process of weighting involves emphasising or reducing the contribution of some aspects of a set of data before arriving at a result, giving them more or less weight in the analysis. That is, rather than each variable in the data contributing equally to the final result, some data are adjusted to contribute more than others. It is analogous to the practice of adding extra weight to one side of a pair of scales to favour a buyer or seller.[7] A typical example would be a national survey that increases the sampling of an important, but small minority group in order to have sufficient data about it for separate analysis. When the national data are calculated and issued, the results from the minority group subsample would be weighted down to their actual proportion in the universe.

References

1. Harold S. Stone (ed.), *Introduction to Computer Organization and Data Structures* (New York: McGraw-Hill, 1972). See especially the first chapter: *Algorithms, Turing Machines, and Programs*.

ESOMAR. *Global Market Research*. 2014, 122–123 and passim. Available online at https://www.esomar.org/uploads/industry/reports/global-market-research-2014/ESOMAR-GMR2014-Preview.pdf (accessed 23 September 2015).

———. Readership Measurement in Europe. Report on Newspaper and Magazine Readership in Europe. Amsterdam: ESOMAR, 1996.

Gordon, Wendy, and R. Langmaid. *Qualitative Market Research: A Practitioner's and Buyer's Guide*. Aldershot: Gower, 1988.

Gunter, Barrie. *Media Research Methods*. London: SAGE Publications, 2000.

Hand, D.J. 'Sampling'. In *Advising on Research Methods: A Consultant's Companion*, eds, H.J. Adèr and G.J. Mellenbergh. Huizen: Johannes van Kessel Publishing, 2008, pp. 83–104

Hague, Paul, and Paul Harris. *Sampling and Statistics*. London: Kogan Page, 1993.

Hague, Paul, and Peter Jackson. *Do Your Own Market Research*. London: Kogan Page, 1998.

Head, Sydney. *World Broadcasting Systems*. Belmont: Wadsworth, 1985.

Head, Sydney, and Christopher Sterling. *Broadcasting in America* (6th Edition). Boston: Houghton Mifflin, 1990.

Jenkins, Peter, and Richard Windle. 'The New Listening Panel'. *Annual Review of BBC Broadcasting Research Findings* no. 11(1985): 37–44.

Kahneman, Daniel. Thinking, Fast and Slow. New York: Farrar, Straus and Giroux, 2011.

Kirk, Jerome, and Marc L. Miller. *Reliability and Validity in Qualitative Research*. Thousand Oaks, London and New Delhi: SAGE Publications, 1986.

Klapper, Joseph T. *The Effects of Mass Communication*. New York: Free Press, 1960.

Laking, Anne, and Mick Rhodes. 'Q.E.D: Research for a Second Series'. *Annual Review of BBC Broadcasting Research Findings* 9(1983): 118–120.

Lewis, Tom. *Empire of the Air*. New York: Harper, 1991

Little, R.J.A., and D.B. Rubin. Statistical Analysis with Missing Data. New York: Wiley, 1987.

Lensveldt Mulders, G.J.L.M., R. Lugtig, and J. Hox. 'Assembling an Access Panel: A Study of Initial Nonresponse and Self selection Bias'. In *Access Panels and Online Research, Panacea or Pitfall? Proceedings of the DANS Symposium, Amsterdam*, eds. I. Stoop and M. Wittenberg. Amsterdam: Aksant Academic Publishers, 2006.

List, Dennis. *Radio Survey Cookbook*. Adelaide: Australian Broadcasting Corporation, Audience Research Department, 1990. This was the original publication but now a more current version (*Know Your Audience: A Practical Guide to Media Research*) is available online at http://www.audiencedialogue.net This is a much recommended site for media research resources and training.

Lynn, Jonathan, and Antony Jay. *The Complete Yes Prime Minister*. London: BBC Books, 1989, pp. 106–107.

Lunt, P., and S. Livingstone. 'Rethinking Focus Groups in Media and Communication'. *Journal of Communication* 46 no. 2 (1996): 79–98.

Mark, Desmond (ed.). *Paul Lazarsfelds Wiener RAVAG-Studies 1932*. Wien: Guthmann-Peterson, 1996.

McKee, Neill. *Social Mobilisation and Social Marketing in Developing Communities: Lessons for Communicators*. Penang: Southbound, 1992.

McQuail, Denis. *Audience Analysis*. Thousand Oaks, London and New Delhi: SAGE Publications, 1997.

Menneer, Peter. 'Towards a Radio "BARB"—Some Issues of Measurement'. *ADMAP* February (1989): 42–45.

Meurs, L., R. van Ossenbruggen, and L. Nekkers. 'Rotte Appels?' In *Ontwikkelingen in het marktonderzoek: Jaarboek MarktOnderzoekAssociatie*, eds, A.E. Bronner, et al. Haarlem: Spaaren-Hout, 2009, 34.

Moores, Shaun. *Interpreting Audiences*. Thousand Oaks, London and New Delhi: SAGE Publications, 1993.

Morgan, David L. *Focus Groups as Qualitative Research*. Thousand Oaks, London and New Delhi: SAGE Publications, 1997.

Morgan, David L., and Richard A. Krueger. *Focus Group Kit,* 6 volumes. Thousand Oaks, London and New Delhi: SAGE Publications, 1997.

Morse, Janice M. (ed.). *Completing a Qualitative Project.* Thousand Oaks, London and New Delhi: SAGE Publications, 1997.

Moser, Claus A., and G. Kalton. *Survey Methods in Social Investigation.* London: Heinemann Educational Books, 1971.

Mytton, Graham. *Listening, Looking and Learning.* Lusaka: University of Zambia, 1974.

Omiyale, W. A Decade of Innovation: Lessons from the Confirmit 2013 Market Research Technology Report. Available online at https://www.confirmit.com/ (accessed 23 September 2015).

Poynter, Ray. *The Handbook of Online and Social Media Research: Tools and Technologies for Market Researchers.* Chichester: John Wiley, 2010.

Pukelsheim, F., and B. Simeone. On the Iterative Proportional Fitting Procedure: Structure of Accumulation Points and L1 error analysis. Available online at opus.bibliothek.uni augsburg.de/volltexte/2009/1368/pdf/mpreprint_09_005 (accessed 20 March 2012).

Reiss, Pamela. 'Continuous Research for Television and Radio: The 1980s Approach'. *Annual Review of BBC Broadcasting Research Findings* no. 8 (1981–1982): 13–26.

Reynolds, Rodney A., Robert Woods, and Jason D. Baker (eds). *Handbook of Research on Electronic Surveys and Measurements.* Hershey: Idea Group Reference, 2007.

Robson, Sue, and Angela Foster (eds). *Qualitative Research in Action.* London: Edward Arnold, 1989.

Rogers, Everett M. *Modernisation among Peasants: The Impact of Communication.* New York: Holt, Rinehart and Winston, 1969.

Rosenbaum, P.R., and D.B. Rubin. 'The Central Role of the Propensity Score in Observational Studies for Causal Effects'. *Biometrika* 70 (1983): 41–55.

———. 'Reducing Bias in Observational Studies Using Subclassification on the Propensity Score'. *Journal of the American Statistical Association* 79 (1984): 516–524.

Rusu, Sharon, and Graham Mytton. *IRIN Evaluation.* New York: OCHA, 2003. Available online at https://docs.unocha.org/sites/dms/Documents/IRIN_Evaluation_FINAL_version.pdf

'Special Edition: Communications, Computers and Networks'. *Scientific American,* 265, no. 3 (September 1991): 30 passim.

Stoop, I. 'Access Panels and Online Surveys: Mystifications and Misunderstandings'. In *Access Panels and Online Research, Panacea or Pitfall? Proceedings of the DANS Symposium, Amsterdam,* eds. I. Stoop and M. Wittenberg. DANS Symposium Publications 4. Amsterdam: Aksant Academic Publishers, 2006, pp. 5–17.

Silverman, David. *Interpreting Qualitative Data.* Thousand Oaks, London and New Delhi: SAGE Publications, 1993, p. 147.

Silvey, Robert. *Who's Listening?* London: George Allen and Unwin, 1974, p.14.

Søgaard, Viggo. *Research in Church and Mission.* Pasadena: William Carey, 1996.

Twumasi, P.A. *Social Research in Rural Communities.* Accra: Ghana Universities Press, 1986.

van den Berg, Heloïse, and Henk van Zurksum. *Now Listen and Pay Attention.* Hilversum: NOS, no date.

van Hamersveld, Mario, and Cees de Bont, *Market Research Handbook* (5th Edition). Amsterdam: ESOMAR, 2007.

van Ossenbrug, R.T. Vonk and P. Willems, 'A Comparison Study across 19 Online Panels (NOPVO 2006)'. In *Access Panels and Online Research, Panacea or Pitfall? Proceedings of the DANS Symposium, Amsterdam,* eds. I. Stoop and M. Wittenberg. DANS Symposium Publications 4. Amsterdam: Aksant Academic Publishers, 2006, pp. 53–76.

Vogt, W. Paul. *Dictionary of Statistics and Methodology.* Thousand Oaks, London and New Delhi: SAGE publications, 1993.

Weisberg, Herbert F., Jon A. Krosnick, and Bruce D. Bowen. *An Introduction to Survey Research, Polling and Data Analysis.* Thousand Oaks, London and New Delhi: SAGE Publications, 1997.

Wimmer, Roger D., and Joseph R. Dominick. *Mass Media Research: An Introduction* (3rd Edition). Belmont, California: Wadsworth, 1991.

INDEX

ABOUT THE AUTHORS

Graham Mytton is an independent media research consultant and trainer based in Dorking, UK. He began his media research career in Tanzania as a student in 1967. He carried out extensive audience research for his doctoral thesis on the role of mass media in nation building in that country before moving to Zambia in 1970, where he conducted audience research for the national broadcaster. From 1973 to 1976, he worked as a reporter, presenter and producer in the African section of the BBC World Service working on programmes such as *Focus on Africa* and a weekly documentary. He also worked on current affairs programmes on BBC Radio 4, a UK domestic radio network. From 1976 to 1982, he was Head of the BBC's Hausa language service for West Africa. From 1982 to 1996, he was Head of Audience Research for the BBC World Service, and finally he created the World Service's first Marketing department, becoming its Controller before leaving it in 1998 to work as an independent audience research specialist and trainer. He was a founder member of the Pan African Media Research Organization, and was awarded the Piet Smit Achiever Award for 2012 in recognition of services to media research in Africa. He is Honorary Fellow of the Bangladesh Marketing and Social Research Society.

He has carried out extensive research projects in Africa and Asia including national surveys in Gambia, Sierra Leone, South Sudan and East Timor. He has led training programmes in media research in 37 countries. He is the author of several books and articles on audience research, broadcasting history and African media.

Peter Diem is an independent media research consultant. He is also the Editor-in-chief of the Austrian Internet Encyclopedia 'Austria-Forum' (http://austria-forum.org). He studied Law and Political Science in Austria and in the USA. In 1964, he became a consultant to the Conservative Party of Austria as an adviser on market research. After a short period in book market research (1977–1978), he started to build up TV and Radio Research for ORF, the public service network of Austria. He was Head of the Audience Research Department of ORF until 1999. For three years, he held the position of chairman of GEAR, the Group of European Audience Researchers. After his retirement from ORF, Peter Diem started a career as an online market researcher. He built up online market research for GfK Austria and its CEE subsidiaries.

Piet Hein van Dam is an independent media consultant, helping data- and technology-driven start-up companies to grow and make it to the next phase. From seed to seasoned. With a PhD in nonlinear dynamics, Piet Hein evolved to business developer type CEO. He spent more than 10 years at Unilever and KPMG Consulting in international business development functions. In 2005, he became the managing director of Motivaction International, a Dutch market research company. In 2011 he joined internet start-up Wakoopa as CEO. This passive metering company grew exponentially and joined Netquest in 2014, where Piet Hein took on a new function as Chief People Officer. Piet Hein is a regular speaker at conferences and author of several articles on behavioural data collection. He is holder of six patents and several scientific publications. At Unilever, he was awarded with the Golden Jubilee Award for Excellence in Research (1997) and in 2008 he received the Deloitte Award for the 50 Best Managed Companies in the Netherlands. He loves traditional sailing boats, books and cooking. He lives in Amsterdam, with his wife and two kids.